FLIGHT FOR JUSTICE

THE TRIAL IS nothing but a distraction. There is no safety without justice, and Darby, Kathryn, and the gals are back, fighting the villains of Global Air Lines. Bill Jacobs is released from prison and the game changes. The stakes increase when Covid is unleashed on the world. Darby's fight is one for the integrity of the pilot profession and the safety of passengers, but little does she know how deep the corruption runs within the FAA and Global. Will she survive? Twists and turns you will never expect in this fight for justice. The 7th novel in the Flight for Series.

Aviation Advocate!
Inspiration. Motivation. Plane Stuff.

"Sometimes truth is scarier than fiction"
By Karlene K. Petitt PhD

at
Flight To Success
www.KarlenePetitt.com

FLIGHT FOR JUSTICE

KARLENE K. PETITT

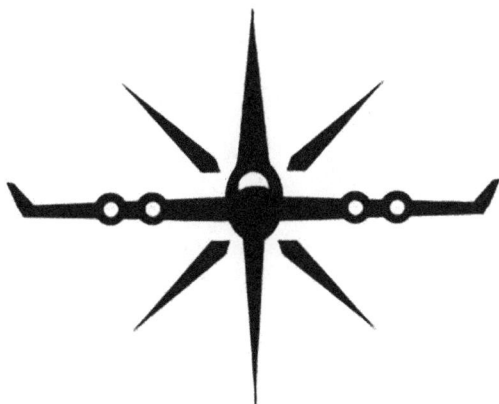

JET STAR PUBLISHING INC.
SEATAC WA

"The skies are not as "friendly" as they seem... A nail-biting, yet very satisfying court drama, along with all the action, twists, and betrayals you've come to expect from a Petitt thriller!"

Captain Eric Auxier, best-selling author

Capnaux.com

"Darby finally has her long-awaited trial. It's full of twists and turns and surprises. Buckle your seatbelts and hang on!"

Captain Kathy McCullough, Retired.

Author of *Breakfast in Narita*

Darby is feisty, brave, funny, resilient, loving, and smart. I've read all novels in this series and too much appears real... How much, I wonder? You decide. With the FAA's focus on mental health, I wonder if they, too, are reading. I hope so!

Carol Singleton, Flight Attendant

Author's Note:

THERE HAS BEEN more truth than fiction in the Flight for Series. While I surmised what would happen if airline management degraded the industry, I also wondered how long it would take to mentally break the pilot. Then, three years after I published my first novel, *Flight for Control*, a Germanwings pilot intentionally crashed his plane killing everyone on board. All accidents in *Flight for Control* were also based on actual events.

I then wrote about substandard airline training in *Flight for Safety*. Shortly thereafter we saw Air France 447 fall into the ocean in the same manner as to the events in the novel. What the reader may not know, was the merger between Coastal Airlines and Global Air Lines was Northwest and Delta. The atrocious training events in *Flight for Safety*, were ongoing at Delta. More so, both Delta and the FAA knew of the faulty equipment that took down AF447 but did nothing until after 228 people died. I had written a blog post about that AF447 accident and how to fly out of a stall. Little did I know at the time, but that blog would become a central theme in the challenge of my mental health and perhaps the core reason to silence me.

I enrolled in Embry Riddle Aeronautical University to earn a PhD in order to better understand aviation safety. The ensuing novels, *Flight for Survival* and *Flight for Sanity*, were inspired by Delta's subsequent actions to silence me for all that I learned regarding Safety Management Systems (SMS) and Safety Culture that contradicted Delta's operation. More than silence me, Delta management attempted to destroy me and permanently remove me from the industry, similar to the action Global took against Darby in the novels. *Flight for Truth* was Darby's and my fight to return to the flight deck, despite a bipolar diagnosis.

Flight for Discovery included what we learned and how Delta attempted to bury me, with verbatim deposition testimony presented in the novel. There was no way Coastal or Delta would go to trial. Yet they did and the fight for safety turned into a fight for justice.

Now we have *Flight for Justice*. While I changed the names, the trial deposition testimony is verbatim. The only character's testimony that differs slightly is Neil. His testimony was my husband's, except for the job offer. The FAA's complicit behavior is fact. The FAA administrators owned by Delta is fact. ALPA's participation and events are fact. The legal system and transferring of judges and purchased arbitrators are fact. A doctor forfeiting his medical license is fact.

The central theme of all the novels is the destruction of the pilot job with autonomous planes on horizon, and my effort to fight for the pilot job and improve training and thus aviation safety. While many do not believe autonomous aircraft will become a reality, when you read about the non-interruptible autopilot, the patents, and the Airbus ATTOL system in this novel, all of that is fact. The training events and near-death experiences all occurred at Delta. Even the pilots falling asleep on short final was true. Despite winning my legal battle in Petitt vs Delta, nobody was held accountable; therefore, I ended up walking away from my airline career.

Perhaps the death of my airline career and Darby living my story inspired the ending of this novel. But the lack of accountability at Delta and the FAA's complicit behavior inspired the next. *Flight for Revenge* is coming soon and will be the first completely fiction novel. For all those involved in the Delta action against me, and those who looked the other way, you should be incredibly grateful that I am *not* crazy.

Captain Karlene Pettit, author

DEDICATION

I DEDICATE THIS novel to my husband, Dick Petitt. He not only lived through Delta's attack against me but was my rock through the legal drama that followed. When he read this novel, he cried. Not at the chapters I would suspect, but during the trial chapters. He said that it saddened him remembering all that I had endured. Tears of compassion are rare these days. One of the many reasons I love him with all my heart.

FLIGHT FOR JUSTICE

KARLENE K. PETITT

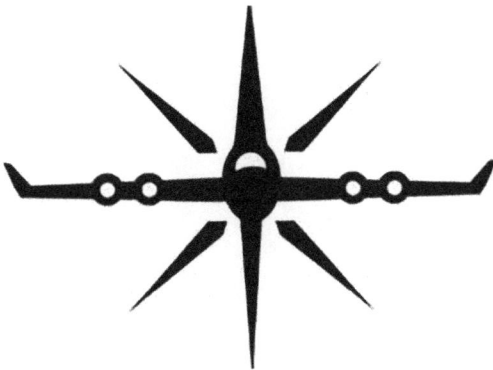

JET STAR PUBLISHING INC.

SEATAC WA

PROLOGUE

MARCH 10, 2019
ENROUTE TO ATLANTA

CLOSING HIS EYES, the first officer said, "God I'm so fucking tired." Then he opened them as quickly as they had closed and leaned forward to force himself awake. Resting his arms on the glareshield, he stared into the night sky speckled with the brilliance of a thousand stars. He sucked a deep breath. His head hurt. His eyeballs hurt. *Just living the dream,* he thought.

Miles below was nothing but blackness with a scattering of lights. The world around them was asleep, as they, too, should be. Instead, the 757 droned on. The roar of the engines mimicked the white noise his wife played for their toddler to help him fall sleep. He now understood the power of that repetition, as it was having the same effect on him.

"Coffee?" The captain asked glancing his way. "Or do you want to catch a quick nap."

"If I fall asleep now, you'll have to land this beast on your own."

The captain reached to his right and picked up the handset. He pressed the forward attendant's push-to-talk switch. "Beth, could I bother you for two coffees black." After a pause, he said, "Looks like 5:45. We'll be starting down short of an hour."

Within minutes, the flight attendant rang the flight deck and the first officer stood and opened the door. He thanked her for the coffee and handed one to the captain. Climbing back into his seat, he sipped the bitter, bacteria-laden brew. "I hate drinking this shit. Especially before arrival. Keeps me awake when I want to sleep."

"We're almost there," the captain said. He was silent for a few moments then said, "I hope that woman lives." Many more minutes of silence followed, and then he added, "That was my first medical divert."

"Guess we're both in the club now," the first officer said. "But why the hell does this shit happen on the first leg of a redeye?"

"Murphy," the captain said stuffing his empty cup into the garbage bag. "Did you get any sleep before we left?"

"None," the first officer said, glancing his way with amazement at how quickly he emptied his cup. "To assign a crew a redeye on the first leg of a trip is not a strategic plan I'd implement. No way in hell anyone could be rested."

"Hell, you should be the most rested coming off your days off," the captain said sarcastically.

"Yeah right. Try to tell my family, and my body, that I need to sleep during dinnertime, after I had a good night's sleep the night before." The first officer drained the remainder of his cup. "I have no problem with this hour if I can sleep in a hotel room first. First leg, that's a deal breaker."

"Until housekeeping pounds on your door, despite the Do Not Disturb sign."

"The very reason I'm an FFDO," the first officer said with a chuckle. "This is not just for terrorists," he added, patting his gun.

"Yeah. Still. I apologize for not shutting this down after removing that passenger," he said. "We could be in a hotel room right now."

"Our adrenaline was too high. We couldn't self-diagnose. Besides, I was with you on the continuation. Gotta complete the mission, sort of shit."

The captain nodded. "Are you sure you don't want to close your eyes?"

"I'm good. Caffeine sensitive. I'll be awake for the duration." He shoved his cup into the garbage bag. "Feel free to close yours. Really, I'm good now."

"Nah, I'll be fine."

The minutes felt like hours as the seconds ticked by over each mile they carved through the sky toward their destination. The captain finally briefed the approach and then said, "See if you can get us lower."

"Control, Global two-niner requesting lower."

"Global two-nine, descend to flight level 220. Contact approach on 127.9"

"Cleared to 220, going to approach," he responded.

The captain dialed in the altitude and selected VNAV and the plane began its motion toward the earth, their destination, and their beds.

The first officer dialed in the frequency and pressed talk. "Approach, Global two-niner is with you out of 320 descending to 220."

"Good morning Global two-niner. You're cleared the Galvin 1 RNAV arrival. You can expect runway 9R this morning. Information ALPHA is current."

The captain dialed in 5,000 feet, and they continued their descent. The first officer acquired the current airport information. The winds were light, and the altimeter was 29.97. Approaching 18,000 feet the captain set the altimeter and said, "Descent checklist."

After they finished the descent checklist, the captain cycled the seatbelt sign to signal the flight attendants that they were passing through 10,000 feet. "Approach check," the captain called. The first officer read it and he responded.

"Global two-niner, turn left to a heading of 140 to intercept the final approach course for runway nine right. Cleared for the ILS nine right approach. Speed your discretion, contact tower on 119.3 over ANDIY."

The captain selected Approach and armed the localizer and glideslope. The autopilot would guide her in. He called, "Flaps 1," and then "Flaps 5," and they slowed. "Flaps 15."

ANDIY was a fix 22.4 miles from the runway on the ILS. Already on the localizer, the first officer pressed talk as they intercepted the glideslope. "Tower, Global is with you, approaching ANDIY for nine right."

"Good morning Global. Winds are 010 at 5, you are cleared to land runway nine right. Speed your discretion."

"Cleared to land, nine right. Global two niner," the first officer replied. "Guess they're not too busy this time of morning. But do they have to be so fucking chipper?" He glanced at the landing checklist. The captain wouldn't be calling for that until he put the gear down.

His eyelids were heavy, but it wouldn't be long until he found his bed. The plane droned on and he closed his eyes only for a moment and then…

"TOO LOW GEAR!" … "TOO LOW GEAR!" the warning screamed.

The first officer awoke and yelled, "Gear down!" When the captain didn't respond, he reached up, grabbed the handle, and pushed the lever down. The noise of the door opening and gear falling into position could wake the dead and it did.

The captain awoke with a start. "What the fuck!" he yelled as he grabbed the control yoke, disconnected the autopilot, fought to flare with the high speed, and was able to slam the main wheels into the runway with the nose following shortly thereafter. Thrust to idle. Max reverse. Max brakes. There was nothing more they could do than pray.

They were fast with flaps only at 15, instead of 30. When the plane slowed enough to make the final exit without going off the end of the runway, brakes smoking, the first officer realized he was holding his breath.

"Jesus fucking Christ," the captain spat. "What just happened?"

CHAPTER 1

MARCH 22, 2019

DARBY SAT AT her kitchen table reading Walter Croft's deposition for the third time. *What the hell am I missing?* She set the document aside, leaned back in her chair and reached for her coffee mug. The contents had turned cold, again.

She carried her neglected coffee to the microwave and stuck it inside then pressed the 45-second button for the second time. She turned and leaned against the counter and stared at the documents spread across the kitchen table, focusing on the notebook she had created. Crossing her arms, she rubbed them to ward off the chill. The microwave beeped, and she jumped. Her nerves were a ball of open wires these days.

Returning to the table with her Crème Brule coffee, she slipped back into her chair and sipped. This time, staring at the massive documents as a group. *What the hell is their game?* she wondered. If she could only figure that out, she would know what to do.

The trial would begin in three days, but Darby could still not believe that Global Air Lines was going through with this. She had to be missing something. If she ever felt this type of apprehension in a plane, there was usually a valid reason. A pilot trusts their instinct, or they die. But there was no reason that *anyone* at the airline should want this case to see the inside of a courtroom.

Darby sipped her coffee, then reached for the notebook. She opened it to the front page and read the list of facts she had acquired in discovery. The email that Vice President of Flight Operations, Rich Clark, had written was at the top of the list. He detailed the exact manner in which he planned to accomplish his task—forcing her into a psychiatric evaluation, called a Section 8.

Next was an email from Clark to George Wyatt, the senior vice president of flight operations, notifying Wyatt *when* Clark would send Darby into Section 8, four months before he came up with the reason. Third, Clark told Darby she was meeting with an HR safety investigator. But Ms. Abbott had nothing to do with flight operations safety. She managed the employee pass travel complaint department. Number four, Clark had stated he conducted an investigation, of which he did not. Five, Clark had invited her to give a safety presentation to senior management *after* they had pulled her from flying by asserting that she was crazy.

There was more on the list, but the first five points were enough for Global to lose the case. Darby had thirteen points in total that could destroy Global Air Lines in court, yet for some reason they thought they could win.

The union warned her not to report any concerns, or the company would get her. The union attorneys, thereafter, advised her to not give the management team anything in writing. She didn't listen to either part of that advice. She had met with Rich Clark and George Wyatt and gave them a written safety report. Clark attacked and she battled in the fight of her life.

The mental health attack was purely premeditated. But why the trial? She got her job back. The Mayo Clinic cleared her. *What the hell am I missing?* She simply could not figure this out, and it was driving her crazy. How can someone battle the enemy while blindfolded? She had no idea.

Darby had filed an AIR21 complaint against Global under the whistleblower law. As it turned out, the union had been complicit and participatory in many ways. Therefore, early on, she had given up on any reliance on their assistance and focused on saving herself and her career.

She opened Rich Clark's tab in her notebook and tapped a fingernail on his name. He had been the vice president of operations at the time. When Wyatt retired, Clark became senior vice president. It was Clark who had set the attack in motion, but Wyatt had approved it. Darby flipped the pages of the notebook to George Wyatt.

Wyatt retired to spend more time with his family, but the next thing she knew he was the number one choice to become the FAA administrator. Those two events were not mutually inclusive. During discovery they also learned that Walter Croft, Global's CEO and chairman of the board, was involved. As was the pass travel lady, a half dozen chief pilots, a whole bunch of corrupt union representatives, and a scummy nail-biting Labor Relations attorney, Joe Wolfe.

With both elbows on the table, she steepled her fingers and brought them to her chin, thinking about what to do next. She was at a loss, and time was running out. Sighing, she dropped her hands and closed the notebook.

Darby had constructed a section for each of the players with notes as to what they did, what she could prove, and at the end was a resolution page, blank. It would be therapeutic to plot the demise of those assholes, especially in the manner of which they had inflicted pain upon her. There was always justice one way or another. But now was not the time.

She drummed her fingernails on the table thinking, then opened the notebook once again to Dr. Wood's section, and the doorbell rang. She startled and looked at the time. *What the hell?* she thought. Nobody she knew would be up at this hour unless it was to fly an airplane. She pulled her robe closed, wrapped the belt around her waist and headed for the door.

Peeking through the peephole, confusion filled her face, followed by a smile. She deactivated the alarm and removed the chain.

CHAPTER 2

DARBY OPENED THE door to her publisher and said, "My God, what are you doing here?"

Purse over her shoulder, Deloris handed Darby her newspaper and said, "Do you have coffee in this place?" as she pushed past her.

"Of course," Darby said noticing the idling taxi in her driveway as she closed the door. She set the newspaper on the entryway table, and they headed toward the kitchen.

"I hope this is research for the next book," Deloris said, nodding to the documents as they entered the kitchen.

"I wish," Darby said, and stuck a Pike Place Market coffee pod into the machine and pressed start. "We can sit in the living room," she said, placing her mug into the microwave.

Deloris touched the notebook and said, "This is beyond belief."

"You got that right," Darby said. "If you would have told me you were coming, I would have been dressed." Darby handed Deloris her coffee and removed hers from the microwave.

"I just arrived from Tokyo. Had a couple hours to kill before heading East."

"And?" Darby said, leading them toward the living room. She knew if Deloris had left the airport, only to face security upon her return, that this visit was more than killing a couple hours.

"I have some news that's better in person." Deloris sat on the couch and set her mug on a magazine. She removed her purse from her shoulder and placed it beside her, patted it, and then said, "I've got two agencies that want your story."

"The Global story? But I thought Global was blocking your company from doing anything with me."

"Oh, they are," Deloris said with a flick of her hand. "But this has the makings of movie. Somebody is willing to fight for it, but only if you win."

"But we have a social media policy," Darby said. "They'll fire me."

"They might try. But not even an NDA could stop Gretchen Carlson in her movie. But we can deal with those details later."

This was exactly what Darby needed. A resurgence of funds. Her legal expenses had far exceeded her salary during this fight. While red was the choice of color on her nails, it was not a good shade in her bank account.

"So, this is good news," Darby said. "Do they want me to write the book first?"

"I want you to write the book first," Deloris said. "It has bestseller all over it."

"When do you want it?" Darby asked.

She wasn't sure how to carve out more time in her already chaotic schedule with her Airbus A350 training around the corner, a trial that was about to start, and she was looking at a full flight schedule to pay for all the fun.

"We can't buy it now. Therefore, we have time," Deloris said. "I just wanted you to know it's on the table. But a winning decision must come first before they do anything."

"What if they win?" Darby asked.

"Would you appeal?" Deloris reached for her cup.

"Hell, yes."

Darby knew if she did not pull this off, Global would continue to play chess with pilots' lives. There was no way she would allow anyone at Global to get away with this if she could help it. She was not the first person they had done this to, she was just the first person who had returned to work and took them to court. She wanted Rich Clark's head on a stake. But losing this trial scared her to death. She wasn't sure there would be a positive outcome.

"Carol also said to tell you hello," Deloris said. "She told me that you need to get laid."

"She said what?" Darby said, almost choking on her coffee.

"Well, specifically she said you need to have sex."

Darby laughed out loud. She loved Carol. She was the best editor she'd ever worked with, who had spent many hours working with her on her books with the most challenging schedules. Carol of all people knew how hard this had been on her.

"Tell her I'll do my best. And please give her my love."

"Goes without mention," Deloris said. Then she sipped her coffee and stared at Darby over the brim.

Uh oh, Darby thought. The words she hated to ask escaped, as she said, "There's something else, isn't there?"

Deloris looked at her watch, set her cup on the table and said, "Yes." She stood and looked at Darby. "They've frozen your residuals."

"What?" Darby said and jumped to her feet. "How? How can they do that?"

"There is a clause about negative publicity, and behavior appropriate to the company blah blah blah." Deloris said. "They said your lawsuit falls into that category."

"What happened to innocent until proven guilty?" Darby said.

"This trial is not about your innocence," Deloris reminded her.

"It's about what the company did to you. Unfortunately, they are innocent until proven guilty. But until that happens, some legal snot in our department put a hold on your residuals. Someone at Global is squeezing you and using us to do it. You could fight it in court, and win. But it would take years, and at what expense?"

"I'm barely surviving the legal battle with Global," Darby said. "I couldn't afford it."

"The only thing that matters is that Global does not win this case," Deloris said. "The rest will get sorted out and we can look for a book deal and movie in the future."

"If Global can get to the executives, what makes you think they can't get to a judge?" Darby asked.

Deloris reached for her purse and said, "I'm going to pray that does not happen."

Darby walked her to the door. When Deloris was gone, she moved the security chain back into place, turned her back against the door, then slid to the floor. Tilting her head against the door, she closed her eyes and tears rolled down her cheeks.

The residuals from her books were nothing to cry about, even though every little bit helped. It was the freezing of funds that showed how much power Global truly had. What if they *had* gotten to the judge? Trial would be the worst thing she could do. Losing the trial would be worse than simply walking away.

She sucked a deep breath and opened her eyes, then wiped her cheeks with her sleeves. But she did not have the motivation to get off the floor. Glancing up, she saw her newspaper. She grabbed it, then removed it from the plastic bag. A white envelope fell onto her lap. Setting the paper on the floor, she inspected the envelope. There were no markings. No name. No address. She opened it and a fear of a new kind filled her every cell.

CHAPTER 3

DARBY'S HEART RACED uncontrollably. She called Tom, but his phone went directly to voicemail. She headed upstairs and slid the note into the copy machine, then made three copies. The sheets were coming off her printer when her phone rang, and she jumped.

"Did you see the memo?" Neil asked.

"No. What memo?" she said. "But forget that, I need to tell you something."

"This one's kind of funny," Neil said, ignoring her.

"Neil, did you hear me?" she snapped. "This is serious!"

Neil was her ex-boyfriend. They had broken up because she wouldn't give up her job for a family, and he didn't think she could do both. But they remained good friends. More like an old married couple the way they argued.

"Whoa," Neil said. "Did I wake you up on the wrong side of the bed or what?"

"I've been awake since oh-God four hundred hours working on legal shit, the fucking story of my life," she said, pulling a hand through her hair. "My editor just told me that they are freezing my residuals, and then I got an effing warning on my porch this morning."

"Holy shit," Neil said. "I'm sorry."

Darby closed her eyes and breathed deep. "No. I'm sorry. You don't deserve this. It's not that big of a deal. Tell me about the memo."

She set her phone on the bed with the speaker on to listen to Neil while she got dressed.

"We almost lost a 757 a few weeks ago. A medical divert in the middle of the night followed by the crew falling asleep on short final." He explained what happened and finished with, "It damn near went off the end of the runway."

"I'm surprised there's a memo so quickly," Darby said, zipping up her jeans. Global normally hid these events. If they avoided them long enough, they could pretend nothing ever happened. She grabbed her socks and shoes and sat on the bed, beside her phone.

"They blamed the pilots for not napping before they flew their evening flight," Neil said. "And they recommend that we stand up, talk, and drink more coffee."

"On short final?" Darby said incredulously, as she pulled on a shoe. "And the FAA approved that solution?"

"Global owns the FAA with Wyatt as the Administrator."

"He's not the Administrator yet," Darby said, pulling on the other shoe. "And, if there's anything I can do to stop him, I will."

"I'd like to help, but there is only one way to prevent that from happening and… well, you know…I've never killed anyone before," Neil said. "But I have read a lot of obituaries with great pleasure."

"I've got a few I'd like to read with pleasure. Speaking of which, how's the girlfriend these days?"

"She's not my girlfriend," Neil said, "she's my fiancé."

"Yeah, don't remind me."

"I'm going to tell you something, but only because I love you," Neil said.

"Of course, you are."

There was a time she had loved him too. Those days were gone, but they had remained good friends. Despite his dumping her because she wouldn't quit flying to raise a family, his fiancé was not only a pilot, but she was also a mother.

"You're turning into a bitch. You need to shake out of this."

"They say life's a bitch and then you become one," Darby said, but his words bit deep.

"Is winning this trial worth it?" Neil said. "I mean you got your job back, so maybe you should just give it up."

"I can't believe you, of all people, would have the audacity to say that to me," Darby snapped. She lifted the phone, turned off the speaker and placed it to her ear.

"I'm just saying that if it's destroying your life, what's the point?"

"Is this because you don't you want to testify?" Darby asked.

"No. Of course not. That's not why I'm saying this. I'll be there for you, It's just…"

"Just what?" Darby snapped.

"Nothing. It's just that I care about you," Neil said. "I've got to go."

Darby said goodbye and threw her phone across the room into a pile of laundry. This legal battle had been a struggle that she'd never expected. He was right, she was a bitch. She just wasn't sure how to maintain the persona of who she used to be. She wasn't happy. She faked it. She had loved flying more than anything, and Global took that away from her. Now the company was trying to bankrupt her. Even if she won, she could still lose.

Darby stood and removed the note from the printer, wondering if Neil had anything to do with it. She folded it and placed it into her purse. Then retrieved her phone and glanced at the time. There was still an hour before she had to be there, but she grabbed her keys and headed for the door.

CHAPTER 4

DARBY DROVE TO Tom's apartment and parked on the street. She knew he was out of town, but he was the reminder that she had goodness in her life. She felt horrible that Neil thought that she was a bitch, but more so that he had suggested she give up the trial. How could he not understand? Tom would understand, but he wouldn't be back in town until evening.

Darby sat in front of Tom's house for fifty minutes thinking, then she drove to the coffee shop and pulled into the parking lot. She sat in her car for a moment to gain her composure. She breathed deep and told herself everything was going to be okay. What options did she have? Not many.

Walking into the coffee shop she saw Linda and Jackie sitting at a table on the far side of the room. Darby waved and headed their way. Forcing a smile that she didn't feel.

"I ordered you a raspberry mocha with whipped cream," Linda said.

"Thank you," Darby said pulling out a chair. She sat and reached for her drink. Then she asked, "Am I a bitch?"

Linda and Jackie exchanged a look before Linda said, "No. Of course not."

"You paused," Darby said, then she leaned forward, dropping her forehead on the table. With her face down she said, half under her breath, "I am a bitch."

"Are you okay?" Jackie asked, placing a hand on her back.

Darby raised her head and sat upright. She looked at her friends, sighed, and said, "I hate being this person fighting all the time. I hate this company. I hate Wyatt and Clark and the asshole doctors and everyone we deposed. They fucking set me up to destroy me, to make sure I would never fly again, and now we're going to trial in three days and I'm not ready for this."

"Yes, you are," Linda said. "You are the strongest person I know."

Darby shook her head. She wiped away a tear that had trickled out, and lifted her cup hoping that sipping her drink would keep her from breaking down and sobbing. She wasn't sure if any of this would ever be okay. "I'm not that strong on the inside."

"The hell you're not," Jackie said. "Despite everything, you're still standing. You will bounce back to the old you. Just give it time. This is almost over."

"Maybe. If they don't kill me first," Darby said.

"I think Clark already tried that," Linda said with a grin. "If I remember correctly, he failed."

"I don't know how much longer I can do this," Darby said, looking at each of her friends with a plea for help. She wanted them to tell her to give it up. To tell her that her efforts were useless. She needed them to tell her that they would love her anyway, even if she wasn't that strong person that they expected to fight dragons.

"As long as it takes," Linda said.

"You're a winner. Winners don't quit," Jackie said with a sing-song voice. "You win, that's what you do!"

Darby laughed and slumped back into her chair and said, "I love you guys."

She sipped her coffee and then said, "I need to show you something."

She set her cup on the table and removed the note from her purse, unfolded it and slid it across the table between Linda and Jackie.

"What's this?" Linda asked.

"A warning for me not to go to trial," Darby said.

"Is it a threat?" Jackie asked, looking at it for a moment. "Or is it someone on your side warning you, like they know something?"

"I took it as a threat," Darby said. Then she read it aloud. "Warning. Do not go through with this trial." It had a juvenile tone to it, but what scared her was it was what she had asked for in her prayers—an answer on how to proceed. If trial was the right thing to do.

"It does say warning," Linda said, "But it kind of sounds threatening to me, too."

"It sounds too nice to be a threat," Jackie said. "It says warning, and that's probably what it is. I mean why is Global going to trial anyway? Maybe someone knows Global bought the judge and is trying to warn you about that."

"Have you talked to Tom?" Linda asked.

Darby shook her head and said, "He won't be home until this evening."

"This kind of freaks me out," Jackie said.

"I need to get a grip," Darby said. "I've been having nightmares that they're going to attack me on the stand with something horrific from my past."

"Like what?" Linda asked.

"I don't know. Maybe I slept with the football team in high school or something."

"Did you?" Jackie asked.

"No. But what if I was so drunk that I don't remember? And what if there were pictures that I don't know about, and they found them?"

This time Jackie laughed. She covered Darby's hand with her own.

"They could find out that you made out with a frog, and it wouldn't matter. Own your truth and live with it."

"Yeah, I think I did kiss a couple toads," Darby said. "But seriously, what should I do?"

"About what?" Jackie asked, with her mouth full of chocolate scone.

"About this," Darby said pointing to the note. "About going to trial. And my publisher told me that they froze my residuals until this is over. If I don't win, I lose them permanently."

"Oh my God," Jackie said. "They can't do that."

"They can't, but they did," Darby said. Then she lowered her voice and said, "Global is behind it. They own the FAA. They own the union. How the hell can I trust they don't own the judge too? Maybe this *is* from someone who knows the truth."

"You're going to be fine," Linda said. "You need to go with the process, kick some ass, and clean up the courtroom with the management team as your rag. You can't fix this. You just must experience it. You'll be fine."

"But what if she loses," Jackie said to Linda. "What if she spends all this money on the trial, and at the end of the day the trial was fixed? Would it be so bad to walk away and just end it now?"

"No, it wouldn't," Linda said. "But Darby has to decide."

"It's not something that I haven't asked myself," Darby said.

"What if you don't win?" Jackie said. "This whole thing has put so much stress on you. I just don't want them to bankrupt you, too."

"The case is simple, and you will win," Linda said. "You gave senior management a safety report. Your airline managers paid a doctor a disgusting amount of money to give you a disqualifying medical diagnosis because of that report. At the end of the day, the FAA, the Mayo Clinic, your flight physician, all knew the truth. You did nothing wrong. So, I don't think you should quit. Go into trial with your head held high and let your attorney work his magic."

"I agree with Linda in part," Jackie said. "But this should never have happened to you in the first place. I'm just saying, you would not be a failure if you walked away."

"This is financially draining," Darby said. "If I only get ninety percent of my attorney fees, and the typical 50K, even if I win, I'll be in the hole."

"That can't be possible," Jackie said.

"The AIR21 law is controlled by the company, and it protects the airline more than the employee," Darby said.

"But this was never about money," Linda said. "It's been about safety."

"You got that right," Darby said. "I just never imagined that I would be gambling over a million dollars on safety in a courtroom."

"You have nothing to worry about," Linda said.

Darby forced a smile. She suspected she had everything to worry about, otherwise Global would not be taking this next step. But Robert Allen was, bar none, the best AIR21 attorney there was. And she had not gone this far for nothing.

"I do need to change my attitude," Darby said. "I was so much more fun when I was playing strip poker and drinking with you before all this happened."

"Murder, death, and plane crashes have a way of changing someone," Linda said, with a tear filling her eye.

Darby reached for her hand and squeezed. Linda's life had changed when her husband died in one of those crashes. She glanced at Jackie and took her hand, too. She also lost her husband in a needless crash. They both moved on and remarried. Jackie had married John McCallister, Kathryn Jacob's old boss from the NTSB. Now Kathryn worked for the FAA and John for the Department of Transportation.

Kathryn had the title but no authority, and John knew more than he was letting on. Linda went back to school, became a therapist, and married a surgeon named Niman. Linda had helped Darby emotionally through this ordeal.

"You need to fight this for safety," Linda said. "Or nothing will change."

"Is this still a fight for safety?" Darby asked. "Or have we shifted to a fight for justice?"

At this point, Darby knew that she could not have one without the other. Justice had to prevail in this case, or passengers would continue participating in a game of Russian Roulette every time they stepped on a plane.

CHAPTER 5

RICH CLARK LOOKED at his Rolex for the second time in the previous hour. He was tired of wasting time with this bullshit. Darby Bradshaw had destroyed enough of his life and had caused him more grief than he'd ever believed possible. With a little luck she'd soon be gone. But this…this was nothing but another time suck. They had already spent three hours reviewing his pending testimony and he wasn't even scheduled in court for another week.

"I know this is frustrating," Wendel said. "But we need to create testimony that will prove Global *had* to take this action against Ms. Bradshaw."

Wendel Kowalski was one of Global's attorneys from the law firm they had engaged. He had also represented Clark during his deposition. Johnson Von Dietrich decidedly no showed, and Clark suspected it was due to the videotaping of that event.

"No, no," Clark said. "I appreciate you both for expert tutelage."

Croft said they were the best and would clear him of all wrong-doing. He should appreciate them, but he detested attorneys more than he disliked female pilots. He simply had to play the game until it was over.

"Thank you," Von Dietrich said. He folded his hands in his lap and added, "Your testimony must show that this was the doctors' decision to send Bradshaw to a mental health evaluation. Not yours. They are the mental health experts and you relied on their assertions. You had no choice."

Clark nodded in agreement, but they were wrong. He had the power to do whatever he damn well pleased because he owned Croft. What he knew would destroy the CEO. Nothing spoke volumes like a good photo and documentation of illegal activities. He and Croft had an understanding.

Flight operations was his with the promise of another promotion at the close of trial. He would then become the CEO of Global's wholly owned subsidiary airline, and eventually at Global when the time was right. When he could finally rid himself of Croft. The buzzer on his desk announced his secretary, and he welcomed the interruption.

"Excuse me gentlemen," he said and answered.

"Captain Wyatt and Mr. Croft are on their way up," his secretary announced.

"Thank you," he said. "Well gentlemen, looks like we might have to end our meeting for today." Clark stood and moved away from his desk.

"Of course," Von Dietrich said and stood.

"Please review these questions and responses we've written for you," Wendel said handing him multiple sheets of paper.

"Thank you, I'll study them as if my life depended on it," Clark said as the door opened.

"It just might," Walter Croft said from the doorway. Then he smiled.

"Mr. Croft," Clark said, then turned toward Wyatt. "Good to see you again."

George Wyatt had been Clark's boss until he retired, to get out of the legal line-of-fire of this trial and ensure his position as the FAA Administrator. A little thing called larceny prompted that early retirement.

"I'm glad to find you both here," Wyatt said to the attorneys as they shook hands. "Where's your lovely little sidekick, Ms. Narcea?"

"Morning sickness," Von Dietrich said flatly.

"That rests my case," Clark said with a chuckle. Narcea was the female attorney they brought in for diversity and inclusion. A total waste of space as far as he was concerned.

Croft assessed Clark for a moment, and then turned to the legal team. "I must provide assurance to the board, that this trial is the best course of action."

"You won't lose," Von Dietrich said with his penetrating dagger-like stare. "This judge is a Republican nominee and an ardent supporter of corporations. You also demonstrated the impeccable professionalism of Captain Clark in contrast to the unprofessional behavior of pilots in front of this same judge with the Samson trial."

"Not to mention Captain Wyatt's nomination to the FAA Administrator's position," Wendel said. "This position will support the strength and integrity of Global Air Lines. His testimony at the confirmation hearing will provide a campaign that the judge cannot overlook."

"But the hearing is three months out," Mr. Croft said, "and after the trial."

"Yes, but his ruling will not be out for months after that," Von Dietrich said. "He will watch the hearing with interest as everyone else in this industry. He'll hear it before he rules on this case."

"Perhaps," Wyatt said, "but I'm concerned that my testimony, and that of Mr. Croft's, might be misconstrued without our cross examination at trial."

Wyatt held a law degree, and his testimony was strong. Strong for Bradshaw. The fact that the CEO of an international airline stated he did not know what an accountable executive meant was suicide. The truth was, Croft didn't know. He was nothing but a glorified accountant that the marketing department dressed up and made the poster boy of the airline. It worked. But Clark also knew that Wyatt's testimony also pointed all fingers at him.

Perhaps the strategy of pointing fingers at the doctors is not such a bad idea, Clark thought.

"Both Wyatt's and Mr. Croft's testimony will be in the form of depositions, since they won't be in court. The judge won't read any of it. The only portions of your testimony the judge may see, will be that of which Robert Allen uses in his final brief," Von Dietrich said.

"There are far too many depositions, witnesses, content, and facts that anything either of you said will be lost in the weeds," Wendel added. "None of it is applicable to causation as to why the doctor placed Bradshaw into mental health evaluation. None of it will matter."

"At the end of the day," Von Dietrich said, "Not unlike the grievance process persuading arbitrators, our office has persuasive power with administrative law judges."

"Good then," Croft said. "Gentlemen, thank you for your time. I would like a few moments with my team."

Wendel and Von Dietrich said their goodbyes and once gone, Croft said, "Thoughts?"

"What they say is true," Wyatt said. "Causation is the only element we are disputing in trial. Allen is focused, but we are both too high in the food chain." He turned his attention to Clark and asked, "Are you prepared?"

"Of course," Clark said. He tossed the stack of papers Wendel had given to him onto his desk. "Let's just get this trial over and continue on with what's important."

"I'm not sure trial is what we should be doing," Wyatt said. "This could be unnecessary media coverage."

"We'll see what happens," Croft said. "I have faith in our legal team."

"What about the board?" Wyatt asked.

"They're taking direction from the Chairman," Croft said, followed by a wide grin.

"How long do we wait until after I'm in position?" Wyatt asked Croft.

"I've been thinking about that," Croft said, walking over to Clark's desk. He glanced at the documents for a moment then turned and sat on the corner of the desk. He pushed his glasses up higher on his nose and said, "We should put this on ice for now."

"We can't," Clark said.

"We can," Croft countered. "Never in the history of Global Air Lines have we seen passenger loads and profits like we have experienced since the MAX crashed. Why risk all that?"

"Because that was the agreement," Wyatt said.

"It was," Croft agreed. "But why mess with a good thing? I never expected results like this."

"I could think of one reason," Clark said. "Wasn't cutting a deal with Airbus enough of a reward? Do you really want to back out now?"

"I'm not saying never," Croft said. "We'll keep our agreement. Eventually."

Clark stared without a word. This was an unbelievably bad idea as far as he was concerned. He did not object to backing out on your deals, it was just who you screwed over, was the issue. More than that, he was looking forward to the climax and next steps.

Croft shifted his attention to Wyatt. "I'm simply saying, that once you're in office you keep the MAX grounded and we can keep this ball rolling."

Wyatt nodded. "That I could do."

"Do you want me to tell him?" Clark asked.

"I'll take care of it," Croft said. "You just make sure you're ready for trial."

CHAPTER 6

KATHRYN SIPPED HER second cup of coffee as she watched arrivals landing to the North. *Not the brightest idea to place the FAA building under the flight path of Sea Tac International Airport,* she thought. Then again, there was not much the FAA did these days that had much thought behind it. The notion of George Wyatt becoming her boss rolled her stomach. He paralleled her ex-husband, Bill Jacobs, in that she suspected he, too, was a sociopath.

It had been years since Bill had orchestrated a crash in the very location where she now sat. A shiver took hold, and she wrapped both hands around her coffee cup to warm herself. Something was up and her discomfort grew daily. She was thankful that Bill was in prison. It worried her to no end, however, that he was spending time with President Drake in the same facility.

They had no proof, but all fingers pointed to the faulty parts in the MAX crashes to be a product of Drake Industries. Bill's name was all over that, as was Drake's.

Then there was Darby.

Kathryn glanced at her watch. This office was not where she

wanted to be. Friday morning coffee with her friends was a much better choice to start her day. She also needed to talk to Darby about the latest Global event. But John had said this meeting was important. Another chill ran through her body. Perhaps it was another near catastrophe, or maybe the pending trial, but something felt horribly off within the world of aviation.

Just as an Alaska 737 approached, her intercom buzzed.

"Kathryn, Mr. McCallister has arrived," her secretary said.

She swiveled her chair toward her desk and pressed a button. "Thank you. Please send him in."

Kathryn set her coffee on the document she was trying to ignore. Standing, she was around her desk to greet John when the door opened.

"Good morning, Kat," John said, pulling the door closed.

"I hope this is important," Kathryn said with feigned look of annoyance. "I'm going to have to answer to your wife as to why I ditched the coffee club this morning."

John chuckled. "I'm more worried what you'll tell Darby."

Kathryn raised an eyebrow and said, "The truth?"

She hated keeping secrets from Darby, but these days she felt forced to remain silent far too often. She hated every minute of the deception she was part of, convincing herself it was for Darby's good. But in truth, she wasn't so sure.

"Maybe not this time," John said, setting a folder on her desk then walking to the credenza to help himself to a cup of coffee.

"What the hell's happening now?" Kathryn asked, returning to her desk. She sat and glanced at the folder John had placed on the edge of her desk, and gently touched it.

John added two cubes of sugar to his cup and then turned towards her. "I don't know what to make of all this."

"Of what?" Kathryn asked, irritated with the drama.

John approached her desk. With his coffee in one hand, he moved the chair with the other to an angle, keeping the door in his vision, and then he sat. That was a new maneuver for John. He was not helping her nerves.

He sipped his coffee, and then smiled. "This is good, what is it?"

"Cinnamon."

Grimacing he said, "I shouldn't have asked."

"Enjoy it and tell me what I should be worried about."

He took a long sip, his traditional delay tactic, then set his cup on the folder.

"As you know, Airbus had planned a two-year extensive flight test program," John said. "But I learned yesterday that they've already successfully concluded their autonomous taxi, takeoff, and landing tests, or what they call the ATTOL project."

"What does that mean, exactly?"

"It means they are one year *ahead* of schedule and have conducted autonomous taxiing, takeoff, and landing of a commercial aircraft through fully automatic vision-based flight tests utilizing on-board image recognition technology. This is a world-first in aviation."

"Then Darby's prophecy is becoming reality quicker than we thought it would," Kathryn said.

John nodded and reached for his cup. "They conducted over five hundred test flights last year, and I'm told approximately four hundred and fifty of those flights were dedicated to gathering raw video data to support and fine-tune algorithms. They also conducted six test flights, each one included five take-offs and landings per run to test autonomous flight capabilities."

"Shit," Kathryn said, fearful of what she'd suspected all along. "I knew that Airbus was exploring autonomous technologies, but you're not saying that…"

"I am," John said not allowing her to finish. "Airbus is researching the use of machine learning algorithms. They're asserting that this technology is to support pilots by enabling them to focus on strategic decision-making and mission management."

"Do you believe that?"

"Not a chance in hell," John said. "They're going to replace pilots."

"Which ties us directly back to the Global attack on Darby," Kathryn said, leaning back in her chair. "She identified the lack of training, forcing pilots to fly fatigued, improper scheduling, all of which led to pilot error and thousands of ASAP reports."

The ASAP system was the FAA approved Aviation Safety Action Program. A kinder gentler FAA that enabled pilots to identify their errors. In exchange for the pilot's self-disclosure, the FAA would not take action against them. The program dictated that the company would analyze the events and create solutions that would include necessary training to prevent similar events in the future. Global had over 25,000 ASAP reports in 2018, logistically making it impossible to evaluate all and solve the multiple problems.

"Darby was correct," John said. He stared into his cup, and then lowered it to his lap and looked up. "Unfortunately, what we thought to be a kill-the-messenger tactic, was not what they were doing when they paid a psychiatrist to permanently disqualify her. I believe that Global management is working with Airbus, and Darby was getting in their way of the bigger picture."

"Do you have any proof of the Airbus connection?" Kathryn asked. This was not something she hadn't wondered many times over. Global cancelling all their Boeing orders and signing exclusively with Airbus had been supposition at best.

"More speculation than proof," John said, exchanging his cup for the folder on her desk. He opened it and handed Kathryn a photo.

"Croft going into Airbus Industries?" Kathryn said, staring at the photo for a moment. Then she handed it back to John, unsure what it meant.

"It wasn't the fact that he entered the building. It was that the meeting was on a Sunday morning with offices closed." John returned the photo to the envelope. "Unfortunately, supposition does not build a case."

"No, it doesn't," Kathryn agreed, but the timing spoke volumes. "Why is Global going to trial? That makes no sense."

Kathryn pushed back from her desk and stood with her back to John, she stared out the window. A Global 757 approached in the distance, but she didn't notice. Her mind was someplace else, trying to figure out what the hell was going on. She turned and glanced at the document that her coffee cup rested upon.

She looked up and said, "They were unable to pull her medical certificate despite their power and money, but what does court do for them? They can't win anything. They're spending more money than they will ever have to pay her so what's their end game?"

"I think they're trying to financially break her," John said. "Or they think the judge will rule in their favor. Maybe they already bought him."

"Despite her not getting some of her attorney fees back, it wouldn't matter if he didn't rule in her favor. She never lost her medical and she's back to flying," Kathryn said, returning to her chair. "She only filed the AIR21 complaint because that damn union was working with the company."

"Global is up to something," John said. "If they weren't, that would indicate complete incompetence of the board of directors."

"That's what scares me," Kathryn said. "But Croft is the Chairman, and that explains so much."

"There's more," John said. "Whomever Tom is working for, ordered him to tell her."

"No," Kathryn said, her hand moving to her mouth. "That would devastate her. Her trial… He can't."

Tom had been one of the police officers who arrived at Darby's house during a break in, and they began dating after that. It was Tom who found the empty prescription bottle and alerted John to the potential of poisoned wine. He was right, and all fingers pointed at Clark for setting Darby up for an apparent suicide after Dr. Wood gave her a permanently disqualifying diagnosis on Christmas Eve. But nothing was as it appeared.

It wasn't until months later that Kathryn learned Tom was not who he'd claimed to be. He was not an officer. He was working for someone. Someone with deep pockets and a great deal of power. John was convinced that Tom was protecting Darby, and therefore, Kathryn promised him that she'd keep quiet. She made that promise to protect Darby.

"He's aware of what it would do to her," John said, "and the reason he came to me. We agreed he'd tell her after the trial. Within minutes of our conversation, Tom received a text, ordering there to be no delay and to tell her immediately."

"Coincidence?" Kathryn asked.

"No." John said with a slight shake of his head. "I had them sweep my office, and we found a bug."

"What the hell?" Kathryn said. She glanced around the space she'd thought to be private. "How did they get into the building?"

"Not here. My home office," John said. "But I did take precautions and swept the entire building, too. Nothing."

"Is this an effort to unravel her during the trial?" Kathryn asked. "And if that's the case, is Tom working for Global?"

"Perhaps, you're right about derailing," John said. "But I have no idea who Tom answers to. If he was on the Global payroll, he would have told Darby instead of me."

"That's a good point," Kathryn said. "Unless it started that way and he's changed his mind because he fell in love with her."

"Perhaps," John said, thinking for a moment, and then said, "I doubt it's Global. He kept the drugged wine away from the police and told me about it instead. But he does have powerful connections someplace."

"John, did you *hear* what you just said? He kept it from the police."

"I just did," John said squeezing the bridge of his nose. "Shit. I trusted that man."

"We all did," Kathryn said closing her eyes to fight the anger she felt with her own betrayal more than Tom's. *Darby will be devastated*, she thought. She sucked a deep breath and shook off the dread. She opened her eyes and said, "I'm going to choose to believe he's a good man."

She had to believe that because anything else would defy her faith in humanity.

John stared at her a moment and then said, "There's more." He glanced at the door and turned his attention back to her. The color draining from his face.

CHAPTER 7

SELF-CARE GOES A long way, Darby thought, pulling on a shoe. Somewhere during her massage Darby decided that she *would* go to trial, despite the consequences. When this all started, she knew the stakes. At the time she was willing to lose her job, her house, her car, and all personal belongings to ensure aviation safety and the safety of her passengers. Now, all she would lose was a shitload of money. She still had her job.

She knew—without justice there was no safety.

Darby slipped the other ruby-red stiletto onto her foot and then extended both legs admiring her pedicure. The color was the same sultry red as her fingernails. Dropping her feet to the floor she reached for her glass of Basil Haden. During her pedicure, she decided that she would not wait until the trial was over to start enjoying her life. Marvin Gaye sang in the background *"Get up, get up."* She smiled and stood.

Swaying to the music, she wasn't sure if alcohol was the best thing to do so close to the decisive battle that was about to occur, but she was not going to let this pending trial take her down any more than it had already. She was long overdue to let her hair down. She had lost her zest for life and decided she would try to find it again.

Darby tugged at her emerald-green, skintight dress and smoothed it over her curves. She had added it to her wardrobe that afternoon with the new shoes. It was mid-length and fit her body like a second skin and was just what she needed tonight. Tom would love it. She reached into the top and adjusted the girls, so they peeked out just a little. Tom would love that also.

Sauntering to the bathroom while swaying to the music, she stumbled and then laughed. Once there, she dropped her head down and then flipped it up for maximum hair fullness, then ran her fingers through it for the final fluff. She added a touch of lipstick as *Aint No Mountain High Enough* began wafting from the living room and she sang with the music.

"If you need me... call me no matter where you are no matter how far..." Puckering her lips, she dabbed them with a tissue and set the lipstick on the counter. Turning left and then right, she assessed herself in the mirror. *Not too bad*, she thought.

"If you ever need a helping hand," she sang returning to the living room.

She stood for a moment staring at the room, biting her lip thinking about how this would work. She moved the armchair to the left of her couch and pushed the coffee table back for more room. Darby then retrieved her crystal glass and twirled to the bar with it, sucking down the water from the melted ice. She reached into the ice bucket and filled the glass with ice. Holding it out with her right hand, she swayed to *Give It Up*.

Marvin Gaye's mix was the perfect choice. An oldie but timeless. She lifted the bottle of Basil Hayden and added two fingers to her glass. She then returned to the living room, found the remote to the fireplace and pressed On. Flames burst into motion. She assessed the room once again, then turned off the lamp. "Perfect," she said.

Flames danced on the ceiling and walls. She grinned at the next song. *Timing is everything,* she thought. Drink in hand she moved with the music.

"Let's get it on…" she sang, swaying her body and sipping her drink at the same time. Then she extended her arm holding the glass out, as if it were her dance partner. She closed her eyes and placed her other hand on her chest and then slowly worked it down abdomen, to her thigh and then…

"Ummm… am I early?" Tom asked.

Darby startled and opened her eyes. "Apparently so," she said with a giggle. She tugged her dress into place again. His broad smile, displaying brilliantly white teeth, moved all the way to his eyes. *Damn he's so cute,* she thought. "Can I get you a drink?"

His eyes dropped to her toes, and then slowly worked up her body until they engaged with hers. "I'll have what you're having," he said.

"You want what I'm having," she said heading toward the bar, "or me?" she called over her shoulder.

"Yes," he said stepping up behind her.

He wrapped his arms around her body and slid a hand where hers had been. The other lifted her hair from her neck, and he placed his lips on her skin. He gently bit, sending a river of chills through her body.

"Both is *not* going to happen if you keep that up," she said breathlessly.

"You're right," he said, removing his lips. His hand lingered, however. "Do we have reservations someplace? I feel under dressed."

"Elliot's Oyster House," Darby said adding ice to a glass. "You're just perfect." She poured his drink with his body nestled up behind her. She then turned facing him. Ignoring his arousal pressed close to her, she looked up into his eyes and held out his drink. "Here you go."

He glanced at it, then brought his attention back to her. His eyes dropped to the top of her dress, and he pulled her closer. If that were even possible.

She smiled and made an effort at taunting allure, blinking her eyes, and he laughed. He kissed her cleavage, then took a step back and accepted his bourbon.

He took a long drink and said, "What time is our reservation?"

"We've got just enough time for a drink, a dance and a long, slow, wet, kiss that could last… uh, maybe thirty minutes," Darby said, taking his hand. She led him to the living room. "The Uber will be here in 45 minutes."

"I was kind of liking the earlier dance," he said with a grin.

"In that case you *are* a little over dressed."

She grabbed the top of his pants and pulled him to her. She set her drink on the coffee table, then unbuckled his belt. She unzipped his khakis, and with a little tug they dropped to the floor. She grabbed both sides of his shorts and slid them down his legs halfway, then stood upright and placed a heel between his legs, stepping on his shorts she pushed them to the floor. She nudged him back just enough for him to step free.

"I don't know what the hell has got into you," he said, stumbling a bit. "But I like it."

Darby reached for his shirt, unbuttoned the top button, and placed her lips on his skin and kissed. She then looked into his eyes and said, "You can blame this on Carol." She returned to unbuttoning and kissing his skin as she did.

"I don't know who the hell Carol is," he moaned. "But you'll have to thank her for me."

Darby grinned. *You and me both*, she thought. She removed his shirt and tossed it onto the back of the black leather couch. Then tilted her head back. Placing her lips to his, she kissed him chastely while pushing him backwards until they could go no farther.

"Sit," she whispered. Placing a hand to his chest, she pushed him onto the easy chair.

"Yes ma'am."

She turned and retrieved her drink then lifted the remote to the stereo. She pressed a couple buttons and restarted *Let's Get it On* and cranked up the volume. Tom sipped his drink, but the grin never wavered. She began dancing with the flames as she sipped her drink, then she returned it to the coffee table.

"I've been really tryin' baby," she sang with the music, slowly sliding a strap off her shoulder, she removed an arm. "Trying to hold back these feelings for so long."

Tom retained the biggest smile she'd ever seen. She loved it. He was happy. That made her happy.

"And if you feel like I feel baby… then come on, come on…" she sang freeing her other arm from the strap. "Oohh… let's get it on…" she sang slipping hands inside the top of dress and then sliding it down her body. "Ahh baby… let's get it on…" Her dress dropped to the floor, and she stepped over the pile of clothes and reached for her drink.

She turned toward him swaying with the music singing, "Sugar let's get it on…" thankful the music was loud enough so he couldn't hear her singing out of tune. Wearing nothing but her four-inch stilettos, she sipped her bourbon and danced toward him with shadows dancing on her body. She set her drink on the table to his right, and he placed his glass beside hers.

Then with a leg on each side of the chair she held his shoulders and bent over pressing her mouth to his. Then she slowly lowered herself onto him. They became one, and that kiss lasted a little longer than 30 minutes. The Uber waited.

CHAPTER 8

TOM HAD BEEN watching the tracking monitor on and off for the previous two hours. The order was to keep tracking until he told her the truth. Darby's car remained parked at a professional complex twenty minutes away. She had not moved since he'd been watching her. Short of driving to the location to see which door she would exit; he could only guess. The order was to plant the monitoring device on her and not the car, but he had refused. Not that this wasn't bad enough. But he did not want to violate her more than he had.

He knew the businesses inside well. Law Office. Pilates. Oncologist. Counseling. Physical Therapy. Massage therapy. Starbucks. A bookstore. She had been to the same location weekly for the previous two months when in town, and yet she never spoke a word. He wondered what she was keeping from him.

As much as he wanted to confide in her, he wanted her to trust him enough to tell him what she was doing. If only he could turn back time and tell her the truth before they had fallen in love. Maybe they would have had a chance. Now he feared it had been too long. Now she would never trust him. And he could not blame her.

Tom sent Darby a text—*Heading to your house. See you soon.*

He grabbed his keys, picked up the monitor and walked out his apartment door.

Darby was full of surprises, and the previous night—*holy shit*, he thought. He stirred, just thinking about the night they'd experienced as he climbed into the car. He wanted a lifetime of that. Then there was dinner. The best time they'd had in a long time. It wasn't as much the food they ate, but the laughter between each bite. He grinned, thinking that he still needed to thank Carol, whoever the hell she was.

Saturday traffic was light, and within no time he pulled into Darby's driveway. He glanced at his watch. They were planning to pick up her attorney at the airport and have an early dinner with him. Tom glanced at the monitor as he got out of his car. She hadn't moved yet, and they had only an hour until Robert's flight landed.

He opened the trunk and placed the monitor inside when his phone rang.

"Tom, is Darby with you?" Kathryn asked. "She's not answering her phone."

"No," he said glancing at the screen then closing the trunk. He headed for her door and added, "She should be back within the hour. I'll tell her you called."

"Do you have a minute to talk?" Kathryn said.

"I'm actually in the middle of something, can we talk later?" he said. He knew exactly what she wanted to discuss, and he didn't have the heart to get into that today.

Darby had been under a great deal of pressure for such a long time. He was glad to relieve the pressure, if only for a night. But something in her changed last night. She behaved as if this battle was just starting and had not been ongoing for the previous three years. Maybe she viewed this as a new fight. In a way, it was.

Despite everything, he was falling in love with her all over again. Falling in love with a different version of the same person. "I'm going to make this right," he whispered, opening her front door. He stepped inside and deactivated the alarm.

George Wyatt was about to become the FAA administrator, despite his participation in the attack against her. Croft was still running the airline. Scumbag attorneys and the dirty doctors roamed the cities. The lying pass-travel bitch, who feigned being an HR investigator, still wreaked havoc on employees. It was all Tom could do to not rid the world of these assholes. Their time would come. And when it did, he wanted to be part of their demise.

Tom opened the fridge and grabbed a beer. He wandered into her living room and sat on the couch. With one leg crossed over the other, he stared at his beer for a moment, and then took a long pull. His phone buzzed. He glanced at the message and closed his eyes for a moment.

Sucking a deep breath, he took another swig of his beer, and then typed, "No." His thumb hovered over the send button for a moment, then he pressed.

It buzzed with the question—*Alone?*

He responded—*Yes.*

He stared at his phone, and then said, "Five, four, three, two," and it rang. He let it ring twice before he answered. "Hello Sir," he said and cringed at the expected outrage on the other end of the line. He took another pull on his beer and stared at the wall as the diatribe rolled off his back. "Yes, Sir… uh huh… I'm sorry I can't do that."

He closed his eyes and listened to the rant, and when there was a break he said, "Sir, let me rephrase, I won't do that." *What could he do to him now?*

The next statement he expected, and Tom said, "Then fire me."

And then fireworks began. Tom held the phone away from his ear as he sipped his beer. He'd had enough. He would let the chips fall where they may. But he was not going to tell Darby anything ever. He was not going to be a part of any of this anymore. Whatever the hell this was. He would live his truth and prayed that his life would be with Darby. But he knew she was in danger.

"I hear you," Tom finally said, then added, "I understand what you want. But you need to understand that I am not going to do that."

"Do what?" Darby said from the doorway.

Tom startled, then smiled at her. He held up a finger and mouthed, "Just a second," and returned his attention to the phone. "Sir, I have to go. The most beautiful woman just walked in."

He ended the call, moved toward Darby and pulled her into an embrace. He placed a finger under her chin and tilted her head toward him and kissed her deeply. "Thanks for a wonderful night last night," he said, and then asked, "Did you have a nice afternoon?"

"I did," she said, hesitantly, and then asked again, "What aren't you going to do?"

"I'm not going on any assignments out of town until this is over," he said, wrapping her in his arms so she couldn't see the lie in his eyes. "Oh, and Kathryn's looking for you."

Darby glanced at her watch and said, "I'll give her a quick call, then we can go."

He was off the hook for the moment. But that note she received with the warning concerned him deeply. He'd had her house under surveillance, so how did they pull it off? Who sent it? Why? He didn't feel it was a threat to her life, but those few words opened a hell of a lot of speculation as to who sent it and why.

CHAPTER 9

PRESIDENT DRAKE CLOSED the flip phone and threw the fucking thing at the wall. The archaic technology did not fuel his anger, at least he had a phone and could make calls without bothering the Warden. It was the message he had just received that infuriated him.

"This fucking prison," Drake said. The trial would start in two days. They were keeping Darby Bradshaw out of the picture, but that was not their only agreement. He'd never expected this from someone he'd worked so closely with and trusted.

Drake called the guard to escort him to the yard before the afternoon break. He wanted Bill Jacobs there, too. Drake walked by the other inmates' cells with cuffs in place. Once in the yard they released them. He walked to the far wall and gazed out at the city. A world he would be part of again soon. The haze was thicker than usual and mirrored his mood.

"Boss," Bill said approaching from behind.

Drake folded his arms but did not turn. "We have a problem. That fucker double-crossed me."

Drake appreciated the fact that Jacobs did not tell him that he was not surprised. He liked Bill Jacobs. The guy had balls. He was also a wealth of information and had helped him immensely in taking down the MAX aircraft. Jacobs also knew Bradshaw, intimately.

"Is there someone else you could get to do the job?" Bill asked. He turned and leaned against the wall beside him. Bill looked across the yard with his back to the city, while covering Drake's back.

"Remember how I replied when you asked if I was afraid China would bring my technology to market while I was stuck in here?"

Bill thought for a moment and said, "I think it was something to the effect that there was nothing a little virus couldn't solve."

Drake smiled. "I've been working on that something for a few months. I just didn't know when to activate it."

"And you do now?" Bill asked.

"I do," Drake said. Jacobs did not probe. That, too, he appreciated. Bill Jacobs was solid. He'd proven himself in his ability to take life for a greater goal. He was also a man he could trust. He then asked Bill, "How would you like a job?"

CHAPTER 10

THEY SAID JUSTICE was quick, but *they* had to be referring to a guillotine. Two years had already passed since Darby had filed her complaint. She was glad it was about to start, but only because she would be that much closer to the end. Regardless, she was surprised how nervous she felt sitting in the courtroom. Her fate to be decided by one man.

She and Robert had worked all day Sunday, followed by a restless night of sleep for Darby. Her nightmares included a mass shooting in the courtroom, compliments of too much melatonin. As much as she was determined to not give a shit and let the chips fall where they may, the outcome was far too important. The truth is, she cared more about the resultant safety than her pocketbook. Dollars could be replaced, lives could not.

Darby took a calming breath and pulled her attention from the window. She focused on the judge as he discussed preliminaries. She portrayed undivided attention, hanging on every word, but was still aware of every plane that departed to the South disappearing into the distance.

This courtroom was on the top floor of the FAA building just south of SeaTac airport. Kathryn's office was three doors down the hall. If Bill Jacobs was playing his games today, nobody would be safe. This was the crash site of Greg's plane, Jackie's husband who died shortly thereafter. She knew exactly where a suicidal pilot would aim today, especially one screwed over by the system.

Judge Patrick Geraghty was presiding. Stately was the best word to describe him as he walked into the courtroom. There was a presence about him like none she had seen in an extraordinarily long time. He was a mixture of authority and calmness with an understated knowledge. He was now schooling the parties on the process, and she could have heard a pin drop.

"I'll tell the parties, I routinely receive these vast quantities of documentary exhibits, which at the end of the day about half of them end up *not* being utilized by either party in their presentation or in their briefs. The parties are forewarned," he said looking between the tables, "that if it's not identified in your briefs, as relevant or persuasive for your case, accordingly, I will give them little or no weight. I'll let you, at the end of the day, tell me what really is important for me to decide when it comes to deciding this case.

"All right. Ms. Bradshaw, under AIR21, a Complainant must show, by a preponderance of the evidence, the employer is subject to the Act and the employee is covered under the Act. It's my understanding that that has been stipulated to by the parties, is that correct?" he asked, looking between the tables.

"Yes, Your Honor," Robert said, followed by Global's attorney, Wendel's, concurrence.

"All right," Judge Geraghty said, returning his attention to the documents on his podium. "Number two, that you engaged in protected activity. I have separately made a finding that the referral to a mental health evaluation was an adverse action. That does not mean that other protected activities could not either be raised or established in this hearing." He glanced up for a moment, perhaps to see if the attorneys were listening, and then returned his attention to the document in front of him.

"Number three, that Global was aware of or had knowledge of the protected activity. Number four, that the employee suffered an unfavorable or an adverse personnel action at the behest of the employer. Number five, the protected activity was a contributing factor in the unfavorable action. It need not be the *primary* reason," he said with emphasis. "It just has to be a factor in an unfavorable action. If the Complainant proves its case of retaliation under AIR21, that she is entitled to relief, unless the respondent demonstrates, by clear and convincing evidence, that it would have taken the same unfavorable action absent that protected activity."

He looked up, and asked, "Are there any specific provisions that either party wants me to take official notice of, as far as the regulations, advisory circulars, anything of that nature?"

"Not at the outset of the hearing," Robert said. "I think those will be highlighted as we go through the process."

Wendel shook his head and said, "No."

"All right," Judge Geraghty said, and continued to discuss the details of the proceedings.

Darby had assumed this would have been a jury trial. When she learned that AIR21 cases were in front of an administrative law judge, she had been worried. Having her case decided by one person who could be bought and paid for, like Dr. Wood, was disconcerting. Robert told her otherwise because he had faith in the system. She wasn't so sure.

She had done her research and could not find a case that Geraghty did not find for the company based on a legal technicality. His admonishments toward various airlines in those rulings identified that he knew what management had done was wrong, but the law enabled him, or perhaps forced him, to rule in favor of the company regardless. The law slanted toward the company, not the employee, and was something Darby would change when this was over.

If this judge was on the fence, she suspected he would give the benefit of doubt to the airline. Robert had said that Geraghty was as straight as they came. Robert had the highest respect for this ALJ named Patrick Geraghty. That had to be good enough for her.

I have truth on my side, justice will be served, everything will be okay, Darby prayed for the umpteenth time over the preceding week.

CHAPTER 11

ROBERT BEGAN. "WE want to start off by briefly referencing the protected activity, because it is unusual in its scope. And will become relevant in terms of what impacts other elements of the prima facie case.

"The parties have stipulated that Ms. Bradshaw engaged in protected activity by, among other things, raising issues regarding pilot fatigue, pilot training, pilot training records and Global's Safety Management Systems, or SMS program, mandated under 14 CFR Part 5.

"We would highlight that one of the primary vehicles for the protected activity was the 45-page safety report first presented to Captains Wyatt and Clark, the senior vice president of flight operations and the vice president of flight operations, respectively.

"The Tribunal has already held that the grounding of Ms. Bradshaw for the compulsory mental health evaluation, which ultimately included a psychiatric examination by Dr. Kenneth Wood, constituted an adverse action."

In response to the contributing factor, Robert reminded the judge that employers rarely admit their discriminatory intent; therefore, they had to rely on circumstantial evidence. This would include temporal proximity, meaning that her reporting and their grounding her following that report were close together, followed by their forcing her into an abusive psychiatric evaluation termed an adverse action. Darby called it what it was—retaliation. When the airline creates false pretext, uses inconsistent applications of company policies, and shifts explanations of their actions, these behaviors support circumstantial evidence.

"With respect to the initial grounding of Ms. Bradshaw and the Section 8 referral, the evidence we present will focus, primarily, on *Global's* contention that the 'sole' reason for directing the Section 8 evaluation was Ms. Bradshaw's statements and her conduct during an Equal Opportunity or EO investigation."

Darby had no idea that that meeting was an EO investigation. Clark had told her she was meeting with an HR safety investigator. He only told her that because she previously refused to speak to Equal Opportunity. Her concerns were safety related.

"We will present evidence that, with respect to the adverse action of the psychiatric examination and its abusive nature, and the ultimate result of an adverse diagnoses—the contributing factor issue is both easier and harder. I say easier, because in Dr. Wood's report, on its face, there's a reflection that Ms. Bradshaw's protected activity contributed to his diagnoses.

"The more complicated question is whether Global should be considered to have been a partner in the adverse evaluation process, and we will submit evidence that Global, by its actions, did assume that status," Robert said.

Darby observed Geraghty. He listened intently without showing any emotion or indication of what he was thinking. If he played poker, he was probably exceptionally good.

"Global has *repeatedly* invoked the Germanwings tragedy, by way of asserting the threat to safe options, should the carrier not prevail in this case. Now, we believe that hundreds, if not thousands, of pilots—of Global pilots—who do not possess Ms. Bradshaw's courage, are now wondering what consequences they might suffer if they report pilot fatigue, deficient pilot training or SMS violations. We, respectfully, submit that such gnawing doubt in the pilot community at Global presents the greater threat to the public interest. Thank you."

Judge Geraghty didn't allow more than a few seconds to lapse after Robert's final words before he turned toward Wendel and said, "Counsel?"

CHAPTER 12

WENDEL GLANCED AT Robert and smiled, then returned his attention to the Judge. That man irritated Darby to no end. He was a gnat on the ass of life, and she so wanted to squash the little bug. To date, she could assert that he was annoying, rude, and made false statements, all of which she had observed in the depositions and from reading his motions. He doesn't tell the truth.

"I appreciate the brevity of Complainant's opening statement. We'll try to be succinct, as well. But I'll start kind of where he ended," Wendel said. "There is nothing more important in this industry than doing everything possible to protect the safety of the human beings, the women, the men who—the boys and girls—who get on airplanes every day.

"And during this case what you're going to hear is evidence, *real* evidence, that the people who work at Global spend every day compulsively thinking about safety, that they make decisions every day that make crystal clear that safety governs before anything else— before scheduling, before revenue, before relationships and certainly and absolutely before concerns about hard feelings or litigation risk.

"Why does that matter? Because at least two reasons—because the evidence that you'll hear in this case is that the Global decision

makers here—Rich Clark, who you'll hear from, head of flight operations, Ann Abbott, a human resource professional with two decades
of experience, Joe Wolfe, an attorney and labor relations specialist,
Robert Dodson, who is here now, another veteran and chief pilot at
Global, two medical professionals—all of them, all of them acted, at
all times, in every way, with integrity and with that principle firmly
in mind—safety first, always safety first!

Safety my ass, Darby thought. Her heart began to speed up. Global
was all about profit, to hell with safety. She listened with disgust,
trying to keep the faith that Robert could shove those assertions
right up their collective asses. But she showed no reflection of her
emotions. She, too, played poker and knew the power of tells. Some
you gave, some you did not.

"Secondly," Wendel continued, "it's important because the stakes
here are so high—one of the few times we might agree during the
week we're spending here together—they couldn't be higher. We'll
demonstrate that the Complainant, through this action and the
allegations against these *good* people who you'll hear from, would
undermine Global's commitment to safety.

"And so we're here to show you that evidence, to ask you to
interpret the law, and to ultimately uphold and recognize that far
from retaliating against Complainant in this case, in a way that
would diminish safety or cover up legitimate safety concerns, Global
Air Lines, when it placed Complainant within its medical review
process—which is defined in Section 8 of its Collective Bargaining
Agreement—acted consistent, consistent with its mandate, consistent
with its negotiated Collective Bargaining Agreement, and consistent
with its primary duty, its *sacred* duty under FAA rules in general,
notions of public policy to preserve safety!"

That sanctimonious little dweeb, Darby thought. Had she described

Wendel prior to trial her analysis would have been that he was whiny and theatrical. Someone who lacked emotional restraint. But today he was on some self-proclaimed pedestal spouting a sacred duty that Global management defied daily.

Darby had often wondered where the hell they found him and how he became an attorney at such a prestigious law firm. Now she realized they must have unearthed him at an evangelistic riverside revival. She glanced at the judge, who still showed no emotion. Darby wasn't sure if he was buying Wendel's sanctimonious load of crap or if he'd heard it all before and allowed it to roll off his back.

"Here's what we're going to present," Wendel continued. "And we should start, really, by pointing out what you, your Honor, stated at the onset of this case. We've stipulated that Complainant engaged in protected activity under the statute when she made her report to Captain Clark and Captain Wyatt. So, this hearing should *not* be about grinding through the specific safety related issues that she raised in that document. Global has never contested—never contested—that Complainant raised those issues, for any reason other than that she, herself, is concerned about safety—as she should be."

What the fuck? They never contested my ass! Darby glanced at Geraghty, hoping he, too, would remember the history and falsity of that statement. Global contested the protected activity every step of the way until the judge finally ruled in her favor only a few months earlier, saying they did in fact violate federal regulations.

Dumbfounded, Darby could not believe how Wendel could sit before an ALJ, in a court of law, and lie. Of course, he doesn't want the hearing to be grinding through the facts of Global's unsafe behavior, falsification of records and retaliatory culture that they wanted kept hidden. Darby forced herself to breathe deep and she buried her emotions.

"Global expects every pilot, every employee, to be committed to safety, and the evidence will demonstrate, beyond any doubt, that Global took those concerns seriously, as it should. You'll hear and see that the heads of Global's Flight Operations met with her. These are not low-level employees… these are the top people at Global! You'll see that Mr. Clark painstakingly went through her report, which is a disorganized, convoluted, rambling report—and you'll see that, you'll have that document—and he tried to parse out the safety issues from a whole bunch of other personal disputes."

Disorganized, convoluted, and rambling? Darby thought. She suspected if she had presented that report in a doctoral course at Embry Riddle Aeronautical University, she would have received an A. They were hitting below the belt. How the hell could they lie in court? If nobody was accountable for their lies, there would be no way anyone could receive justice.

"Captain Clark tried to do his best," Wendel continued. "Why? Because, as he is going to explain, and as Mr. Wyatt—who just, as we know, was nominated to a pretty important job here—testified that Global is always seeking continuous improvement in the areas of safety and he listens to every single pilot when they come up with concerns. So, you'll see that Captain Clark personally reviewed the safety issues that First Officer Bradshaw raised.

"He enlisted others, and he invited First Officer Bradshaw to address Global's most senior safety officers, to both educate *her*, because she didn't seem to understand what Global was doing, and because she had some things that were just wrong— and you'll hear about that—and to allow her to share her ideas."

Fucking educate me? Darby thought. She could not believe what she was hearing. The ignorance of that statement frightened her to no end. She had thought this was going to be a fair trial, but Global was reaching beyond reality to destroy her. And they had very deep pockets. Darby suddenly realized that they may get away with this after all.

"And that meeting happened, and it happened notwithstanding the Section 8 process that we're here about. It happened *after* the Section 8 referral, hardly evidence suggesting a cover up or an effort to discredit Ms. Bradshaw, it's the opposite of that. You'll see the documents that show that Global credited Ms. Bradshaw for some of the ideas that she raised. You'll see that they engaged her in dialogue. And you'll hear—I think you'll hear—the word Safety culture used in this case quite a bit, and that's a vague sort of a term, Safety culture.

"I think Ms. Bradshaw will contend that pretty much everything an air carrier does, from interpersonal relationships to diversity, to compensation, to allegations of unequal treatment, all that impacts Safety culture in some way. And that seems a little bit of an over-broad definition, but regardless of that, what you'll see is that Global is relentlessly committed to Safety culture and you'll see that evidence."

Safety culture is a vague term? She had googled safety culture and 1.6 million items populated. There were over 4,000 books written on the subject, and an FAA search related to Safety culture populated well over three million documents. She felt as if her heart was to break out of her chest with the violent pounding. She took a couple slow calming breaths. *Relax. I have truth on my side, justice will be served, everything will be okay,* she silently prayed.

"There may be an allegation that Captain Clark thought about Section 8 before the meeting, but what you won't see is anything from the meeting date until Ms. Abbott makes her report. And Captain Clark, as any rational person would, under those circumstances, as you'll hear, accepts the recommendation of Dr. Marsh, Global's director of health services. He takes the conservative approach, and he approves requiring Ms. Bradshaw to undergo a medical review, with full pay and full benefits under the contract. And that's the evidence, that's what you'll hear! It has nothing to do with safety, it had nothing to do with her report, it had nothing to do with anything but her conduct during that meeting with Ms. Abbott—and that's a very important distinction.

"You'll hear from Global about its robust—robust—program to make sure that they get reporting of anything and how competent they are that they get accurate and positive reporting from its pilots and from all its employees. You'll hear from all those individuals. You'll see that Global cooperated with Dr. Wood, as they should. You'll see that they wanted and repeatedly told Dr. Wood they wanted him to call the balls and strikes, and not get involved in it. And he worked diligently.

"There will be other issues that will come up, and you'll see it here and see the evidence of all of that. But in the end, you will not—you will find, as you must, that there was absolutely no connection between Ms. Bradshaw's protected activity and what you have determined to have been an adverse action, the placement into Section 8, nor will you see *any* evidence that once Ms. Bradshaw was in Section 8, Global took any steps— *any steps at all*— in retaliation for Ms. Bradshaw having engaged in that protected activity, none at all. We look forward to putting on the evidence. Thank you for patience in listening."

"All right," Judge Geraghty said. "Call your first witness."

CHAPTER 13

PARALYZED IN FEAR after listening to Wendel's overly convincing lies, is not how she expected this trial to begin. Perhaps she should have heeded the warning and Neil's advice to back out of it, as she glanced around the courtroom wondering who had sent her that message. But Darby had never run from anything in her life. She had also never brought anyone to trial. She believed in compromise, that there were always two sides, sometime three, to every story and there was nothing that couldn't find resolution. She wasn't so sure anymore.

Neil found his way to the stand, and the judge swore him in. He was nervous and she understood his feelings more than he knew. Until you have first-hand experience being placed on a grill, unknowing the height of the flames or the number of skewers they would insert into your body, emotions fired on all cylinders. This process was disconcerting to everyone.

She was thankful he was standing up for her. They had been through a lot, but at the end of the day he was solid. She knew his testifying could place his job in jeopardy. However, Robert had assured him that the AIR21 law would protect him, because testifying was a protected activity. All the same, Robert played the game and forced a subpoena on him. Neil was not a voluntary witness, and that gave him a level of protection from Clark and the boys.

After the preliminaries of Neil's background, education, and personal relationship with Darby, Robert began questioning him on the day of her meeting with Ms. Abbott, a time when they were still together. He'd asked her to marry him, but with a condition of her quitting her job. Before month's end he was dating another pilot who was now sitting in the back of the courtroom. Darby forced herself to keep her focus forward.

"How soon after the meeting with Ms. Abbott, did you talk to Darby?"

"Probably about five minutes," Neil said. "She called, and said she was on the way home. She arrived about ten minutes later."

"When she arrived home did you witness any emotional upset?" Robert asked.

"No. She simply said the meeting didn't go quite as well as she thought it would."

"Was there any indication in Darby's appearance or visage, that she had been crying?"

"No, not at all," Neil said.

"Have you seen Darby cry before?"

With a smirk he said, "Oh, yes."

"Do you think you would have been able to tell if she had been crying within the last 10 to 15 minutes?"

"Most definitely," Neil said.

"Prior to this meeting, had anyone told you that Darby might be subject to a Section 8 referral?"

"Yes."

"Objection to those comments as hearsay," Global's pregnant attorney, Ms. Narcea, said. Wendel sat to her side, but this was her witness to cross examine.

"Overruled," Judge Geraghty said. "Hearsay is allowed in these proceedings."

Neil explained how it was common knowledge among the pilots that the company was after Darby. He said, "There was a lot of talk about a target on her back. I was also at her house when her union rep told her he thought they were going to give her a Section 8, the section in the contract that opened the door for a mental health evaluation."

"Were you ever directly asked to do anything to harm Darby?" Robert asked.

"Objection!" Narcea said.

"Overruled."

"Yes," Neil said. "Captain Clark had offered me a job as a pilot. But that job came with a price. He wanted me to give him information on Darby that he could use against her."

"Did you?" Robert asked.

"Objection," Narcea said. "This trial is not about what an ex-lover did to harm his girlfriend."

"Overruled," Judge Geraghty said for the second time.

The pain in Neil's eyes reminded her of how hard that decision had been. But she understood. That decision changed the course of his life. Unfortunately, that had been the beginning of the end to their relationship as well.

"Yes. But nothing that could ever *hurt* her…" he said quickly. Then he said, "But, being offered a job to fly at Global as a low time pilot was a dream I couldn't pass up."

"What did you give him?" Robert asked.

"Nothing important. Just the type of wine she liked or her schedule outside work… stuff like that." Neil quickly added, "I told Darby.

I told her I was offered the job and the conditions. She agreed the job was worth it and trusted that I would never say anything that could hurt her."

Robert questioned Neil as to Darby's knowledge and ability as a pilot. He then established that Neil had listened to Darby's phone call with Dr. Marsh stating this was a misunderstanding, but the situation was out of his hands.

"During the entire mental health evaluation," Robert said, "did any doctor ever contact you?"

"The only doctor I had talked to was from the Mayo Clinic. He called up and asked me three questions. He asked me how long I had known Darby. He asked me if she spoke fast. And then asked me if she had always spoken fast. I told him how long we'd known each other, and I said—Yes, she speaks fast. Yes, she has always spoken fast. "

"Thank you," Robert said. "That's all I have."

Ms. Narcea was now on stage, wearing a tight dress that pronounced a baby was on board. Darby believed that Global had employed her to show the judge they respected women, especially mothers working in a male dominated environment. She was nothing but for show.

"Did you ever contact Dr. Wood?" Narcea asked.

"No, I did not," Neil said with a dumbfounded look. "Why would I contact a doctor who was evaluating my ex-girlfriend?"

"Please stick to answering the questions," Judge Geraghty said, and Neil nodded in response.

"You never wrote him a letter?" Narcea asked, with an irritatingly squeaky voice.

"No."

"You said that your girlfriend was warned about being placed into a Section 8. Who warned her?"

"I did," Neil said. Then he added, "And her union rep, Bud

Johnson."

"And you weren't there for that conversation?"

"I was not there for their first conversation," Neil said.

"You just heard about it through your girlfriend?"

"Correct. But I did hear a conversation on the telephone later."

"I'm not asking about that conversation. I'm asking about the Bud Johnson conversation that you weren't there for."

Could this be any more juvenile? Darby wondered. Neil established he'd heard one conversation firsthand, and not the other, but both conversations established the same fact—ALPO knew what the company was up to and allowed it to happen.

"You also testified that you recalled Dr. Marsh, Global's in-house doctor, saying that this was all a misunderstanding. That's the only thing that you really recall from that conversation?"

Neil thought for a moment, and then said, "That's the main thing I recall."

"And you're absolutely sure that that was the language he used, that he felt it was a misunderstanding?"

"I do. Absolutely on that," Neil said.

"It's not possible that he might have said that it *could* be a misunderstanding?"

"No. He said it was… he said in his … it's hard for me to say exactly what he said, but he did say—*In my estimation, this is a misunderstanding.*"

"So, you don't recall the exact wording, though?" Narcea said.

Ms. Narcea pressed on borderline badgering Neil for the exact wording on the conversations that occurred over three years earlier. He handled it as well as anyone could. Better than most could under these conditions. *God that woman is a bitch,* Darby thought.

"You stated that Captain Clark offered you a job in exchange for information on Darby, is that correct?"

"Yes."

"To harm her?" she asked.

"Yes."

"And you accepted that proposition?"

"I did."

"Then wouldn't it be safe to infer that Captain Clark did nothing to harm Ms. Bradshaw, but it was *you* who accepted a position in exchange for inflicting harm upon her?"

"Objection!" Robert said.

"Sustained!" Judge Geraghty boomed.

CHAPTER 14

DARBY HAD NO idea that sweet little Ms. Narcea could be such a strategic bitch. She twisted Neil's words to imply that Darby could have done something that the company could use against her, and she and Neil were hiding it. However, during her antagonistic cross examination Darby watched the judge closely. She would have bet that he, too, thought it was a ridiculous line of questioning, not worth anyone's time.

The room fell silent, and Darby glanced to her right to see what was happening. Her attention followed the attorney's gazes toward the door. She exchanged a glance with her next witness, and he gave her a slight nod. He shook Robert's hand, then walked to the front of the courtroom.

"Please take your seat," Judge Geraghty said.

"Thank you," John Nance replied, and was subsequently sworn in.

"Mr. Nance, could you tell us what your current employment is?" Robert asked.

"I am the aviation analyst for ABC World News and Good Morning America," John said, in his authoritative broadcasting voice. "I am a self-employed author, wrote a couple of books. And I am also maintaining my business of about 27 years running as a professional speaker, mostly in medicine."

Not only was Nance one of the most stalwart individuals Darby knew, but he was modest, too. *A couple of books? Yeah right,* Darby thought. He'd written over two dozen books, most of which were bestsellers, and some even made into movies. *Blackout, Final Approach* and *Scorpion Strike* were a few of her favorites. But his newest novel, the *Vendetta Crossing*, was amazing. She had the privilege of a sneak peek and couldn't wait for publication.

"Can you tell us about your previous employment?" Robert said.

"Yes. I was an airline pilot with Braniff International from December 5th, 1975, until we collapsed in bankruptcy on May 12th of 82. I joined Alaska Airlines on July 15th, 1985. And retired early from them in 2004."

Nance had also been a United States Air Force officer and pilot commissioned in 1968 and on active duty until 1975, at which time he shifted to the 97th Reserve Squadron at McCord where he remained for a total of 17 years. He had over 16,000 flight hours, with a type rating in the L300, which he claimed to be essentially useless, because that was supposed to be the civilian version of the C141 that never happened. He also held ratings on the DA20 and the Boeing 737. He was a distinguished graduate in the Class of 7108 at Williams Air Force Base. He also held a Juris Doctorate Degree from SMU Law School.

"And you said you were an author, have you written any books related to the Aviation Industry?"

"Yes. Out of the 22 books I've written, I would say probably 17 to 18 of them were about or have the background of aviation in one form of another. They're not all about airlines, but the platform is aviation."

"Have you received any award for your writing?" Robert asked.

"For one of them on medicine, *Why Hospitals Should Fly*. It won the 2009 Book of the Year Award by the American Academy of Healthcare Executives."

"And how long have you known Darby Bradshaw?"

"About 25 years."

"Have you worked with her professionally?"

"Only to the extent that I called her because I had a book that featured the Airbus A330, and I knew she flew the airplane. I needed a lot of help on that because I was not an Airbus pilot. I knew a lot about the 320, I had been in the simulators, but I was getting deep into the systems of the 330 and she was *invaluable* in her help with that."

"Have you read any of Ms. Bradshaw's books?"

"I have."

"And how would you describe the focus of Darby's book?"

"The focus was most definitely on the sanctity of safety, and an awful lot of it is about the difficulty of getting the information on something that's going wrong, systemically, to the people who can do something about it, and the difficulties involved in the human system."

"What have you witnessed with respect to Darby's professional demeanor?"

"An extraordinary individual—would be just my overture to answer that question. Because we try in any high-risk industry to get people to engage, to own the situation on the front lines, whether you're in a managerial position or whether you're in an instructor position, or whether you're just a participant.

"And my impression has always been that she owned the situation regarding safety, regarding the atmosphere and the receptivity of the Safety culture, in her case Global, and this is something that we want. We *want* people to be engaged, we want them to have the ability, as well as the chutzpah, if you will, to say to power—We've got a problem."

"Your Honor," Ms. Narcea said exasperated. "I'm going to object to the testimony of Mr. Nance to the extent he's testifying as an expert on human factors. He's never been disclosed as an expert," she said, placing a hand on her lower back, "and we certainly didn't have any notice that he would be testifying as someone with expertise in this matter."

"If I may respond?" Robert said. "As we discussed the experts in the context of our raising the non-disclosure of Dr. Wood, that the Tribunal has recognized that pilots, through their ATP and experience, have an expertise that's worth testifying about and is recognized by the federal rules. Just because you're an expert, doesn't mean you're giving expert testimony."

Judge Geraghty turned his attention toward Mr. Nance. "Are you an ATP, Sir?"

"I am an ATP, yes," John replied.

"All right," Geraghty said. "Overruled. I'll hear it with some caveats, as I view a large part of this case involving credibility and, therefore, I'm going to consider the testimony, in part, as it relates to Ms. Bradshaw's credibility, since that's been put on the table in this case from the very beginning. Go ahead."

"Now, based on your description of your position at ABC," Robert said, "have you participated in live broadcast interviews concerning aviation subjects?"

"Constantly for the past 27 years, yes."

"Is that a stressful endeavor?"

"I usually describe it as a *high wire act without a net*," John said. "But it's exhilarating if you do it right, and it's very upsetting if you do it wrong. But it's a very high stress situation."

"And have you witnessed Ms. Bradshaw participate in TV interviews?"

"I have. A couple of interviews on CNN."

"And how did she conduct herself in that stressful environment?"

"Very well. As a matter of fact, I was quite pleased of the degree of casualty, which is what you want to show, with which she was able to handle the interviewer's questions."

"Now, you made a reference, a couple minutes ago, to Safety culture," Robert said. "What do you mean by that?"

John explained in detail the importance of safety culture within the airline industry and the implications of retaliation that would destroy safety overnight.

"Have you, in your experience in the airline industry, witnessed retaliation against anyone who reported safety concerns?" Robert asked.

"Yes, I have," John said gravely, nodding as he spoke.

"Have you ever witnessed the use of simulator training, or are you familiar with the use of simulator training as a retaliatory tool?"

"All too often. And I will say, if permitted to, that that's one of the greatest fears of an airline pilot because there is no pilot, no matter how good, no matter how experienced, who can't be busted on a check ride if somebody wants him gone."

Robert asked as to the importance of SMS and safety culture, and John answered.

"Do you have any concern as to the impact on safety culture and SMS programs in referring a pilot such as Ms. Bradshaw for psychiatric examinations?" Robert asked.

"Every alarm bell that I have goes off in something like that," John said, with renewed intensity. "Because if that is done without a great degree of evidentiary rationale, then it sends a message to literally everybody else who knows about it in the flight department, that if you speak up about something, this is what's going to probably happen to you, too.

"So, the idea that you might suddenly become persona non grata and be sent to a psychiatrist and have a stain on your record and something in your file because of having just spoken up, may not square with the facts of what actually happened.

"But this is one reason, in a safety culture, where you've got to be extremely careful, in leadership, and not to do something that sends that message, because you will harpoon the willingness of other people to come forward. This is an incredibly serious situation," John said.

"Thank you," Robert said. "No further questions."

CHAPTER 15

JUDGE GERAGHTY SHIFTED his attention from Nance toward the opposing table and said, "Counsel?"

Ms. Narcea smiled. "I am also an SMU law grad, so I will say, *Go Ponies*." Her attention then dropped to the paper she held, but quickly returned to the witness.

"So, earlier you talked about doing live TV broadcasts and how it's a very high stress situation. Do you believe that flying an aircraft, as a pilot, is the same level of stress, where you're responsible for thousands of lives, as a live TV broadcast?"

"Well, I don't think there's any comparison. The live TV broadcast doesn't have lethal potential, well, it may have in some respects, but no, I mean you're in an airplane you're right there responsible for all those lives."

Darby wished she could have answered that question. Live television was far *more* stressful than flying. A pilot was trained to fly an airplane. It was a scripted play, and she knew her roles and how to respond to any questions when asked. On television, she had to think on her feet and deal with the unexpected and hope she didn't look like a fool. A pilot prepared for flying, but there was no preparation for a live interview when there was no idea what to expect.

"Well, you also testified about retaliatory simulator training?" Ms. Narcea said.

"Yes."

"You've never had any personal experience with simulators at Global, have you?"

"Not at Global Air Lines, no," John said.

"You talked earlier about safety culture and the fact that you should, you need an evidentiary rationale for a Section 8 mental health evaluation?"

"Correct," John said.

"Don't you believe that an airline should err on the side of safety, and while they're gathering all that evidence the pilot should be pulled from flying aircraft?" Narcea asked.

"I believe that an airline—*any* airline—has a responsibility to be incredibly careful on two counts. Number one, with investigating anything that might have a component of mental or emotional instability, certainly must not be swept under the rug. But secondly, because of what I was talking about, the extreme sensitivity of all the pilots to the nuances, if somebody is seen to have been pulled into a psychiatric evaluation and the *only* overt reason for that seems to be that he or she presented a safety concern, you have tripped off in the other direction. There's a delicate line here, not a clear shiny white line, but one that flight managers must be very, very careful about. There must be something more than just a single point reason that is raised to call somebody in for that, it's a very serious analysis," John said.

"I'm going to object to that as non-responsive to the question," Ms. Narcea snapped. "I was asking if an air carrier has been notified of concerns for a pilot's mental health evaluation by an employee, and you said that you should have an evidentiary rationale. Should the carrier pull the pilot while they're gathering that evidentiary rationale?"

"I'm not sure that I would answer that the pilot should be pulled, but certainly it should be pursued."

"And when they're pursuing it, do you think the carrier that has notice that there's concerns about that pilot's mental safety or mental health, that that pilot should be allowed to continue flying?"

"I think that has to be evaluated in each case, not an automatic thing," John pressed back. "As a matter of fact, if it's not evaluated in each case, and becomes automatic, then it probably is going to miss, in one form or another, realities. So, am I responsive to you on that?"

"Not quite, but we'll move on," Ms. Narcea said with a derisive smile. "Based on your understanding of safety culture, if an airline has concerns about a pilot's mental health, is it incumbent on the airline to look into those concerns, even if the pilot is ultimately exonerated?"

"Asked and answered," Robert said.

"It has been asked and answered," Judge Geraghty agreed. "But I'll allow it this last time."

"Okay?" Ms. Narcea said, and then stared at John with a closed-lip smile.

"All right," John began. "I'm sorry, did you ask it as a yes or no? I apologize, but would you give it to me again?"

With feigned exasperation, Ms. Narcea lifted the paper and read. "So, if an air carrier has been notified of mental health concerns of a pilot, is it incumbent on the air carrier to investigate those concerns, even if that pilot is ultimately exonerated, correct?"

"Yes," John replied.

Darby wanted to scream. This line of questioning was so out of context because there was no legitimate complaint. There never was. And that in a nutshell was the problem with all of this.

CHAPTER 16

JOHN NANCE STEPPED off the stand as Captain Joe Galen entered the room. They shook hands at the door, exchanged a few words that brought a smile to both their faces and John walked out the door. Joe and John were friends and had been for many years. Darby smiled with the knowledge that good people found each other. And despite the unfathomable characters at Global Air Lines, there were some incredible people in the aviation industry keeping passengers safe. These men were two of them.

"All right. Please, take a seat," Judge Geraghty said. "After you're seated, Sir, please provide your full name and contact information. Joe complied, and then the judge asked, "Are you a pilot?"

"I am," Joe said in easy going manner.

"Please give me your FAA certificates and ratings," Judge Geraghty said.

"I have an Airline Transport Pilot License, Flight Instructor, Flight Instructor Instrument, and Flight Instructor Multi-Engine type ratings," Joe said in a slow methodical way with a perpetual smile on his face.

"In what?" Geraghty asked. He, too, was a pilot, and Darby wasn't sure if this was more a curiosity, or if he graded witnesses by their experience level.

"A320, Boeing 727, 737, 747, 747-400, 757, 767, 777, BE300, ahh...Cessna 650, DC3, DC9, DC10, DA50, which is a Falcon 5900, and Lear 45. I have a Flight Engineer License, turbo jet, turbo prop. Ground Instructor License and Advanced Instrument." Joe thought for a moment and then said, "I think that's it."

"Total time?" The judge asked.

"Just short of 32,000 hours."

"How many in jets?" Judge Geraghty asked.

"About 29,000."

"Okay," Judge Geraghty said with a nod and looked toward Robert. "Counsel?"

"Could you give us some background on your training?" Robert began.

"I started in 69 with the Boeing Company as a flight crew instructor. I worked there seven months, I was right out of college, taught in the ground school. Got laid off when Senator Proxmire shut down the SSTs, so I went back to the Midwest and flew mail for the Postal Service. Came back to Boeing in 72. Worked in flight crew training, again, until 1974.

"I went to the Middle East, lived in the Middle East about two, two and a half years. Came back, went to work for a non-sked airline, and there became the director of training, it was a 121 airline. Let's see, from there, went to Hughes Air West. At Hughes Air West, I did ground training with them as well as fly. They merged with Republic, and I did some training at Republic in cockpit resource management.

"Then on to Coastal Airways, became an instructor and check airman on the DC9. In the meanwhile, in 1979, I started a training facility in Seattle. And I had an organization that trained, on a contract basis, small airlines. I owned 727, 737 and Lockheed Electra simulators. So, I've been involved in training all my life, basically."

"How long have you known Ms. Bradshaw?

"Over 23 years, probably."

"And did you have any involvement in her application to Coastal Airlines?"

"I wrote a recommendation letter for Darby to Coastal," Joe said.

"And why did you write a recommendation letter for Ms. Bradshaw?"

"Well, Darby came to my school, I can't remember the exact year. I just can't remember. But she came and told me she wanted to get a type rating in the 727, 737 and a Flight Engineer's License. And I asked her about her qualifications. She had... I'll never forget this— she had 472 hours total time. So, I explained to her that the likelihood of her being able to complete one of those programs would be questionable, because of her experience level. And she says, 'Well look, I'll pay you even if I don't make it. And I'll be the best student you've ever seen in your life.'

"And at the time, there was talk in the industry about trying to get lower time pilots into cockpits sooner and they were experimenting with multi-crew training ideas and so forth. And I just wondered if you could take a 472-hour general aviation pilot and get them qualified in transport category jet. So, I was kind of curious as to whether we could do it anyway.

"So, I told Darby at the time that, 'We'll take you on, but you have to complete an instrument training course with us in instrument scan technique and flight management skills, and if you do that, and pay for it, of course, we'll give you a shot at the 727. And if that goes well, we'll do the 73 and then we'll see about the Flight Engineer License.' And that's, basically, what we did," he said with a slow smile, clearly thinking back to the day. He then said, "It was amazing. And she did it."

"And you say it was amazing, did you fly with her?" Robert asked.

"Well, I gave her instruction, but I've always felt that when a person goes through the training, they need to have a viewpoint of different instructors, because every instructor has their own talents and unique and specific skills at being able to impart information. So, I probably did, maybe, 50 percent of her training through that program, and I had two other instructors there that probably worked with her, as well.

"But what was funny, and I don't mean funny ha, ha, but what was interesting was, when the FAA came in to give her the check ride—and this I remember distinctly—they went into the briefing room, her and the FAA inspector out of the Seattle office here. So, they're in there for about 20 minutes and the inspector came out and he says to me, he says, 'Joe, can I talk to you for a second?' I said, 'Sure.' So, we go into my office, and I said, 'What's wrong?' And he says, 'I can't give her a check ride.' And I said, 'Why not?' He goes, 'She doesn't have enough experience.' And I said, 'Well, John, she has a private pilot license, and she has a medical, you have to give her the check ride.' And he said, 'I'm going to call the office.'

"So, he called the office, at the time his office was over in Boeing Field. And he came back in, and he says, 'Well, I'll tell you what, he says, I have to give her the check ride. You're right.' He says, 'But if she messes one thing up, you know, it's over.' I said, 'John, if she messes one thing up, fail her, that's your job, you have to do that anyway.' So, he says, 'Okay.'

"So, they went in the sim. And a normal check ride for a type rating should take two to two and a half hours. So, it got to two and a half hours, and I'm thinking, uh, oh, this is not good. About two hours and 45 minutes, they came out, went in the briefing room. Then he comes over to my office and said, 'Can I talk to you for a second?'

I said, 'Yeah.' So, he comes in my office, and he closes the door."

Darby smiled listening to the story. She remembered that event well but had no idea what had been going on behind closed doors with the FAA. This was all new to her, and she listened with fascination.

"He says, 'How did you guys do that?' I said, 'How did we do what?' He says, 'Man, I've given check rides to 10,000-hour captains who were not near as good as that.' He said, 'That check ride was flawless.' I said, 'Well, John, why did it take two hours and 45 minutes?' He said, 'Because I couldn't believe it, I just kept piling it on and she handled everything.' He said, 'I gave up.' He said, 'You know, we're going to pass her.'

She had been prepared because of the instruction she had received from Joe. Unfortunately, today there was a huge problem with the concept of taking low time pilots and doing what they did with her back in the day—the instructors today are more administrators than educators. More so, the planes are far more complex today such that flying is no longer the primary skill but memorizing and pushing the correct buttons.

"Have you discussed important flight safety issues with Darby during the years you've known her?"

"From time to time, sure," he said glancing at Darby with a smile.

"And what was her demeanor during these discussions? Was she ever fretful, upset?"

"Well, I'd say Darby is passionate about safety. Darby is a very unique individual. She's not like a lot of people." He glanced at the judge and said, "I'm sorry, I don't mean that in a bad way. What I mean is she has a capacity that most people could never achieve. And I've always wondered how she did it.

"When she came to me she was nannying a handful of kids, worked, attended college while flying, and with a very, very low flight time accomplished getting not one type rating, but two, and an Engineer's license, going on the line for a freighter, goes out and writes a book about aviation safety, and earns a B777 type-rating, while fighting a company that basically, essentially, created an event that could have trashed her whole career. Darby is a very, very different, unique person."

Joe held Geraghty's attention with each word he spoke. The judge was now seeing Darby Bradshaw beyond Global's assertion of her needing a mental health evaluation.

"Darby is passionate about safety. That's the thing that she has latched onto," Joe said. Then he paused, and added, "You know, is it bad to be different? Well, let me tell you, it's people that are different that change the world, whether we like it or not."

CHAPTER 17

RELAXED ON THE stand, Joe sat in his element with an audience listening to his stories called experience. His eyes twinkled when he smiled, and nothing appeared to daunt him. He was one of those aviators who'd lived life, cheated death, and could smile at the memory of it all.

"You referenced a merger. Do you have any experience with differing airline cultures?" Robert asked.

"Oh, yes. I've been involved in four mergers in my career. And they're all interesting, because you're trying to put different cultures together."

"Have you had professional dealings or social interactions with many Global pilots?" Robert asked.

"Well, quite a few," Joe said, with a slow nod. "I have a lot of friends that fly for Global. And I have many friends that flew for Coastal, that amalgamated into the Global culture."

"Based on the information that you've received from them, can you describe to me your understanding of the difference, if any, between culture at Coastal and Global?" Robert asked.

"I'm going to object," Ms. Narcea said. "This isn't based on personal knowledge, at all, it's all secondhand information he's received from individuals *about* Global's culture."

"Counsel?" Judge Geraghty said to Robert.

"We've heard about his extensive experience and also his training experience, and the use of simulator checks to retaliate. This man is immersed in the airline industry and the airline industry culture," Robert said extending a hand toward Joe. "And whatever value the testimony may have, it's relevant and it's really for the Tribunal to later ascertain the level of value to attribute to it."

"I don't think we've heard anything about his experience *at* Global, because he's never been employed by Global," Ms. Narcea argued.

"Well, the fact that he hasn't been employed by Global, doesn't necessarily sway me," Judge Geraghty said. "Has he been identified as an expert?"

"You mean in terms of our disclosures? Robert asked.

"Yes," the judge said.

"No, he has not been identified, beyond and we were relying on as was previously discussed with the Tribunal to the effect that pilots acquire experience that's relevant with respect to their ATPs and their decades of experience in the industry," Robert said.

"That's as pretty liberal interpretation of what I had understood it to be," Geraghty said.

Darby fought a smile. The judge was correct, and Robert was pushing the ATP experience to far more value than Darby ever thought it was worth. She loved it. But even that idiot Rich Clark held an air transport pilot license, and he was one of the biggest tools that existed. Regardless, that rationale was getting them what they wanted.

"He's not really testifying about his pilot experience. He's testifying about safety culture," Ms. Narcea argued.

"Well, airlines have cultures and those cultures matter," Robert said. "And this is something that's, in effect, identified in 14 CFR

Part 5, and has been relied upon by Global as a defense, that they have a robust reporting culture. And what we're trying to elicit from this witness is based on the information he has, that it's not as robust as has been represented."

"I'm going to allow it, but I'm allowing it because the bar is so incredibly low at these administrative proceedings. Whether or not I give it weight, is a different matter," Judge Geraghty said, "Okay. Go ahead."

Darby looked at Joe and winked. He returned it with a grin.

"Would you repeat the question, please?" Joe asked, pulling his attention back to Robert.

"Based on your professional experience, and the information you've received over the years, can you comment on the comparative airline culture of Coastal and Global Air Lines?"

"It might be easier to comment on culture in general between any airline," Joe said.

"Why don't we begin with that?" Robert said.

Joe began sharing the history of culture utilizing experiences from the Middle East as compared to America. He used examples of meeting for dinner in Tehran, how Persian's behave compared to Americans, and spoke words such as *normals, Inshallah, God willing,* and even explained the three stages of culture shock. Robert interrupted at one time and asked how he would describe Coastal's safety culture, and Joe told him he was getting to that. And he did. Eventually. Joe spoke of airline cultures coming together and knocking on different doors from each airline.

Robert realized the can of worms he'd opened. Ms. Narcea listened with a line etched between her brows. The judge listened without expression. She was surprised nobody cut him off, which only meant they found his stories as interesting as she did.

"Now, what would happen at Coastal is, the Chief Pilot would say, *'You know what, Joe, we're going to check into that.'* And a week later, two weeks later, I'd get a call—*'Hey Joe, we ran this past Standards, we ran it past Training, and we think it's a good idea and we're going to implement it, and I think it will be done by, maybe, three to six months. Are you okay with that?'*

"I'm going to object, again," Ms. Narcea said. "There is no personal knowledge of this. I mean this is all based on ..."

"Well, that *is* specific knowledge," Joe said interrupting her.

"He's talking about Coastal up until now," Robert said.

"He's talking about what happens with a door at Global and a door at Coastal, and he was never employed at Global!" Ms. Narcea pleaded.

"Well, I haven't got to the Global door *yet*," Joe said, out of order.

"The objection ..." Robert said.

"Wait a minute," Judge Geraghty said. "I'm hearing as to Coastal. It's my understanding there's some understanding of Coastal. We'll see what happens when we talk about Global."

"Okay," Robert said.

"And counsel," Geraghty said, to Robert, as if a father were to scold his son, "This is more than ATP testimony." He turned his attention to Ms. Narcea and said, "You have leeway, counsel, on cross-examination."

Joe explained that the Global door would be closed, and management may not respond. Robert then brought forth a letter Joe had written on Darby's behalf to give to Dr. Wood as a long-term character reference. Darby had gathered numerous letters of support and provided them *to* Dr. Wood, but he never used *any* of those in his report, and never contacted anyone. Narcea argued that Joe's letter was hearsay, but Judge Geraghty admitted it as evidence.

"Did Dr. Wood ever contact you?" Robert asked.

"He did not."

"Did a Dr. Hanover, who we've stipulated was the neutral medical examiner in this proceeding, did he contact you?"

"Yes, he did."

"And what did you discuss with psychiatrist, Dr. Hanover?"

"Well, as I recall, the conversation centered around Darby, of course, what I had observed in having trained her and known her over the years. Did I see any signs of emotional stress at any point? And I related that no, I did not. He wanted to know if she became emotionally upset, crying, under high stress conditions. And I do recall telling him that what we put Darby through in the simulator would make a grown man cry and she never shed a tear."

CHAPTER **18**

JOE'S CROSS EXAMINATION

THE JUDGE PASSED the baton to Ms. Narcea. She smiled sweetly at Joe and then said, "So, this type rating event, where you described at the beginning of your testimony, and the referral for a mental health evaluation, there was a 20-year gap between those two events?"

"Oh… I suspect probably so," Joe said, with a smirk.

"We talked about this earlier, but you were never employed by Global, correct?"

"Correct."

"You never received a paycheck from Global?" Narcea asked.

"Oh, I've received money from Global, just not a paycheck."

"I don't know what you mean?" Narcea said.

"I have stock," Joe said.

"Okay," Narcea said with a glare, but her fake smile never wavered. "Can you just answer me, yes or no, you have never been an employee of Global?"

"And I hope that stock keeps going up," Joe said. Before she could object, he added, "No. To answer your question, no."

"Okay. Thank you." Narcea glanced at her notes and said, "So, you don't have any personal knowledge of how the merger affected the two cultures between Global and Coastal?"

"I was not subjected to it personally because I was not there. My knowledge comes from all the friends. When I say friends—people I knew. I had lots of conversations with pilots that went through the experience, so that's the extent of my knowledge."

Narcea confirmed for the record that Joe was never employed by Global, never knocked on that culture door, and never took a check ride at Global. She established that he did not see texting in the simulator and was not present during a retaliatory line check. He had no first-hand knowledge of anything, only knowledge of what others had told him.

"Okay. And you don't know whether she received an oral following that simulator training, do you?" Narcea said.

"Sounds like I don't know much of anything, doesn't it?" Joe said with a slow smile.

A smirk crossed the judge's face, and some chuckles emitted from the back of the courtroom. Joe pleasantly smiled at Ms. Narcea. She simply flipped through a binder.

"Please read the last line on paragraph four, of the letter you wrote to Dr. Wood."

Joe located the spot after some discussion and read. "Rather than push this employee aside through the mental stability gate, they may well be better off listening to what she has to say, I don't know."

"So, you told Dr. Wood that you *didn't know* what an airline should do in a situation that was presented by Ms. Bradshaw, is that correct?"

For God's sake, Darby thought.

"I never... Say that again," Joe said, slightly confused by her question.

"In this letter to Dr. Wood, you told him that you didn't know what an airline should do when faced with a report of a pilot's mental health?"

"Well, you could interpret it that way, I suppose, but…" Joe began.

"Is that what you wrote—*I don't know*"? Ms. Narcea demanded, cutting him off.

Darby knew exactly what the wicked bitch of the law firm was doing. She manipulated the context of his letter. But Judge Geraghty was intelligent, and if he wanted to understand the semantics of this, he would. Darby also knew that people listened to what benefited them. *Please, God*, Darby silently prayed, *don't let Global own him.*

"Okay. When I say, I don't know, it's manner of speaking," Joe said. "And I thought, at the time, knowing what I know about Darby, that to accuse her of being mentally unstable, because she was trying to bring a safety issue to the forefront, was unreasonable. And I did feel that the company, from what I had seen, was creating a situation for her that was unfair."

"Why did you say, I don't know?" Narcea challenged again.

"Just a manner of speaking. I grew up in a family that had many sayings. My grandmother told me, always—*You get like the people you live with.* It's just a way of speaking."

Ms. Narcea stared at Joe for a moment. Then said, "You've never performed a mental health evaluation of a pilot, have you?"

"Well, I've been involved with a lot of pilots that had some mental issues, I can tell you that," Joe said.

"Can you give me a yes, or no?" Ms. Narcea snapped, and then said, "Please."

"Yes, with qualifications."

"So, you've actually performed a mental health evaluation of a pilot for an air carrier?" she asked with a sarcastic tone of disbelief.

"In a sense, not on a professional level," Joe said, "but yes."

"What do you mean not on a professional level?"

"Well, we had a pilot at Coastal everyone called Randy Runoff. Randy would see angels on the wing of the aircraft. The company wanted him to be gone in the worst way. He had run off the runway twice, because he believed that the use of reverse was too loud for the passengers."

Ms. Narcea placed fingers to her forehead while he spoke.

"I know this is irritating to you, but you asked the question, and I have to explain it," Joe said. "So, the company asked me, '*Is there anything we can do with Randy?*' When I'm talking about the company, it was the Fleet Captain and the Director of Training. So, I thought about it. Randy was having problems in a DC10, it was costing a lot of money, he was not qualified. So, I went to Randy, we talked, and I suggested he retire. Which he evaluated his choices and did."

"So, you're saying your recommendation that he retire was a mental health evaluation?"

"Well, when he saw angels on the wings, I don't know what else you'd call it," Joe said.

"You're not a licensed psychologist?"

"I don't have to be, to know that that's a little—"

"Can you please just give me yes, or no? It would really help things," Ms. Narcea said, interrupting him again.

"Well, you have to ask yes or no questions," Joe said, pleasantly.

"Are you a licensed psychologist?"

"No."

Ms. Narcea's ensuing questions were repetitive. So much so, that Judge Geraghty finally said '*the question was asked and answered at least a half dozen times.*' She explained she was setting up a question. Geraghty allowed it, with a sigh. Likely regretting the leeway, he had promised.

"So, even if the pilot is removed with pay," Ms. Narcea said, "while the airline is investigating the credibility of this accusation, you think that the pilot should still be allowed to fly, while there's pending concerns about a pilot's mental health?"

"Well, I think if a pilot had a vendetta against another pilot, and they said that—*hey, this guy is a nut job*—well, if I'm in a supervisory position, I have to take that seriously, but I also have to immediately get corroborating evidence that that's the case and it's not just a vendetta of one pilot against another."

Amen to that, Darby thought.

CHAPTER 19

LUNCH

THEY FINALLY BROKE for lunch, which was not an easy task in the FAA courthouse. The FAA headquarters was a secure building, and nobody could wander. With only one chaperone and a couple dozen people in need of an escort to the ground floor cafeteria, it took time with one elevator. Half the group left first. Then they returned to get Darby, Robert, Linda, and Jackie.

The rules at lunch were—*do not discuss the case.* But that's all she'd been discussing for years, and perhaps the reason for her attitude of aggravation. Being friendly was an effort these days. But this was the final stretch. Unfortunately, not unlike a marathon, that last mile was the most difficult when you didn't know if you could finish. She knew she would get there; she was simply unsure as to what shape she would be in when she crossed the finish line.

Robert found a table to himself so he could focus. The two pilots who'd stopped by for the morning session left. Tom had a meeting, but would return for the afternoon session, and Linda and Jackie found a table in the corner. Kathryn never made it. Darby grabbed a sandwich and joined her friends. The Global people filled a table with a handful of attorneys and Robert Dodson. Dodson was a Global Regional Director and a Chief Pilot.

Linda and Jackie were talking about some tiling project and Darby only half listened. She stared at Dodson as she bit into her turkey wrap. Dodson was the kind of person that you trusted, but who could stab a knife into your heart while never losing eye contact and all the while retaining the sincerest smile. As the knife plunged in, you still couldn't believe it was happening. Robert even liked Dodson. Of course, everyone did, unless he had screwed them too.

Dodson's high level of participation in her mental health diagnosis bothered her to no end. She pulled the toothpick out of the other half of her wrap to take a bite and twisted it between her fingers. She thought about the email Dodson had sent her, telling her that he was fishing off the Florida Keys and drinking cocktails with little umbrellas.

He had asked her about the contract. But what appeared to be his befriending her, was nothing but the action of a spy, trying to get her to write something that he could share with management. Something they could put in a file to get her later. She never trusted him and remained guarded.

Darby looked at her toothpick and then to Dodson. She grinned as she bit into her wrap. Knowing exactly where she'd like to stick the pointy end of his little cocktail umbrellas.

"Darby," Kathryn said from behind.

Darby jumped and dropped her sandwich. "You scared the shit out of me," she said.

"Sweetie, I'm sorry," Kathryn said, pulling out a chair. "Where were you just then?"

"Fantasyland," Darby said, "torturing Dodson."

Kathryn chuckled, and said, "I am most certain that he deserves it."

"I could see something was working on you," Linda said, "but I didn't want to interrupt."

"Just homicidal fantasies," Darby said with a smirk. Then she asked Kathryn, "Are you going to make it this afternoon?"

"I hope so. But there's an issue I've been dealing with."

"Does it relate to this case?" Darby asked, noting the shift in her gaze.

None of her friends would be testifying on her behalf. They had all spoken to the neutral doctor and their comments were in his report. Kathryn, however, had read her safety report and was in the know from a safety perspective. Regardless, the FAA prohibited her from testifying. They were blocking the one person who knew her the best.

Darby wanted to believe the FAA was not working for Global, but daily events proved otherwise. They were about to elect Wyatt, Global's retired SVP to the FAA administrator's position. The very man who authorized the attack on her. The old FAA administrator, who enacted SMS, and had been highly involved in the oversight of the MAX aircraft, looking the other way, retired to Global's board of directors. The relationship between the FAA and Global was incestual.

"I saw that look," Jackie said. "It does."

Kathryn said, "Maybe. I'm not sure how it connects, but please let me tell you tonight."

"I honestly don't have room for one more worry in my head," Darby said. "Just tell me, do I need to know about this before we finish today?"

"No," Kathryn said.

"Okay, then. I'll be at your house after court," Darby said.

"Jackie and Linda, would you join us?" Kathryn asked. "I'd like you to hear this too.

"I wouldn't miss it," Linda said.

"I'll leave the baby with John," Jackie said. "Cuz, I'd bet a million bucks he already knows."

CHAPTER 20

DAY 1 TRIAL CONTINUES
DAN WALKER DIRECT EXAMINATION

WALKER WAS TESTIFYING via Zoom. The questions opened like all others, and he shared his experience and flight hours. What was unique about Walker was that he had worked as an ALPO Chairman for six years, and then became the Master Executive Council contract administrator, for 12 years. He'd been an advocate for all pilots, not just Darby. He resigned his position during the merger because the Master Executive Council chairman flat out lied to him, dropping all the Coastal grievances after the merger. Despite telling him otherwise. That MEC chairman went on to become the next ALPO National president.

Robert established that Walker had known Darby for ten years and they had flown the A330 together.

"And how would you describe her performance?" Robert asked.

"I would say it was excellent, I mean nothing outstanding that I would remember as derogatory, just the same as every other pilot."

Now that was lame, Darby thought. Excellent, but nothing outstanding? The same as every other pilot? Robert asked him about his familiarity with Darby receiving a Section 8 referral. He then testified that two people from HR had interviewed him.

"Okay. Can you recall what their questions were and, perhaps more importantly, what your answers were?" Robert asked.

"Well, they asked me did I feel I had ever been subjected to any sort of retribution while at Global. And I said yes, but also at Coastal, and they asked me to describe how, or why I felt that way. And I described, you know, circumstances that led me to feel that way."

"Could you share with us the circumstances that made you feel that way?" Robert asked.

"Well, in May of 2010 I was a witness at an arbitration for a pilot who had been discharged by Coastal, while I was the contract administrator. I had been involved in the defense of that pilot. The attorney representing the pilot eventually asked me to be a witness in the case.

"We ended up prevailing in the case and the pilot got his job back. And it was my feeling that the company… it was my impression that the company was not happy that the pilot got his job back and with my testimony. I had recently been qualified on the A330 and had a qualification line check but received three additional line-checks and a random drug test shortly after the resolution of that case. And then there was a fifth line check that the check airman didn't show up for. The way I interpreted what happened in that short period of time, five line checks and a random drug test seemed to me to be unusual."

"And did you talk to Ms. Bradshaw about these circumstances?"

"Yes."

"Do you have knowledge of other pilots complaining that they had been subject to retaliatory line checks?"

"I'll object," Narcea said.

"Yes, I have anecdotal information on that, yes," Walker said, despite the objections.

"It's not based on personal knowledge," Narcea said.

"Overruled," Judge Geraghty said.

"I'm sorry, I didn't hear your answer?" Robert said.

"I said, yes, I've seen things posted on public web boards from some pilots."

"Okay. Very good," Robert said. "And at the end, going back to your interview with HR, do you recall how they concluded their interview of you?"

"The last thing that was said from the company on that call was that I was directed not to discuss it with anyone else, and I complied with that."

He explained the difference between Coastal and Global's fatigue policy. At Global, if the board determined you didn't get paid, you wouldn't. But Coastal's board also had problems.

"Okay. Have you ever heard the term: 'Good Ol' Boys Club,' used at Global?"

"Yes."

"Can you describe the context and your understanding of that phrase?"

"Yeah. I've also heard the term at Coastal, as well. And the context would be 'friend of the family,' so to speak. If you're a known entity, if you're a friend of whoever happens to be in charge, you can get in. I've never been a member of the good ol' boys club. It refers to, like I said, being friends, with whoever is in charge. In my experience, it's been, you know, you're not part of the in-crowd."

Global had asserted Darby made gender discrimination claims in her report because she discussed the good ol' boys club, despite that her reference was regarding culture. Within no time, the judge turned the questioning over to Global. Walker testified that he told the OSHA investigator that he had no personal knowledge of Darby's Section 8, and that he himself had filed up to 30 ASAP reports with no retaliation and Global never referred him to a Section 8 evaluation.

Walker's back-pedaling during most of his testimony surprised Darby. Throughout his assertions he continually identified similar behavior at Coastal. Then, there was the ASAP program. Those reports did not identify a reporting culture under an SMS. Granted, ASAP reports were a component of an SMS, but did not replace the requirement for a bona fide reporting culture designed to identify errors and safety concerns beyond self-reporting.

Walker was not as forthcoming as he was during their communications. However, after all he'd been through, she could not blame him.

CHAPTER 21

CAPTAIN JEHN WAS on the stand, and one of the few pilots that did not fear coming forward. He was as deeply concerned for the safety at the airline as she was. Darby had always appreciated flying with him. They'd had great discussions and she always learned something new from their aviation banter.

"Could you describe the training you received for the A330?" Robert asked.

"It's a little bit like being put through a toothpaste tube," Craig began. "I was Anchorage based on the 747-200, which was the only airplane that did not come over to the Global fleet from Coastal. There was a whole group of us that were the last, kind of the rear-guard staffing of the 747-200, and a great majority of us went straight to the 330, particularly the captains. There were probably 50 to 60 captains that went into the A330 training program.

"So, the reason I mention this is that I had contemporaries, we had similar backgrounds, and I know for me this was my first glass airplane. The 747-200 was a 1970s technology analog, hydro-mechanical airplane. And the A330 is still, arguably, one of the highest technology, wide-body airplanes flying. It certainly was at the time that I got on it.

"And so, this was quite a transition. This was the most difficult thing I've ever faced, as far as a training environment. The subject matter was more difficult because when we went through training, the emphasis was not on understanding the airplane as much as it was a rote procedures process. With rote memorization of processes and procedures, sequence of button pushing without, nobody necessarily fully understood what it was we were doing or why."

This had been Darby's primary concern. The lack of understanding was why airplanes crashed. Notwithstanding that the manuals were incorrect, and instructors were not paying attention, texting in the back of the simulator, and falsifying training records.

"And that made it very difficult for all of us," Craig said. "And I think we all shared the sense that when we came out the other end of that pipe, that we were really ill-prepared to be turned loose out into the system. There just seemed to be a push to get us through, jump through the various hoops and get through.

"I remember being in the procedure's trainer with my partner. A procedures trainer is like a simulator, but it doesn't move, it's got a lot of the same cockpit panels, some of them are functional and some are not, but it's for establishing patterns, pattern work in the cockpit. And I remember sitting in there and said, *'What does this do when I do this, or why am I doing this?'*

"And the instructor's response was, *'Stop asking questions, be the monkey, hit the lever, get the banana.'* That is a verbatim statement of what we were being told. We were not encouraged to learn about and understand why the equipment did what it did. *'You don't need to know that'* was a phrase that was given to us frequently in the course of that process."

Craig told the judge that he had never been so uncomfortable in an airplane as he was in his first year as a captain on the Airbus

A330, and that he was not alone in those feelings. Robert had also established that he and Darby had known each other for 20 years and they had flown the 747 and A330 together.

"Now, how would you describe her operational performance?" Robert asked.

"Oh, she's very confident, steady hand, good stick, good hand flying capability, knows her stuff."

"How frequently have you discussed flight operations issues with Ms. Bradshaw?"

"It's pretty much the topic of conversation on almost every conversation," Craig said.

"And do you recall some of the topics she raises with respect to flight operations?" Robert asked.

"Oh, it's run the gamut," Craig said. "It's been many years, you know. But there's usually training related things, procedure related things, what's the best way to accomplish something, and sometimes it's about procedures within the airline, sometimes it's more about the Airline Industry. I know that one of the things we've talked about is the All Attitude Upset Recovery Strategy, at Global, that's one of them."

"Okay. Do any of the conversations include safety compliance?" Robert asked.

"Yes."

"And to your perception, were the issues that she raised and discussed rational, irrational, researched, what was the quality of the conversation?"

"Always excellent, actually," Craig said. "It's always well researched and interesting ideas about—depending on the subject matter— whether it's about a training or a process or what happened on some accident that we're familiar with, you know, the recent 737 MAX accidents are an example of that. Also, Air France 447, which of course is a frequent reference point, since we both flew the 330 and were qualifying on it at the time when that occurred."

"Can you describe her demeanor as she discussed these safety compliance issues?"

"Interested, concerned," Craig said. "I think you used the term, asked about *rational*, yeah, absolutely. Just a peer-to-peer discussion, I guess."

"After she had been referred for a Section 8 Mental Health Evaluation, did she call and talk to you about that referral?"

"Yes, that's been discussed," Craig said.

"And how would you describe her demeanor, behavior, as she discussed those issues?"

"You know, it's a remarkable thing about Darby, I've said, I've known her almost 20 years and talked about a lot of things, and as a result of that I consider Darby a trusted friend, and I think she feels the same way about me.

"All the things that she went through, I think about myself going through something like that, and I can't imagine, at some point, not feeling the need to vent or to lash out, or to just have somebody to talk to and say, you know, I just don't know if I can keep doing this anymore, or you know, this is really getting me down, or you know, those bastards, you won't believe what they did to me this time—and I never heard anything like that come from Darby, ever, not once. And I think that is remarkable."

Darby glanced back at Linda and Jackie. They both retained neutral expressions. Even Kathryn had listened to Darby and shared many tears with her. She trusted Craig and valued him as a friend, but his life was full of his own challenges and did not need to add her dismay to it, too.

"Have you ever discussed SMS with other pilots at Global?"

"Well, a little bit. Usually when I say SMS they say, '*What is that? Is that part of the airplane?*'"

"Well, to the extent you have knowledge of SMS, to what do you attribute having obtained that knowledge?" Robert asked.

"Because I know Darby."

Craig testified he never received training on SMS. Robert added to the record a dozen safety concerns Captain Craig Jehn had with Global. Story after story he shared events. Then Robert asked him about his nominating her for the ambassador award. Global, thereafter, had pulled her before the company upgraded her nomination to the next level due to her exceptionalism as an employee.

Judge Geraghty was seeing the Global puzzle come together. She would not be surprised if he threw away his Global miles and flew only on Alaska or United in the future. It was now Ms. Narcea's turn to challenge Craig, and Darby prayed that he could weather that storm.

"Captain Jehn, you testified that you had submitted Ms. Bradshaw for a Chairman's Club Peer to Peer Award, and that it had been nominated and upgraded on June 20, 2016, correct?"

"I'm not sure of the date on that," he said.

"Well, you can flip to it, if you need to. It's on the back," Narcea said.

"I see June 13th, it looks like, as a date that's on here," Craig said.

"And so, your nomination of Ms. Bradshaw was upgraded *after* she was referred for a Section 8 evaluation, correct?"

"I have no idea," Craig said.

"You don't know when she was referred for her mental health evaluation?" Narcea asked.

"No," Craig said.

"It was March 2016," Narcea said. "Then your nomination would have been upgraded after her Section 8 referral."

"I'm not following what you're saying," Craig said.

"Is counsel testifying?" Robert asked, and Darby wanted to laugh.

"So, you don't know when she was referred for the Section 8?" she asked again.

"No, no, I don't know," he said, scratching the back of his head.

"Okay. No further questions," Narcea said.

That was it? Darby thought when the Judge released them for the day, telling everyone to not discuss their testimony. They would reconvene at 0800 the following morning.

Darby leaned toward Robert and whispered, "Why was that cross examination so short?"

"Craig was the first of Global employees to have direct knowledge to substandard training," Robert said. "They could challenge him on assertions, but it would only dig a deeper hole. They cut their losses and ended it."

CHAPTER 22

EXHAUSTED, DARBY ARRIVED at Kathryn's house, but could not motivate herself to get out of the car. Linda and Jackie were already inside, and she wanted to be with her friends. But she wasn't sure she could handle any more drama for the day. Day one of trial zapped her and she was only an observer. Perhaps getting some sleep was not the worst idea before she testified.

She closed her eyes for a moment, sucked a deep breath, and then opened the car door. Forcing a smile in an effort to change her mood, she walked up the path. A quick knock at the door and she opened it and went inside, trying to shrug off her exhaustion.

The warmth of Kathryn's home embraced her. Only Kathryn lived here now, with the kids off to school. But Darby could still feel their energy. Change was a good thing, so they say. That was the thing about life, it changed with time. Everything changes. Even people. But her friends were here forever, and she loved them.

"Hey," Darby said, as she entered the kitchen. Linda and Jackie were sitting at the table with an open bottle of wine between them, and glasses in their hands.

Kathryn embraced her. "I'm so sorry I could not get there today," she said. "Please sit. Let me get you a glass."

As Darby sat, Kathryn placed a glass in front of her and Linda filled it.

"Thank you," Darby said, and raised it. "To the final stage of hell, may I break through the fire with only first-degree burns."

"Yeah. No," Jackie said. "To friends, where love is thicker than blood."

"I love that," Darby said, placing a hand to her heart. Her eyes watered, and she used a napkin to dab under them. They all clinked glasses and Darby drank a large gulp of wine.

Kathryn placed deep dish lasagna on a placemat before them. Then she returned with grilled cheese sandwiches, made from homemade French bread.

"Oh my God," Darby said, eyeing Kathryn. "Double comfort food? Seriously?"

"If whatever it is to bring on a feast like this," Linda said, digging into the lasagna, "I don't care."

"I'm going to gain ten pounds just by looking at it," Jackie said.

Darby then scooped a heaping pile of lasagna onto her plate, and she reached for her sandwich and bit into it. Closing her eyes, she moaned as she chewed. She had not tasted anything this good in a long time. "These calories are more valuable than therapy," Darby said with her mouth full.

"Don't over think it," Kathryn said with a laugh. I just had too much bread and cheese in this house and didn't trust myself." She set a Caesar salad on the table and joined them.

They talked about the trial despite orders not to, but none of her friends were testifying. Besides, she had no doubt Global's legal team was stuck in a dark hole strategizing after the day's testimony as how to counter it.

Darby finished her sandwich and did as much damage to the

lasagna as she could handle, accompanied by a large serving of salad. "That was delicious," she said, placing a hand over her stomach. She then stood and began to pick up plates.

"Leave those," Kathryn said, reaching for a third bottle of wine.

"We should at least rinse them," Jackie said.

They all quickly cleared the table and rinsed the dishes that made it all the way into the dishwasher. Perhaps everyone was delaying the inevitable. But it only took ten minutes to clean the kitchen together and they moved the party to the living room.

Darby sat on the floor in front of the gas fireplace. Linda and Jackie were on the couch and Kathryn was sitting in the easy chair looking extremely uncomfortable. They all stared at Kathryn, each wondering what happened and what she was about to tell them.

"I feel like we're your kids about to get lectured," Darby said.

"I wish it were that simple," Kathryn said staring into her wine.

Darby exchanged looks of concern with Linda and Jackie, while they gave her time.

Kathryn finally looked up and said, "The President of the United States is going to pardon former President Drake."

"How can that be possible?" Darby said.

Former U.S. President Drake owned and operated Drake Industries, the largest manufacturer of airplane parts in the world. For his part in the conspiracy to commit murder, he went to prison. The world had always speculated that he ran for Presidency to control taxes to protect his company. But Darby believed his real motivation was to own the aviation industry with autonomous aircraft. No better way than to do that than to become the president who appoints the positions for the controlling agencies within the FAA and DOT.

"The president can pardon anyone," Kathryn said. "They never proved Drake killed anyone; they had just enough evidence to convince a jury that he was participatory."

"A jury of his peers that didn't like him," Darby said.

"But that recording you found can't be overlooked," Linda said to Kathryn.

"That's what got him," Darby said. "But still…"

President Drake had attended college with Lawrence Patrick, the former CEO of Global Air Lines. Patrick learned the airline business while at Coastal Airways, and then he became the CEO at Global and merged the two airlines. The recordings Darby found were enough to implicate Drake, or at least prove he was an accomplice. Lawrence Patrick died driving off a bridge, a couple FAA employees died, as well as a pilot friend of Darby's. Mr. Patrick's death gave Walter Croft the CEO position at Global.

There was always speculation whether the deaths were suicides or accidents, but the recordings indicated motive. Drake went to prison. San Quentin, a low-level security prison, which was nothing but a token sentence. Bill Jacobs, Kathryn's ex-husband, was shortly thereafter transferred to the same prison.

"There's more," Kathryn said, her face paling. "They're pardoning Bill, too."

"What the fuck!" Darby said jumping to her feet. "They can't!"

Jackie began to cry, and Linda's face drained of all color. Bill had tried to kill both Kathryn and Darby after they discovered he was behind a series of plane crashes. Crashes that killed both Jackie and Linda's husbands.

"They can't do this," Darby said, shifting her weight from one foot to the other. She placed a hand to her forehead. "And the kids. Oh my God, they were so young when this happened. Kat, do you think he'll try to get to them?"

"I don't know what he'll do. I'm sick about this. John told me last Friday, but I couldn't believe it. I spent all weekend trying to find out if it was true. I talked to the girls. They promised to stay clear if they see him and call me immediately. Then today I spent the day trying to stop it, to no avail."

"Bill had something to do with setting up the Boeing 737 MAX crashes with Drake from prison," Darby said. "He had to be working with Drake. How can they just let them out? The FAA, Global, and the union are all involved."

Linda patted the couch between she and Jackie. "Please, come here for a minute," she said to Darby. "Please."

With her heart racing, the soothing effect of the wine now gone, Darby sat between Linda and Jackie. She was breathing hard, trying to control her emotions. She never had a panic attack before, but this felt like one. It was hard to catch her breath.

Linda squeezed her hand and said, "You cannot be accusing everyone like this, as if it's some big conspiracy. They will use your words against you."

"But it's true," Darby said. "It's all tied together. It has to be."

"I think you're right," Kathryn said. "But so is Linda."

Darby finally controlled her breathing and then placed her hands over her face, leaned forward, and began to cry. Linda rubbed her back, and Jackie placed a hand on her leg. Darby wanted to push them away, but she didn't. She wasn't crying for herself. Her tears were the result of a broken world, and what pardoning criminals said about justice—there was none. She cried in fear of what would happen to Kathryn and the twins with Bill out of prison.

"Oh my God," Darby said, and sat up. "You need to get a restraining order."

"As do you," Kathryn said.

CHAPTER 23

TRIAL DAY 2
STEVE HOLMS DIRECT EXAMINATION
MARCH 26, 2019

DARBY PUSHED THE news Kathryn had presented the night before out of her mind. She swallowed three Advil to eliminate her wine-induced, legal system nightmare-provoked headache from getting any worse than it was. She had a horrible night of sleep. Bill Jacobs chased her with a poker through her house and she couldn't scream, as hard as she tried. Tom stood in the yard and watched, surrounded by tombstones with her friends' names etched in the stones.

Shaking those thoughts from her mind, she breathed deep. She would be testifying after Steve and needed to keep it together. She needed to focus.

Judge Geraghty placed the proceedings back on the record, and Robert called the first witness of the day. Steve Holms, a Global pilot, who had merged from Coastal to Global with Darby. They had a 30-year history, as he had been one of her first flight instructors. Steve had over 22,000 flight hours with 19,000 in jets.

He had also worked as an ALPO representative and defended Darby early in her career when Global had been after her for a blog post she'd written about Air France Flight 447, a flight that fell into the ocean due to equipment failure, which the pilots lacked the training to overcome. As it turned out, Global and the FAA both knew that there was a problem with the pitot system that ended that flight, and 228 people's lives. Yet they did nothing until after the fact.

The goal with Steve's testimony was to confirm the warning that Darby had a target on her back. Miss Abbott, the pass travel lady, had stated Darby's concern was paranoia. But not if she had been warned.

Robert handed the letter of counsel to Steve that Global had given Darby regarding her Air France 447 blog post. "Tell us your involvement, if any, with respect to this, the issuance of this letter of counsel, and any aftermath?"

"I represented Darby in this case," Steve said confidently. "There was a pre-meeting with Oliver Miller, the chief pilot and regional director at the time, and Lee Stevens, the assistant chief. We started the meeting with the four of us, and then we brought in Darby and this letter was presented to her."

Steve explained his history of pilot representation in disciplinary proceedings, representing pilots for three years as a captain representative.

"Was the company response to Ms. Bradshaw's blog consistent with your prior experience?"

"Not exactly," Steve said. "Normally, if a pilot is disciplined, does something wrong, it usually falls into different categories. If you do something wrong and you're unaware, and someone brings it to your attention, and they correct it then there is not an issue."

"In the aftermath of this meeting, did you express any concerns to Ms. Bradshaw?"

"Yes, I did. I said, *They're gunning for you. This is heavy-handed, you have a target on your back, keep your head below the ridge line.*"

"Did you discuss this matter with Captain Miller?" Robert asked.

"Yes, I did. At the pre-meeting, I asked, you know, is this a minor deal, medium deal, or a big deal where it's going to be a big problem. And his indication, at that time, was, *'Hey, it's not that big a deal, we just want to make sure she's aware of the policy on social media.'* So, we had the meeting and I said, *'You know, this seems a little heavy, you know, are you guys going to give her a line check or, you know, take any other action?'* and Miller told me, at that time, he said, *'No, no, we don't do that, that's not how we deal with discipline.'* I said, *'But you put a letter in the box, which is inconsistent with other counsel, with other pilots.'"*

"Why did you bring up the issue of a line check," Robert asked. "Do you mean line check as a disciplinary action?"

"Correct," Steve said.

"Hold on, counsel." Judge Geraghty said. "In your experience, has Global used a line check as a disciplinary means?"

"I have talked to other pilots that have gotten line checks, several of them. So, the policy is they don't do it. When you normally get one every 24 months, but get many in a short period of time, that is inconsistent with what they say the policy is."

The testimony continued as Steve explained his efforts to warn Darby's union representatives after he left the position. He knew what the company was doing and went out of his way to voice his concerns to Oliver Miller, who downplayed them.

"Have you, in the last few years, reported a safety event to the company?" Robert asked.

"Yes, I have," Steve said.

He described his transition from widebody aircraft to a Boeing 737, and the many flap issues he noticed, as well as serious discrepancies in the flight operations manual and operations on the narrow body aircraft. He made a report that pilots were not extending flaps. He gave it time after he reported, months in fact, yet the company was still having thousands of incidents with the flaps not being set.

He wrote to ALPO safety. He wrote to flight safety. He even talked to chief pilots, to no avail.

"I want to know," Judge Geraghty finally said, "can you tell me, you talk about this flap check not set, how was that significant to either takeoff or landing?"

"Without the right flaps, you're going to die!" Steve exclaimed.

Chapter 24

ROBERT FINISHED QUESTIONING Steve regarding Global's safety issues, and then they took a quick break. Upon return, it was Global's chance at him.

"Earlier, you testified about hearing, and I guess, *secondhand*, from people, that they had experienced *alleged* retaliatory line checks. Who, specifically, told you they had experienced retaliatory line checks?" Ms. Narcea asked.

"I heard from several people, but if you want a name, Captain Dan Walker."

"So, Dan Walker told you. Anyone else?"

"Several other people, I don't remember names."

Steve was protecting the other pilots. Not unlike Walker, Robert had subpoenaed him, therefore he gained an element of protection. Yet, there was no protection for those pilots named in court. That was the problem with the Global culture—nobody was safe.

"So, the only two people you can recall are Dan Walker and Darby Bradshaw?" Narcea said feigning disbelief.

Steve was discussing line checks when Narcea asked if line checks were considered discipline. Robert objected, and Darbty didn't understand why. But Geraghty overruled him and Steve had to answer.

"Yes, they are. You fail a line check, you can be fired," Steve said.

"Well, that's if you fail it, but just the act of a line check isn't disciplinary," Narcea said.

"When you get a line check, you are being looked at by the company. If it's not during the normal 24 months with the regulatory procedure, then it's considered a disciplinary action in my mind. Being an instructor, you could almost fail somebody every single time by putting pressure on someone. That's not the role of the instructor, but it can be used as that. I would see a line check, many line checks within that 24-month period as being retaliatory and disciplinary."

Narcea pressed Steve as to who scheduled line checks and finally said, "So, if you don't know who schedules the line checks. You don't know what factors are used by those individuals to determine if a line check is needed?"

"At Global, if you had a failure in training then there's increased check rides that go along with that. If there's a safety event that the company feels needs to be part of remedial training process, there would be a line check, but it would be associated with an event.

"But the 24-month, or the initial check, when you're first checking out on a piece of equipment, that's when you'd get the line check. So, you'd get the training, you get a line check, you're good to go. And then you're going to get one every 24-months, unless you're in a special training program or you've had an event that the group of people that go through the event, which is the FAA, the company and ALPO, determine that you would go and get a line check."

To say Steve jumped down her throat would be an understatement. He knew his stuff, he was assertive, and he didn't mix words. He also clearly communicated—don't challenge me because you can't win. Narcea got that message loud and clear. Steve's cross examination was over. But that meant Darby would be next.

CHAPTER 25

LUNCH

JUDGE GERAGHTY ORDERED an early lunch break and Darby was glad for the temporary reprieve. She removed her phone from her purse to text Kathryn and widened her eyes at the text message that had arrived earlier that morning.

She sent Kathryn a message —*Busy during lunch. Starting my testimony at 12:15.* She sent a similar text to Tom. She found Linda and Jackie in the restroom and showed them the message she had received—*My name is Dan Hanley. I was diagnosed bipolar for reporting safety concerns. Please call if you're interested.*

"Are you going to call him?" Linda asked.

"I think so," Darby said. "I hear about other cases all the time. Usually, it's always too late to do anything. But something about this…yeah, I'm going to call."

Darby stayed in the courtroom to avoid the noise of the cafeteria, and Linda and Jackie headed downstairs. She closed the courtroom door and pressed call.

"Dan, this is Darby Bradshaw," she said when he answered.

"Thank you for returning my call so quickly," he said. "I heard about your case from a Global pilot who said they paid a doctor to claim you were bipolar. It sounded like my case."

"I'm actually in trial today," Darby said. "What happened?"

"September 11th happened. Flight attendants were concerned that security measures the company promised were not being implemented and they wanted me to say something to management. So, I approached lower-level company management and the union, and in more words or less, they said, 'Watch it, Dan, these guys are nasty' and told me that if I took it to the next level of management I would 'get hurt.'"

"Wow," Darby said. "I was warned too, by the union."

"I guess that's how they roll."

"What airline was this?" she asked.

"Delta."

"Dang. I heard those guys are bigger assholes than Global," Darby said.

"Later I was told that the company thought that I was a big-mouthed, loose-cannon whistleblower, and they wanted me to go away."

"What did you do?" Darby asked, wandering to the back of the courtroom.

"I knew that I had to protect myself because of the blowback, and the union informed me that they were not going to follow me into this very far."

"I'm sorry," Darby said, sitting on the edge of the table. "ALPO didn't help me either."

"Yeah, great union we have. So, I knew I was on my own and I set about developing an extensive paper trail and recorded phone and face-to-face conversations and established a witness list of close friends."

"That's good," Darby said. "I had a good paper trail but no recordings."

"Well, I had seen other pilots terminated based on trumped-up psychiatric evaluations. So, I saw a psychiatrist and psychologist in Atlanta to confirm the soundness of my mental health because I had been warned by the ALPO attorney that if the company could not terminate me on professional grounds, they would do it via a psych eval."

"Me too," Darby said. "I was so naïve, couldn't believe doctors could be bought to do such a thing."

"I wish it weren't possible," Dan said, "but it is. I wrote letters and emails and made recorded phone calls, while sending in Captain's reports that were stonewalled. I decided to write the CEO of Delta Airlines a letter stating that, due to the constraints imposed on the union while Delta was in bankruptcy, it was precluded from representing the pilots. My union leader in New York convinced me to let him forward the letter to ALPO attorneys for review."

"Oh my God," Darby said. "I was convinced to see my ALPO representative attorneys before I gave my safety report to senior management, too. Did they help?"

"Hell no, in a later phone conversation with both the ALPO attorney and grievance committee chairman they both said that they agreed with the contents of my letter but advised me not to send it to the CEO. When I asked why not, the grievance committee chairman said, *'Go ahead and send that letter in if you never want to fly another Delta airplane again in your life'*.

"My ALPO attorneys tried to convince me not to give the report in writing," Darby said. "I didn't listen."

"I listened, to an extent," Dan said. "I filed several reports that brought the FAA in but was immediately removed from the flight schedule. The company wanted to arrange meetings but would not allow me to bring an attorney in since ALPO would not represent me."

"They grounded you because you contacted the FAA?" Darby said. "I wish you would have known about the AIR21 whistleblower law at the time. It could have helped."

"Hindsight," he said. "Delta put me on the sick list without my having seen an aeromedical professional. When I was running out of sick time and I called my chief pilot who encouraged me to submit to the Employee Assistance Program to guarantee continuance of my pay, which I did. I knew at that point in time that I had more than enough evidence and witness testimony to nail both the FAA and Delta."

This felt so much like Global when they denied her the disability insurance payments unless she asserted that she was bipolar. She had refused. Her paperwork stated 'no diagnosis' but she till requested the insurance because Global had refused to allow her to fly due to a false mental health assertion. They denied her.

"I flew to Chicago to meet with an AME and the employee assistant rep. The AME asked me if I would be willing to speak with a mental health professional to which I agreed. My visit to the Alexian Brothers Behavioral Health Hospital wound up to be a three-day ordeal after which a psychiatrist who had only seen me for 30 minutes diagnosed me as being bipolar."

"Holy shit!" Darby said.

"Grounded for life, I fought it for five years, but the government department of transportation inspector general closed my case without interviewing a single witness or reviewing my evidence. My intent during this time was not to get my job back but to expose the illegal methods employed by the FAA and management to rid the ranks of unwanted pilots."

"You and me both," Darby said. "I've been hounding the Illinois medical board for Dr. Wood's license for years now, to no avail."

"Well get this," Dan said. "In 2006, I learned of a Coastal Airlines DC-10 Captain Field McConnell, that Coastal, the FAA *and* ALPO were attempting to railroad off the property by forcing him to see a quack shrink in LA named Dr. Joseph Elmer. I contacted Field and told him not to go as it was a setup. A few days later he retired early."

"I was told by a good friend, a Global pilot, the same thing," Darby said. "But my attorney advised me that I had to follow the contract or kiss my job goodbye. If the contract said I had to go, and I refused, I was in the wrong. I also wasn't fearful he would fail me, I suspected he might. But I knew that the truth would protect me."

"How's that working for you?" Dan said with a chuckle.

Darby smiled. "Well, I was fortunate enough to have a few chain-of-events occur simultaneously that even if I was crazy, the doctor probably would not have ruled against me."

"How's that?"

"Some guy in the FAA warned my AME to not get backed into a corner because Global was the *baddies*. My AME passed me onto the Regional Director who gave me my medical. When the FAA deputy flight surgeon challenged the Regional Director, at the direction of Global Air Lines, this guy stood his ground. My AME would have folded. The Regional Director was a retired General and had the wherewithal to stand up to the challenge and do the right thing.

"He ended up investigating his own decision. After his report, the FAA medical appeals board cleared me a week *before* the neutral examiner decided my fate. Of which Global had told him to do again, no expense spared. Because Global interfered with the FAA, *and* delayed the doctor's decision, it backfired. The neutral doctor could not go against the Mayo Clinic *and* the FAA medical appeals board, even if he wanted to. Timing was on my side."

"That it was," Dan said. "Well, in 2007, Field informed me

that he thought the 911 aircraft had been electronically hijacked and remotely controlled to their targets through employment of a system called the uninterruptible autopilot that enables a remote source to take complete control of the aircraft autopilot and flight management computer."

"The *what?*" Darby said.

"The uninterruptible autopilot," he repeated. "This was my *aha* moment as I did not believe the hijackers were qualified to fly the Boeing 757 or 767 aircraft but did not know how the aircraft struck their targets with such precision and on the first attempt."

"Huh," Darby said. She didn't necessarily buy into that theory, but when a person's opinion became a mental health issue, that was something everyone should fear.

"Well, Field and I worked together for several years attempting to enlighten the public of the existence of this system. I created a grassroots network called the *Whistleblowing Airline Employees Association,* launched a website and blog, and even hosted a podcast for many months to draw attention to lapses in aviation safety and security and other issues."

"When we're done can you text me that link?" Darby asked.

"Of course," Dan said. "I'm planning to create a grassroots effort this Fall called 911 Pilot Whistleblowers whose purpose is to show that the 911 aircraft were electronically hijacked and electronically controlled."

"How do you know that autopilot exists?" Darby asked.

"During the process of this investigation, we learned that the uninterruptible autopilot had, in fact, been patented in 2006 by Boeing, but we have witnesses who will confirm that it was developed and produced in the mid-90s well prior to 911."

"I'm speechless," Darby said. "I don't know what happened with

911, other than close to three thousand people died. But there were too many holes in stories, errors made, and nobody held accountable for those systemic failures. I also know that the industry has profited from those deaths since, in many ways."

"That they have," Dan said. "Forcing passengers to put their baggage in cargo for a significant fee, items prevented through security, but purchased on the other side at twice the price, to carry on the plane. It goes on and on."

"Have you seen the patent of the uninterruptible autopilot?" Darby asked.

"I have."

"Drake Industries would not be named on it would they?" Darby said.

"Actually… they are. How did you know?"

CHAPTER 26

DARBY STARED OUT the window thinking about what Dan had said. She hadn't known anyone had returned to the courtroom until Linda touched her arm and startled her. She turned toward Linda, as everyone was moving into their respective positions.

"How'd your call go?" Linda asked.

Darby lowered her voice and said, "Scarier than hell. I'll tell you after we're done here."

She approached the stand and sat as nerves, like she had never experienced before, took hold. It was an odd feeling to be sitting on stage. Not so much like a fish in a bowl, but more like a lobster in a tank waiting to be selected, boiled, and eaten.

The judge swore her in, and she provided her flight experience. Then Robert opened with Global's safety culture report. Wendel, who had replaced Ms. Narcea for her questioning, immediately objected to Robert's first question.

Darby became a silent observer as the argument between attorneys grew to an all-out verbal battle. This was not such a bad way to get acclimated to the stand. She sat there and watched, without being the center of attention.

"You're talking about the 43- or 45-page report?" Judge Geraghty finally interjected.

"Forty-five-page report, yes," Robert said.

"I'm going to allow this. If I understand the testimony, part of the testimony is Dr. Wood provided voluminous amounts of information and dug into this airman's records, and relied on portions of that report, at various times, to render an opinion—of which I have not read. I've purposely *not* read all that stuff, because I want to hear what he has to say.

"But I'm going to give leeway if he dug in and provided this information. I'm not a doctor and I can't dispute his opinion about bipolar or whatever, but I *can* evaluate the facts that are in that report and any rationale he uses to come to a conclusion.

"I can't question his conclusion, but I may be able to question some of the facts, if they're correct or erroneous, to how he comes to that conclusion. So, I'm going to give you some leeway. She has the burden at this stage. Go ahead," Judge Geraghty said.

Robert reread the question and Darby thought about it for a second and then responded.

"The issue was not to pick apart Global," Darby said. "It wasn't even to make a complaint about a *specific* issue. Global had a culture of manage by threat."

Darby explained her motivations and that she simply aligned examples of a negative safety culture with behaviors initiating from the time of the merger to the time of her reporting. She testified that the report was an ethnographic study encompassing several years.

"My first experience on Global property, a scheduling manager said that there were four reasons that if you got an inverse assignment, you didn't have to take it."

Darby explained that an inverse assignment was when the pilot was on their days off and the company had nobody else to fly. Global could force the pilot to take the trip, except for the four reasons they couldn't—a childcare problem, they couldn't get to the airport, they'd been drinking, or were fatigued.

"The manager said '*Don't ever call in fatigued. At Global Air Lines, fatuigue is the other F word, it would be better to call in drinking.* Then I asked, '*At six in the morning?*'"

Darby explained the difference between Coastal and Global's training philosophy, not dissimilar to the doors that Captain Joe Galen had explained in his testimony. Coastal had empowered their instructors to create the changes needed. Global told instructors to mind their own business, and if there was a better way management would already be doing it.

She glanced at the safety report. Global had allegedly dissected Darby's safety report and asserted there were EEOC issues buried within it, and the reason Global requested her to meet with Ms. Abbott, the equal opportunity and pass travel manager. However, Darby had refused when Rich Clark told her to meet with EO. He lied, telling Darby that Abbott was an HR safety investigator. It was all a ruse, and she told the judge as much.

"Throughout your career, at any of the other airlines you were employed, did you have any personal issues that could have been Equal Opportunity issues?" Robert asked.

"Probably daily," Darby said with a grin. She failed to add that many could have been her initiation to avoid incriminating herself. The choice back then was to join in the jokes or become the brunt of them. But none of the humor ever bothered her. She never filed an EO or gender-based complaint at any airline and Robert asked her why not.

"Well, some of the things, like the guys putting naked pictures of women in compartments on the 727… well, I know they didn't do that to get me. I was the first woman at many of the airlines I flew, and at the time I came into *their* world. Those pictures were already there. And it also wasn't offensive to me, therefore I kind of dealt with it in my own way. One night I put my own pictures in the cockpit," Darby said with a grin.

She had cut out pictures from *Playgirl* magazine and replaced the photos of boobs with pictures of little guy parts. "The real issue is that women are such a small minority, that if a woman said anything, she's ostracized in this industry. Even today, you hear all the *'Me Too'* stuff in every other industry, except the airlines. Not that it's not going on here, it is. Women just don't say anything about it, or their careers are over."

"What has been your experience with respect to Global's diversity within the pilot force?" Robert asked.

"I think Global is at 4.6 percent women, well below 7 percent worldwide. From what I learned, many of those women aren't even working today. While I was working on my MBA, I had taken a diversity course. I had emailed Walter Croft, who was the chief financial officer at the time, now our CEO, and asked him what they were doing related to diversity. That was around 2008. He sent me to another Global executive, who said they *'had a difficult time with diversity at Global Air Lines at the leadership level, but they were starting a focus group.'* Which I thought to be odd because focus groups for diversity started in the early '70s.

"I look at diversity far different than gender, race, or religion," Darby said. "In a safety orientated business, you want differences that you can bring to the table to problem solve. In my frame of reference, diversity is different thoughts, different people, different experiences."

"What was your overall objective in submitting this safety report?"

Robert asked.

"We were coming up on the mandated regulatory compliance of SMS. Safety Management Systems. Global had an SMS in place but we weren't following it, and Global did not have the safety culture to support an SMS."

The presentation she gave was based upon her safety report and titled, *Global Air Lines Ethnographic Study*, because it was an eight-year lookback that provided examples and standard practices that conflicted with the FAA's defined safety culture necessary to support the federally mandated SMS regulation.

Rich Clark, however, identified her lookback and those examples as her inability to let things go from the past. After Clark's deposition, Darby realized that he more than likely had no idea what ethnographic meant. Regardless, stupidity should not be a defense.

"Before you continue, I've got a question," Judge Geraghty said. "Structurally, I'm trying to understand where you're going with this. Where does the Director of Safety fit in all of this?"

"The Director of Safety would be somebody that I would go to if pilots were having say, a pushback problem due to a tug, something on the airplane. SMS is the CEO's responsibility."

Darby explained that there was a need to have the final authority in the flight deck—the captain. But with crew resource management, the captain must be willing to listen, and expand his team to the flight crew, flight attendants, ATC, and ground crew. Risk mitigation was the key. SMS was similar in that the accountable executive, that person of authority, must expand his team throughout the organization. Employees must be free to communicate, share concerns and be able to report if there was a problem, free of retaliation. Global's negative safety culture was evident, if for no other reason, they had retaliated against her for providing a safety report.

Darby explained that she had asked her Regional Director, Robert Dodson, who the accountable executive for SMS was and he thought she was talking about social media. That statement was eye-opening, as was his response when she offered him a safety management systems book. Dodson said he didn't read because he didn't have time, which opposed a safety culture of continued learning.

"Has your question been answered?" Robert asked the judge when Darby was finished.

"One follow-up," Judge Geraghty said. "Who's the accountable manager under SMS?"

"The CEO," Darby said. "Walter Croft."

CHAPTER 27

JUDGE GERAGHTY OPENED the door for Robert's ensuing line of questions. The perfect segue, as Robert handed Darby the transcript from Walter Croft's deposition. She could have told him what Croft had said without it, but Robert wanted her to read it verbatim.

"When asked what his understanding of SMS was, what did Croft reply?" Robert asked.

"He said, *'I don't know, I'm not a pilot or a technician.'*"

"When asked what Croft's understanding of the components of SMS was, what was his reply?"

"He said, *'I don't know the components off the top of my head, I have no idea.'*"

"When he was asked what his personal involvement in SMS compliance was, what was his response?"

"He said, *'I don't have one.'*"

"He was asked if he knew that he was the accountable executive," Robert said. "Can you read me his response?"

"Yes," Darby said. He said, *'I don't even know what accountable executive means.'*"

"And were you aware, at that time, about his knowledge as he describes in this testimony here?" Robert asked.

"Objection!" Wendel cried.

"Basis?" Judge Geraghty asked in a non-emotional tone.

"He didn't read the whole testimony," Wendel complained. "He cherry-picked lines within the testimony. And if he asks the witness what… he can't use this testimony to ask this witness that question! He can ask the witness what she *knew* about Walter Croft's involvement in SMS, but to read parts of a deposition transcript and then ask the witness '*did you know about this particular testimony,*' which obviously hadn't been given in 2016, when she was trying to contact him, in fact, the SMS program, I think, wasn't even mandated until 2018. It's not a proper use of deposition testimony."

Wendel forgot Darby had witnessed Croft's entire deposition and could testify to it. He also voiced his objection in a whiny-ass, two-year old, non-comprehensive plea. He was wrong about regulatory requirements—if the FAA approved any program, mandated or not, the airline was required, by law, to follow it.

Judge Geraghty listened patiently to Wendel's objection. When Wendel came up for air, the judge calmly asked, "Anything else?"

"I think I went too far by about four minutes already," Wendel said. "So, I'll stop there."

"Okay," Geraghty said. "Overruled. You can address it in cross."

"Based on your knowledge of SMS," Robert said, "does this testimony reflect non-compliance by Global with SMS?"

"Objection, foundation," Wendel said.

"Sustained," Geraghty said.

"If I may state for the record," Robert said, "it's under 14 CFR Part 5, Global is required to train its employees and, in effect, make its employees knowledgeable of the requirements of SMS. It states it, right in Part 5. So, every Global pilot ought to be competent, every Global pilot, *by law*, ought to be competent to answer these questions. Especially the CEO."

"Counsel?" Judge Geraghty said, shifting his attention to Wendel.

"First of all, again, you have to read all the testimony. Mr. Croft is not a pilot. Secondly, this witness hasn't been offered as an expert in the SMS system in 2016. There's no record reflecting any of those positions here in this case. And if counsel wants to argue later on legal issues about SMS, he can do so.

"Last, what is the relevance to the claims in this case of any of this testimony? It has *nothing* to do with Ms. Bradshaw being placed in Section 8 as a result of complaints about, or protected activity about safety, nothing, whatsoever!" Wendel exclaimed, almost panicked. "So, all those reasons, I think your objection, which you've already granted, should be continued."

Geraghty returned his attention to Robert. "Rephrase your question. I mean I'm tracking you for the SMS and where you're going with the SMS route, but rephrase."

Judge Geraghty was no fool to safety. He'd been an FAA prosecuting attorney, and he was a pilot. He fully understood language and safety ramifications. There was no way the jury would understand a fraction of what was happening here. Judge Geraghty was another story. He could pick the fly shit out of the pepper. She thanked God for providing him for this battle.

Robert brought forth an email that Darby had written to Mr. Croft, and passed between Rich Clark and George Wyatt, Clark telling Wyatt that Darby had invited Croft to her presentation. He was quite appalled.

"And why did you invite Mr. Croft to your SMS presentation?"

"Because he was the accountable SMS executive."

"Did you provide Dr. Wood with this email?"

"I did not."

"Okay," Robert said, "the next reference from Dr. Wood's report reads—*In this email she invites the future CEO to attend a meeting arranged by others, without asking them. This is another example of the impact of an expansive mood. Also note that she addresses Mr. Croft as 'Walt' undo familiarity as associated with mania,'* (spelled here u-n-d-o).

"Did Dr. Wood ever bring up the inappropriateness of referencing Mr. Croft as Walt?"

"I don't think so," Darby said. "But if he had, I would have corrected him."

Robert then brought forth an email from Rich Clark to Darby and said, "It reads, *'It will be necessary for HR to become involved, along with EEOC, prior to meeting with Captain Wyatt and me.'* Now, had you requested that HR or EO become involved?"

"No."

"When that suggestion was made to you, how did you respond to Captain Clark?"

"I told him I wanted to focus on the safety issues."

"And if you can move up to the email thread before that, from Rich Clark to George Wyatt, approximately, three months before your meeting with Ms. Abbott," Robert said. "It reads, *'Here we go. Just FYI, I will brief HR and handle this with kid gloves. She could be a candidate for a Section 8 after this meeting goes through.'* At that timeframe was *anyone* suggesting that you had a mental health issue?"

"No. The only suggestion was from my union that if I brought my safety report to Captains Wyatt and Clark, that they would utilize the Section 8 against me."

"Move to strike, non-responsive," Wendel said.

"Overruled," Judge Geraghty said.

"Why did you not want to speak to HR or EO representatives at this time?" Robert asked.

"Because I've never talked to HR or EO in my career, and I was not going to start now," Darby said. "I didn't know why they were behaving the way they were. It was just a violation of safety culture, identifying we were not going to meet our SMS compliance. Actually, we were in full violation of our current FAA approved SMS program. So, why they did what they did didn't really matter, because it was in violation of FAA regulations."

CHAPTER 28

AFTER A QUICK break Robert brought forth additional emails identifying that Global's attorney, Martha Jones, had advised Rich Clark that it was okay to meet with Darby because she *did not* have any safety information—only safety culture information. Apparently, Martha lacked the knowledge that safety culture was safety information, thus she allowed Wyatt and Clark to meet with her, and the *only* reason she had an AIR21whistlblower case.

Darby then explained her motivation for authoring the paper was because Global did not have the safety culture to support an SMS. Robert questioned Darby about providing the safety report to the union.

Darby told the judge how she met with a union attorney who advised her against giving anything in writing. The only reason she had met with the attorney was because her captain rep was concerned that something was going to happen to her if she moved forward. He said—'Please, at the very least, talk to the attorneys.'

"Did the union's attorney have any comments on your report?" Robert asked.

"She tried to convince me *not* to give it to the management team, but I didn't want to run out of time or be taken out of context. Most importantly, there were multiple pages of references. So, I asked her if she would just read it and let me know what she thought. She said it was very well written, but she still didn't want me to give it to them."

"Did she tell you why?" Geraghty asked.

"Yes, she did. She said that *'they were very corporate and scary, and it was just the attorney in her, that she didn't like to put things in writing.'* They being Clark and Wyatt."

Robert directed her to a page in her report and said, "Okay. And those bullet points, starting with two on the bottom of the page and the three on the other page, did they relate, in any way, to pilot training and competency?"

"Absolutely."

Wendel objected with force. He did not want these events on the record for a reason—they were damning to Global because they were scarier than hell. Judge Geraghty requested the basis of his objection and Wendel stated they already stipulated to protected activity and that the document spoke for itself. Geraghty overruled him and Robert continued.

Robert read the list of concerns embedded in Darby's report that identified a lack of understanding and near catastrophic events. Wendel objected on the rule of incompleteness and cherry picking, but the judge overruled him. Wendel objected based upon foundation. The judge overruled that too. Wendel was losing it. He even objected to Darby's knowledge that nobody followed up on the events in the report. He then objected six more times in the next ten minutes, and the judge overruled each time he did. After establishing a lengthy list of federal violations, inadequate training, and lack of safety culture, Robert asked Darby what she had told Ann Abbott at the meeting regarding potential accidents. Wendel objected.

"Your honor," Wendel interrupted, "I'd like a fifteen-minute break." Even though they had only 45 minutes remaining for the day.

CHAPTER 29

DARBY RETURNED TO the stand the following morning, and stared out the window, watching a KLM Boeing 747 turn a base leg on approach. The robin egg colored Whale stood out against wispy white clouds that painted the early morning sky. She smiled, thinking of the good old days. There was a line of three other aircraft in sequence for approach to another runway.

Shifting her attention toward the courtroom she smiled at Tom. He gave her a slight nod with a grin. She was fortunate to have him in her life, and happy he was sitting here today. She would not have survived all this without him. He was her rock, and she loved him.

Global's legal team eventually strode into the courtroom as if they owned it. Within no time they were on the record again. Robert began questioning her about her experience with that pass travel lady, Abbott, the person that Rich Clark feigned was a safety investigator. Global had promoted her to a manager two weeks after her report against Darby.

Robert advised Darby to not tell the judge what to think, just give him the facts and he would come to the same conclusion. She wanted to tell him that this woman was a lying bitch. Instead, she would do her best to create the picture so he could see the truth.

"Did you ever make a comment to Abbott about being physically harmed?" Robert asked.

"Never," Darby said.

"Based on your interview and face-to-face with Ms. Abbott did you have any reason to believe that she was emotionally upset?" Robert asked.

"She didn't really show any emotion. She showed, perhaps… confusion and blank stares sometimes. In hindsight, and after listening to her deposition testimony, I probably scared the hell out of her."

"Did you say anything that would scare her?" Robert asked, surprised by her response.

"Well, not knowingly at the time, because I thought she was a safety investigator. But when I found out that she had never interviewed a pilot before, that she was afraid of flying, takeoffs and landings were the worst part, and she said she couldn't sleep the night after we spoke, I was surprised she didn't sleep for a week after what I told her."

"Did you discuss any near catastrophic events with Ms. Abbott?" Robert asked.

"I did. There were four in particular," Darby said, keeping her eye on Robert as she spoke. "One of them was a 737 where the pilots got behind the approach, and thought they selected TOGA, takeoff go-around power, to go around. But they disengaged the autopilot instead, and continued flying directly toward the ground. When they finally realized what was happening and pulled the nose up, they were at 186 feet AGL, and a 2,000 foot per minute descent."

"186 AGL?" Judge Geraghty asked for clarity on the record.

"AGL. Above Ground Level," Darby said, having turned his direction. "And 2,000 feet per minute into the ground meant they were within seconds—10 seconds—of impacting the homes at the end of that runway and killing everyone on board."

Darby returned her attention to Robert and said, "And I told her this was a training issue. The captain who made the go around procedure to fix it, was the same captain who had declared an emergency because he lost his auto flight system. But that captain didn't lose the automation, he took off with it failed and continued."

"Is that a problem?" Robert asked. "Taking off without an autopilot."

"It shouldn't be. However, if a pilot feels uncomfortable flying the airplane, like this captain did, he should have gone back and landed. He didn't. Instead, he flew into RVSM air space without an autopilot, and that was illegal. And it was the first officer who flew, not him."

"Wait a minute. Reduced Vertical Separation Minimums, I believe," Judge Garrity said.

"Correct."

RVSM airspace provides only a thousand feet of vertical separation. Because that separation was so close, regulations required an autopilot. Even if air traffic control gave the pilots permission to fly into that airspace without an autopilot, doing so was a violation. If there wasn't enough fuel to fly at a lower altitude, then the pilot needed to return or land someplace. Any airline could schedule a time, a week out, to fly into RVSM airspace without an autopilot, but it had to be a preplanned event. Neither the captain, nor Global dispatch knew these rules.

"The company turned this event into a workload management video. I saw so many things wrong with this, I looked up the captain's name and I emailed him."

Darby reached for a glass of water and took a drink and then continued. "I heard about the 737 almost hitting the ground, but that captain emailed me the actual numbers. That's why I know precisely where they were and what altitude. He's also the chair of the Human Factors Committee, and he gathers the data. He emailed me and told me that *'Global pilots, as a group, cannot fly Level 0, nor can we fly Level 4, so says ASAP.'"*

She turned her attention to Judge Geraghty and said, "Level 0 meaning there is no automation and is a completely manual flight. No flight director, auto thrust, or autopilot. And Level 4 is a fully automated aircraft, what we would consider going into NextGen. He also said, regarding his flying skills, that he flew 1,500 sorties in the military and the necessity for him to declare an emergency for manual flight was a personal wake-up call. Yet nobody woke up."

Darby faced forward and spoke directly to Robert. "So, what the company identified was, that we have an entire group of pilots who can't fly our aircraft. And here, this captain, who is writing all the training procedures for this—had to declare an emergency.

"So, they used him to create a video and called it workload management. What they were really saying is—pilots, we know you can't fly, so if something happens just declare an emergency. This was a big point of my meeting with Dr. Wood. As it turned out, Global had given Dr. Wood the transcript to the workload management video, but I forwarded the emails from that Chairman to him after the meeting, and he never put them in my report."

Darby continued with her testimony detailing the events that were nothing less than life threatening to unsuspecting passengers. In one situation, a check airman, originally from Coastal, was in the right seat, and a new-to-type Global pilot was in the left seat taking his final ride as an A330 captain. Darby was the required third pilot, due to the length of their trip. They had over 259 passengers whose lives were in the hands of God, as both those captains argued over how to operate the aircraft.

An arrogant captain who lacked knowledge in the left seat was arguing with a check airman in the right seat. Darby believed that this check airman feared he could lose his job if he failed the captain, because of Global's culture. They were high on approach. They were fast. This was the left seat captain's check ride, but the check airman in the right seat was pushing buttons and helping him fly. The check airman was giving lessons on descent rate with flaps and speed brakes. The captain in the left seat was explaining that on a previous plane he couldn't use speed brakes and flaps at the same time.

The new captain was arguing but lacked experience and understanding. The check airman was also a distraction and caused much of the problem. The new captain argued, but he pulled full speed brakes to increase the descent. They came close to being a statistic.

"So, the captain disengaged the autopilot," Darby said. "And he's shooting down toward the glideslope, excessive rate of descent, and they flies through the glide slope. Then he pulls back on the stick, and while coming up to the glideslope, the power is increasing.

"On the A330 the thrust levers don't move, but the power on the engines was increasing as I could see it on the instruments. The nose was pitching up and the power was coming up and yet, we were still bellying into the ground. Headed toward the ground, the plane is screaming *Terrain!* And both those captains just sat there, neither responding. They were simply passengers sinking into the ground and not knowing why, and not doing anything.

"I saw the problem and yelled, *'Speed brakes.'* The captain jammed the speed brake lever forward, the airplane popped back up to the glideslope, caught it, and within seconds we were landing. A very firm landing, but alive." Darby rubbed her arms to ward off the chill, remembering how close to death they had come.

"So, everyone deals with their near-death experiences differently, and my heart was pounding so hard." She took a breath, then said,

"This left seat captain decided he's going to take charge of the cockpit. So, he tells me to get us a gate and then the right seat captain tells him—'*No, we don't do that. What if there's only two pilots?*' The other guy argues that the third pilot always communicates at Global." Darby turned to the judge and said, "If we fly domestic, we only need two pilots, not three like this trip." She took a drink of water and continued.

"So, they're arguing over who talks on the radio. And the left seat captain yells at me, '*Get us a gate!*' So, I called the ramp in Atlanta and asked for a gate. The agent said, '*Sweetheart, where are you?*' I stood up and looked out the window to see the taxiway, told her, and she said, '*Wait 'til you come around the corner and call me back*'.

"The captain yells at me again because apparently, they already had a gate, and I was supposed to only tell ramp we were coming in. The next thing he does is to shut down the right engine for a single engine taxi. But we're going to make two left turns, first onto the ramp and then into the gate, and now we don't have any power on the right engine. The first one is an easy left turn, but we get up to the gate and stop. The gate is on the left, at 90 degrees.

"The A330 manual states no pivot turns. I'm just sitting there wondering what they're going to do. Despite multiple options, including being towed in, he runs the power up on the left engine, holds the brakes and pivot turns. Once the engines are shut down, the check airman shook his hand said, '*Good job, get out of here, and go catch your flight.*' He signed him off."

CHAPTER 30

ROBERT WAITED A moment to allow Darby's testimony to sink in as he read his notes. The judge had to know that this was definitely *not* an EO investigation.

"Was there an A330 event in Boston that you told her about?"

Darby explained the confusion of technology for those new to flying the Airbus, supporting Captain Jehn's testimony. The Airbus had two approach modes, each having a different purpose. One was like the Boeing where the pilot selected approach and told the airplane to fly the ILS and glide slope.

"On the Airbus the computer also has an approach mode for the phase of flight," Darby said. "Therefore, you must tell the computer, *I'm going to fly the approach*. So, you select approach in the flight management system to put it into approach mode."

Darby explained that on approach they typically used selected speed, managing the speed by pulling the speed knob and turning it to accommodate ATC requests. But on final, the pilots give the speed control back to the airplane by pushing the speed button in, called managed speed. When the pilot gives the plane control, the speed is based upon phase of flight. If the pilot does not put the plane into approach mode for landing, the power comes up and increases speed.

"So, these pilots on the A330 were flying into Boston, the first officer was the pilot flying," Darby said. "They selected manage speed, the power came up, I think it was 250 knots the first time. But they go around because they don't understand why the speed increased. Then they do the exact same thing on the next approach, getting the exact same results, but the second time the speed goes to green dot."

Darby explained that green dot was a little green dot on the air speed indicator, indicating the best lift over drag speed, clean. Meaning with no flaps. She guessed it would have been about 210 knots.

"They went around three times," Darby said. "But, on the last approach when the captain said to go around, the first officer said, *No'* and kept flying the approach. When they got close to the runway, I want to say just under twenty feet, the plane announced, '*Retard, retard' and* that was the first time the first officer thought to pull the thrust back. They almost went off the end of the runway they were so fast."

"And you gave this account to Ms. Abbott?" Robert asked.

"I did," Darby said.

"Did you give her an account regarding a flight into Taipei?" Robert asked.

"Yes. I was flying with one of the new Anchorage captains that Captain Jehn told us about. ATC was bringing us in close, almost on a 90 degree right turn to the outer marker. The weather was solid IFR. We couldn't see anything out the window. We were busy, so prior to our final turn, we hadn't had a chance to clean up the flight plan.

"Cleaning up the flight plan is nothing more than when you get a vector, you delete the waypoints behind you, to remove the clutter on your map. I was the pilot flying, and we're coming in and the approach was set up. The captain says, '*Oh, I forgot to clean up the flight plan.*' I said, '*Don't worry, just leave it.*' He said, '*Oh, no, I've got it*'.

"Suddenly there was a ding, ding, ding. He wiped everything out, in front of us, too. When I say *everything*, our map was gone, and we lost all situational awareness it provided. But I had raw data—my glide slope, and my localizer. And at this point I could see all the little blips indicating other traffic out there, but the pilots are not speaking English. I have no idea where they are going, or what they're doing.

"He did this just as we were approaching the marker and so we went high. This was one of those moments of decision. Do I continue? Do I go around? Is the missed approach in the box, or did it go away too? It was one of those times that all the questions slammed into my brain at hyper speed and I decided quickly, we were going to land.

"So, we're not supposed to exceed 1,000 feet per minute descent over the marker for a stable approach. But we needed about 1,200 feet per minute to recapture the glide slope. I knew where we were, what was occurring, and I was capturing the glideslope and decided continuing would be the safer course of action. Going around was the unknown. So, I continued.

"Then just before 300 feet above decision height, without any visual, I took a breath and said, *'We're on glide slope, on localizer, missed approach altitude is'* … but it was gone, as well as our minimums. But I remembered what they were and told the captain. We immediately broke out, saw the runway, and I landed the airplane. At touchdown he said, *'Why did it do that?'*"

Darby explained that this was due to a lack of training, and these were not isolated events. This was standard performance stemming from a cultural problem within the training department, as well as the entire organization. Push the button and be the monkey mentality.

Darby said, "When I was talking to Ms. Abbot and giving her these examples of what is happening, and how critical this is, I had no idea that she was afraid of flying."

"I object to the entire testimony as non-responsive," Wendel said.

"I don't even remember what the question was, but it was, I think, what did you tell Ms. Abbott. It was a long time ago. And I object to the characterization and the hearsay about what Global did and knew in 2010."

"It's noted," Judge Geraghty said.

"Did Global modify its training in the aftermath of the Air France?"

"Objection! Objection!" Wendel yelled, but Darby continued to answer.

Then the judge interrupted her. "Hold on. Basis for the objection?"

"Foundation." Wendel said.

"Overruled," Geraghty said.

"Causation," Wendel said. "I mean they might have changed it, but the witness doesn't have a foundation whether anything was changed. Well, we haven't heard the foundation, yet, as to why they might have changed or any connection between the tragedy of Air France. If they lay the foundation, she can testify about it, in my opinion, but otherwise it's just speculation."

"Do you have knowledge of Global's training program?" Robert asked Darby.

"I do because I went through the training program. And Dr. Wood has knowledge of the training program, because Global management gave it to him, and their changes, as well."

"Wait a minute. Did those changes occur *after* Flight 447?" Judge Geraghty said.

"Yes," Darby said.

"Okay, continue," Judge Geraghty said, with another deep sigh.

"And did you receive the modified training?" Robert asked.

"I did not."

"And would that be unusual that your instructor did not provide you with the modified training?" Robert asked.

"Objection, relevance and speculation," Wendel spat.

"This all goes to communications with Abbott," Robert explained. "It's all going to be followed up with all these things that you brought to the attention of Abbott, and brought to the attention of—"

"I mean she talks fast, but it's only a three-hour meeting," Wendel said.

"I don't hear an objection," Robert countered. "I just hear sarcasm and hostility there."

"Well, hold on," Judge Geraghty said. "Connect it to the interview with Ms. Abbott."

"Did you discuss, with Ms. Abbott, any omission from your training?" Robert asked.

"I did," Darby said.

Without training, people died. What she was about to say implicated the FAA. What the judge would do with that information was the question. What he could do was another story.

Chapter 31

NOBODY HAD TO die, Darby thought as she explained to the court how she had told Abbott about Air France, and her lack of training. Darby had told the regional director and chief pilot that she had not received her stall training. A response to that oversight should have been to get her trained and query who else missed it. They did neither.

Air France flight 447 was a catastrophic accident that killed 228 people. The Airbus A330 literally fell into the ocean like a leaf because the pilots lost their computers. But it wasn't that simple. The pilots stalled the aircraft, and were ultimately helpless because they did not understand what was happening or how to deal with it.

Prior to the AF447 crash, the only stall training conducted was to watch how the plane couldn't stall. With all systems working, the Airbus would not stall. However, when the plane lost all computer capability, it behaved like a real plane, training was a necessity.

After 228 people died, an airworthiness directive, called an AD, was issued mandating a fix to the pitot system, a component that required airflow for the computer system functionality. The pitot tubes had filled with small ice balls called grapple. The system is heated, and time would have melted that ice, but because the pilots were fatigued, in the clouds, and disoriented, they overreacted.

Darby wrote a blog about how to fly out of a stall. Something that was missing in training. She didn't know at the time that Global had had 14 of those exact same events. She learned this because she found documentation of those events in her medical report from Dr. Wood.

The airline knew this system failure had been ongoing. The pilots all wrote ASAP reports; therefore, the FAA knew. But there was no fix in place at the time of the failures. Safety management systems should have prevented such an accident. SMS demanded problem identification, risk assessment, and a solution before people died. In this case, Global knew of the potential, but did not train for the event. The also FAA knew, but the agency did not issue an AD to fix the component *before* the crash, despite their very own regulations.

Robert then established that she had told Dr. Wood her safety concerns, with the intent to prove that her safety report contributed to his diagnosis of her. Then he shifted to her Skokie, Illinois, visits, on three separate occasions. Each meeting had a flavor of its own.

The first visit he challenged her background and asked about birthdays of distant relatives she'd never known. He was interested in her nannying while attending college and taking flying lessons. He'd asked if the mother had expressed her milk so Darby could feed the babies. Visit two, she tried to explain to Dr. Wood that manual flight was not an emergency, that it was a basic skill. That became a debate.

"The third time you met with him, what did you discuss?"

"Alcohol, drug abuse. He asked me if … his statement was, '*Oh, this is a good question for you West Coast people, what are your political and religious views on suicide?*'"

"Did he use the phrase, '*For you West Coast people?*'" Judge Geraghty asked.

"He did," Darby said turning his direction.

"Okay," the judge said, writing a note.

Dr. Wood had asked her about her gambling, drinking and experiences. By experiences he meant supernatural. By this time Darby suspected he was on a mission but would only play the game until he could bill no more. She never expected a fabricated diagnosis.

This doctor was also the top expert in the HIMS program, named for the Human Intervention Motivational Study, which is a substance abuse treatment program that evolved from a 1975 study that focused on airline pilots with alcohol use disorder. However, Global used that program as a tool of retaliation.

At the time Darby had decided she would have some fun and test his motivation. Was he giving her an actual evaluation of which her behavior with Abbott could be atributed to alcohol use, or was he told to just get rid of her?

When Dr. Wood had asked if she drank, she said, *'Yes.'* He asked her what she drank, and she said, *'Bloody Mary's for brunch, but I also like mimosas. I like a cold beer in the hot tub. Margaritas with Mexican food, on the rocks with salt. I like nice scotch or bourbon at the end of the day. A red wine with a steak dinner, a cab, shiraz or merlot. And champagne for celebrations is always good. But I like it dry, not sweet.'*

Dr. Wood had stared with his eyes wide open and mouth agape. Darby realized that, as the head of the HIMS program, there was nothing more that he wanted to do, than stick her into the program. Well after her meeting with him, she learned he had forced a pilot into the program who had a glass of wine at lunch, with a low-level DUI, but otherwise rarely drank. Therefore, why not her?

Any doctor should also know that excessive drinking could lead to memory loss, which Dr. Wood claimed she experienced. Yet, in her 354-page medical report, he never mentioned anything about drinking. Not one word because that wasn't their plan.

CHAPTER 32

THANKFUL TO BE off the stand if only for a short reprieve. Global was squeezing in their surprise witness before they finished with Darby. Global had flown him in from Skokie, Illinois. Unfortunately, Robert had never deposed Dr. Wood because Global did not list him as an expert witness. He wasn't on *any* list to even testify until ten days before the trial commenced. Of course, they notified Robert late Friday night, enabling only five business days to address it.

Today, attorney Johnson Von Dietrich sat beside Wendel. He had more skill with the written word than Wendel. But unfortunately for him, the intense stick-up-his-ass demeanor would lead to an early death—caused by either a stress-induced illness or by pissing off the wrong person. Von Dietrich continued his argument, as Darby doodled a picture of Dr. Wood in the resolution section of her notebook.

"We heard from the ABC News Airline Correspondent," Von Dietrich said with intensity, "who certainly was not disclosed and did not prepare an expert report in this case. The Tribunal allowed all of that under, I believe, the inherent idea that pilots, and their very nature, possess expert knowledge. *Certainly,* the same is true of a psychiatrist with 30 plus years in the airline industry, who is one of the key witnesses in the case.

"Dr. Wood has got the right to testify. And again, I would just underscore, at the very end, he's not an expert witness. This seems very straightforward to me. He's a *fact* witness who did expert things as part of the facts of the case."

"All right, call the witness," Judge Geraghty said.

Dr. Wood was a licensed Illinois physician, Board Certified in General Psychiatry, and by the American Society of Addiction Medicine. He attended medical school at the University of Chicago. His internship was at the University of Iowa, and psychiatric residency had been at the Michael Reese Hospital in Chicago. Then he served two years in the Army and then returned to be the assistant chief of the Adult Inpatient Service at Northwestern University Hospitals.

"When did you first start working with pilots?" Von Dietrich asked.

"In about 1983, the hospital I worked at was approached by Delta. And the requirement for Delta to send pilots to our hospital was they wanted it only to be an evaluation, and they wanted one psychiatrist and one nurse assigned. So, I volunteered, and that's the way I began."

"So, I'm clear," Judge Geraghty said, "Was this hospitalization due to substance abuse?"

"Yes," Dr. Wood said, "and Dr. Charles Chesanow, who is the chief psychiatrist at the FAA, told me that I've done more evaluations of pilots than anyone else at this point in time."

A proud moment for him, Darby thought, but a disgusting thought as to how many pilots he had harmed in his career. Chesanow was high up in the FAA, and perhaps the reason Dr. Wood was identified as their big gun.

"Do you recall the first time you then spoke on the telephone with anyone from Global?" Von Dietrich asked.

"Well, I had spoke with… uh there was a conference with… uh, this basically was the telephone call that Mr. Wolfe was alluding to. They described the situation in which the manager of the EO, or department head, had gone to have an interview with First Officer Wolfe."

"I'm sorry, First Officer Wolfe?" Von Dietrich said.

"First Officer Bradshaw. I'm sorry, First Officer Bradshaw. And she had raised a number of issues, one of which was the concern that people at Global were in some way going to hurt her or cause an accident, where she or others would be injured. They also talked about that there were memory problems. That the exact nature of those memory problems weren't clear to me at that time, but that they would talk to her, over years, that there would be discussions with her and she would appear to understand what they wanted to happen, and then she wouldn't remember."

Judge Geraghty said, "You said during this first conversation they were talking over *years* this occurred?"

"No. In other words, they're talking about the fact that over years there's this question of a memory problem," Wood said.

"Over years," Judge Geraghty said again. "What do you mean by *'over years*?"

"That in previous, that the maybe the background," Wood said. "I can explain it. For the majority of—"

"Well, I'm *only* interested in what you were told in that telephone call," Judge Geraghty said. "You said, *'over years,'* okay?"

"Right. That the…the majority of pilots have very little contact with the Chief Pilot's Office. She'd had multiple contacts in which they had counseled her over a number of years, and that information which they felt they had communicated to her then kept coming up again and again. Does that help?"

"It does," Judge Geraghty said. "And that happened during this first phone call?"

"Yeah," Dr. Wood said.

"Continue," Geraghty said.

Testimony continued and Dr. Wood stumbled through his answers. Darby took notes the best she could, but he was a bumbling idiot.

"Doctor, let me understand," Judge Geraghty boomed, grabbing Darby's attention. "Are you saying that she put something on the blog and thinks she's doing it right. Then finds out later, from management, that they disagree, and then she immediately removes that. That that's indicative of some sort of mental health problem?"

You go judge, Darby thought.

"That's not … that's not. It's that later she says it never happened. That's the point. In other words, if it's that the concern that she did something that violated the media policy, she calls completely fraudulent, that's the problem, not the initial part."

There was never a denial of the post. The denial was the violation of social media with a newspaper publishing it. Darby wasn't sure if he was one of those people that believed what he wanted to and created a narrative to fit his thought pattern, or if Global convinced him of something other than the truth. But then again, why the hell was he sitting here defending himself? He had to know that this did not look good for him. *Or did he?*

CHAPTER **33**

WHEN A DOCTOR discusses a *strategy* with company management during a mental health examination, everyone should take notice. Darby prayed the judge would find this suspect. She had no doubt that Global's legal team would attempt to diffuse this too, but based on the first email, that tactic wasn't working. Von Dietrich stuck another email in front of Dr. Wood, hoping perhaps the second time he could come up with a better answer.

Despite all the evil that Dr. Wood had been complicit with by trying to destroy her for money, she could not help feeling embarrassed for him.

"Could you provide, in the context of *this* e-mail, what you meant by the term 'strategy'"? Von Dietrich asked.

"Okay. The question is… the question I'm trying to answer is… over time is First Officer Bradshaw changing the amount of time flying, and the number of times she is piloting the plane? Okay, that's the question. So, I'm trying to develop… so, I say the strategy is to draft time against cumulative hours and cumulative flights. That's the strategy to try to answer *that* question."

What the hell did that have to do with my mental health? Darby wondered. Being on reserve and not flying was not a mental health issue, but often an excellent mental health survival tool. Besides, he went back to her Coastal Airlines days and added those years in, when she was a simulator instructor and not allowed to log those hours as flight time.

"This is an e-mail from yourself to Joe Wolfe and Robert Dodson on July 15th, 2016. And if you look at the end of the second line, you say, *I've thought of a strategy which has the possibility of confirming her opinion and refuting it.'* Again, if you could provide the context of *this* e-mail and what you meant by the term, 'strategy' in this e-mail?" Von Dietrich asked.

"A procedure, an algorithm, in other words I'm trying to obtain a quantitative measure to answer this question, which served to… this question I struggled with through the whole … for months… I mean, you know, there were a tremendous number of e-mails back and forth. But again, it's an attempt, I mean this is a strategy to deal with a specific question. Unless I don't understand the question, that's—"

But Von Dietrich cut him off and said, "I'd like to turn, for a while, to your report, which is Joint Exhibit L. We're going to look at your report, which is Joint Exhibit L."

"Don't ask any more questions," Judge Geraghty said. "I want to read this." While he read, the courtroom remained silent. He made some notes and then told Von Dietrich to continue.

That report had haunted Darby for months, made her sick and then she dissected it to the piece of fiction that it was. Now they were discussing Abbotts's fabrication of why she said Darby did not want to meet at the airport, and Dr. Wood's assessment of her alleged paranoia.

"Wait," Judge Geraghty said. "I'm looking at your report on page 62 and the example that you give, the extract dealing with the Abbott manager interview. And you say in the note here, *'It's because she was afraid leaders would find out she was talking to me and start asking questions.'* You were aware, at the time, that this was an EEO investigation or an investigation into allegations against management, were you not?"

Dr. Wood stared without making a response.

"Let me rephrase it this way—" Geraghty said. "In this response here, you're saying that that's a paranoid stance that a person who is taking action *against* the people that hired them, that she may not want to find out that she's reporting on management?"

"The management is sending Ann Abbott to interview her," Dr. Wood said. "So, finding out that she's being interviewed seems, I was unable to see why that would be something they would find out, since management is sending them, sending her. In other words, it's like wait… these people are sending you and you don't want them to know that you're talking to me. That's the part where it seemed suspicious of people's motives."

Abbott had said she wanted to keep the meeting away from operations and later asserted it was Darby's decision, because Darby was afraid managers would see her. Judge Geraghty saw the illogical stance of that, yet Dr. Wood now turned that into Darby's illogical behavior. Apparently, doctors could skew anything in a manner which served them.

"Doctor, did you ever interview the person that you're relying so heavily on in this, Ms. Abbott?" Judge Geraghty asked.

"No, I never interviewed her."

"Why not?"

"Because I was basing it on the idea that I wanted the contemporary data. In other words, this was her contemporary report, based on what happened. So, basically, I was trying to go with what are the things that are contemporaneous to the event and focus on that."

The very reason he sat in a Chicago hotel room with attorney

Wolfe and the Regional Director, Dodson, for more than ten hours getting briefed. *Contemporaneous my ass*, Darby thought folding her arms but not allowing her passive expression to change.

"And I apologize," Judge Geraghty said. "Did you ever present what was given to you, the statement that Ms. Abbott, the contemporaneous report that you're relying upon, did you ever give that to Ms. Bradshaw, to give her an opportunity to explain her version of events?"

"We discussed—."

"Not discussed. Did you give it to her?" Judge Geraghty said.

"No, you're right," Dr. Wood said, "I did not. I alluded to different items."

CHAPTER **34**

D ARBY STOOD IN the cafeteria off to the side, with a bank of windows to her back. She was on hold with a mortgage company because of the need to refinance her house. There was no way she would be able to pay Robert for this trial on her salary alone.

Kathryn, Linda, and Jackie sat at a table a few feet away eating lunch. She smiled at them and held up a finger that she'd be there soon. Robert was at a table by himself, preparing his cross examination. Dr. Wood and Regional Director Robert Dodson sat together across the room, the closest table to the door. A *good strategy* she thought, being by the door to escape. They were deep in conversation. More than likely reminiscing about the good old days from their time in the hotel room together with Global's attorney, Joe Wolfe.

Someone was getting screwed in that hotel room, and it turned out to be her.

"Hey," Darby said, when the broker finally answered the phone. She stuck a finger in her other ear and turned her back to the noise of the cafeteria and faced the windows to talk. The Global attorneys were standing on the outside patio deep in discussion. They did not look happy.

"WHAT ARE WE supposed to do now?" Von Dietrich snapped. "I told you the risk did not outweigh the benefit of bringing him." He stood with his hands on hips, legs spread, simply to keep his anger in check. This was a huge mistake.

He glanced at Dianne Dickerson, Global's in-house attorney, who had sat in the back of the courtroom with a team of five listening to all testimony and texting information back to headquarters. A playbook was being created behind the scenes, as illegal as that was. Now she spoke to someone on her cell phone, while her group stood engaged in her every word. Her face a slight shade of red, theirs of question.

"It wasn't so bad," Wendel said, splaying his hands. "Wood stood firm on his diagnosis. All we needed was the judge to think Wood believed his diagnosis to be true. Regardless how ridiculous it was, I think we accomplished that."

"Geraghty is not an idiot," Von Dietrich said.

Von Dietrich had no choice but to bring Wood to trial. Those who paid the bills had the power and the final decision. He made every effort to tell them it was not a promising idea, but Wendel had agreed to the decision and that was all that it took. Wendel agreed with *anything* that leadership wanted. The fact his father-in-law was a founder of their law firm gave him power he did not deserve.

"I don't think that it was *that* bad," Narcea said. "But I am a little concerned about Robert Allen's cross examination."

Von Dietrich shifted his attention to her but made no response. He wished Narcea would go home, have the baby and get out of his hair. Having a pregnant attorney did not have the effect they thought it would. That, too, was not his idea.

"We get through the afternoon," Wendel said. "It'll be fine."

Von Dietrich wasn't so sure. But he also knew that in the end, it didn't matter. Other than the fact that he had a reputation to uphold. He glanced at Dickerson as she came their way.

"We have company," Von Dietrich said quietly.

"Gentlemen," Dickerson began. "Plans have changed. We're meeting with Rich Clark tonight. Don't make dinner plans, I'll have something brought in. It's going to be a long night."

CHAPTER 35

SYMPTOMS OF MANIA include uncritical self-confidence, grandiosity in an expansive mood, these symptoms cause the patient to not recognize and not acknowledge inconsistencies in reporting events. The description of events in the manic patient's histories often dramatically modified to fit a narrative congruent with the patient's elevated mood state, thus, a marker of mania is a pattern of contradictions in reporting events, and a refusal to acknowledge the presence of an error in judgment or an error in behavior. From this viewpoint, inaccurate reporting, which serves to support a grandiose expansive mood is one of the many behaviors that characterize mania—so described Darby's mental condition in Dr. Wood's report.

Now it was time for Robert to do his magic. As it turned out, Dr. Wood first spoke to Wolfe, and then he had a conference call with a large group. He recommended to that group that she should see a psychiatrist, who turned out to be himself, for the sizeable amount of $74,000.

Despite Robert tying up the payoff with a bow, to do a dirty deed for Global, the law technically only addressed what came before Dr. Wood. Not what came after. However, what came after gave credence to what came before. The judge had also said there could be more adverse actions. Perhaps this was what he meant.

"Did you ever request that Global provide you with any published open-door policy?"

"I don't remember asking."

"Given your focus on the, I'll call it "cognitive dissonance" or the "dissonance" you're talking about," Judge Geraghty said, "if that issue had come up, is that something you, in the normal course, would have asked for?"

"Likely. There were so many issues," Wood said, "with so many different details and so many things to check on, I don't know that I... so the answer is likely. Did I do it? I'm not sure."

"Okay," Geraghty said. "Counsel?"

"What were her symptoms?" Robert asked.

"Well, there are two ways to look at it. There's two, the micro viewpoint, where I'm totaling up each one. And then the major ones, which were very prominent. One was, let me talk about the two major ones. Those two major ones were not enough to make the diagnosis, though, you needed everything."

Dr. Wood told the court that Darby thought she could be the CEO of the airline, or the director of training. That was not exactly the conversation, but it was a good sound bite for crazy. Darby had the recordings, however, that proved him to be extrapolating and twisting the facts. Not that she couldn't be the CEO or the Director of Training, but that wasn't the point.

"Now, then I returned to it again," Dr. Wood said. "After a discussion, to say, *'Okay, you know, tell me more about this?'* And she gives more details of how she can do it. This sounds grandiose to me. And it's also the word, earlier in the interview, she makes the point that I used the word 'worry,' when she really was concerned. So, she's very particular about words. And she was, by the way, absolutely right. I misused the word. She's absolutely right, it was and should have been concern, and not worry. But the point is, she's very particular about, and she said, *'Seriously.'* And if a person says, *'Seriously, I can be the CEO of the airline,'* that sounds like they say, *'I believe it.'* So, that's one."

Darby had told Dr. Wood she didn't worry. That if she had a concern, she would take action because worrying was a wasted emotion. He had argued that point. However as a result of what she has experienced since that time, worry had become part of her vocabulary.

"The second point has to do with the idea that to have mania you have to have elevated energy. You have to be able to do, you have the energy to stay up, you have the energy to engage in activities which are well beyond normal. And the question is what's normal? So, during the interview she talked about that she nannied three kids under three. Okay. And she also, simultaneously, went to night school and got a 3.7. GPA. And she also took flying lessons.

"And I asked her, *'Did you get any help?'* And she said, *'No, not really.'* I don't know any woman who could do that. I don't know *any* woman taking care of three under three that isn't exhausted, let alone going to school. Oh, and I asked her if the kids' mother expressed her milk to feed the babies, and she was very upset about this.

"So, basically, she's doing all of this, I think that's well beyond what *any woman* I've ever met could do. And she acknowledged that in the transcript. She acknowledges, *'I don't recommend that, and I don't really know how I did it.'* It was sort of a puzzle. But she doesn't close the loop and say, there's something unusual about this. So, there are these four elements, back then three under three, going to night school, getting a 3.7, taking flying lessons, and no help. I don't think that that's within the normal range of a person's energy."

"Could it equally be just a determination that she's gifted?" Judge Geraghty asked? "Do you know her IQ, for example?"

"Wait. I don't know if IQ matters with three under three. Three under three is exhausting. No help means no help. In other words, this is a clinical judgment. If you can show me a large cohort of women, or ever talk to a woman who was able to do that and not be wiped out, then we have different cultural experiences." Dr. Wood's volume escalated as he spoke. He took a breath and then yelled, "This is well beyond what any woman I've ever met could do!"

His outburst reminded her of the movie, *A Few Good Men,* when Jack Nicholson's character shouted, "You can't handle the truth!" Then he confessed his sins.

Judge Geraghty stared at Dr. Wood for a few moments, then he looked Darby's way. Their eyes locked and she shrugged. *What can you say to that?* she thought.

"The pilots are defensive," Wood said. "So, if you're going to make the diagnosis and you just ask them you want to just ask them the symptoms, it's easy, it's *'No, no, I don't have it.' 'Did you, your speech?' 'No.'* Okay. So, you have to look in the history to see are the symptoms there, manifest, in a way other than the direct examination."

Darby looked perplexed, trying to follow Dr. Wood's nonsensical testimony. Much of which was difficult to understand. She glanced at the judge, but he gave no indication of his thoughts.

"And that's what I believe I did," Dr. Wood said. "Now, others can have another opinion, that's perfectly legitimate. The data is there, I tried to give all the data based on everything, so that it could be determined. And others found it not convincing. Well, I can accept that, because others have opinions that are not the same as mine!"

CHAPTER 36

SEATAC THE ROASTER

RAISING THEIR GLASSES, Kathryn toasted with Robert, Tom, and Darby. "To success." Glad she didn't miss the show.

"To de-feathering the quack," Darby said as the waitress arrived with their appetizers.

"That's one I've never heard," the waitress said, setting a platter of chicken wings on the table. "I don't think these little guys will ever fly again, either."

Darby laughed and said, "I like the way you think."

"What are we celebrating?" the waitress asked, setting sauce for the wing on the table.

"Just a good day," Robert said, lifting his beer. "We're not at the final celebration yet."

"Okay, come back when you're ready for the real one," she said. "For now, is there anything else I can get you?"

"We're good," Kathryn said. She reached for a carrot stick and Darby selected a wing. They both headed for the ranch dip at the same time. Both pulled back. Both tried again. Then Kathryn looked up at Darby, who was smiling and winked.

"How do you think it's going?" Tom asked Robert.

"Excellent," he said. "But it's far from over. They get their chance at Darby tomorrow, then they bring their witnesses that we already deposed. But Global doesn't have a case and they should have settled by now. I'm also surprised they put Dr. Wood on the stand."

"Aren't you supposed to prep witnesses?" Kathryn asked. "At least tell him what you plan on asking. That was embarrassing."

"That you are," Robert said. "I'm not sure if Wendel has done an AIR21 case before. Maybe he's never even gone to trial."

"But Von Dietrich questioned him," Kathryn said.

"Point taken," Robert said. "But Wendel is running this thing, and not well, I might add."

"I have no idea what they are going to ask me," Darby said, licking sauce off her fingers. "Their deposition was kind of worthless."

"Answer with yes or no, and if there is a grey area, ask if you can explain," Robert said. "He may let you or not. If he asks an open-ended question, have fun with that."

"That drives him crazy, doesn't it?" Darby said with a grin. "Honestly I don't think he has the attention span to keep track."

Darby reached over and held Tom's hand. His look of adoration was authentic, but Kathryn knew that Darby would never forgive his deception. Kathryn prayed that she would never be the wiser. Hopefully one day the story of how they met would be a cute story that they told the grandkids. But time was running out for that.

"Tom, what do you do for a living?" Robert asked.

"I work on the other side of the legal system," Tom said. "Trying to catch the bad guys and throw them in jail."

"Speaking of which," Darby said. "When this trial is over and all the evidence is out, will Global have to hold everyone accountable? As in…they all get fired and or go to jail?

"The law doesn't mandate it," Robert said. "They could continue on status quo."

CHAPTER 37

DARBY WAS READY to be attacked by opposing counsel when Judge Geraghty said, "Before we get started, I have a question. Is CAT III considered level 4?"

"Yes Sir, it is," Darby said.

"Is Global certified to fly CAT III approaches," Judge Geraghty asked.

"Yes, sir they are," Darby replied.

Darby realized by looking at the blank stares among the attorneys, her friends, and even Dodson, that nobody knew what she and the judge had just established. Judge Geraghty had thought about the previous day's testimony that Global could not fly level 0 or level 4. He had heard the underlying meaning and put the pieces together—the FAA certified Global for a procedure that has been identified by the ASAP program, that the majority of Global pilots do not have the ability to perform.

Then Wendel went to work. After the first hour of his questions, figuring out why he asked what he did was not difficult after listening to Dr. Wood's assessment of her mental health. Therefore, driving Wendel crazy was easy. She was glad he had switched roles with Von

Dietrich. The problem, however, was that she, too, believed if a pilot had a mental health issue that they should be grounded. How she expressed that and not give Global credence to what they did to her, would be the challenge.

"Would you characterize yourself as very knowledgeable about many aspects of safety?" Wendel asked.

"I make an effort to learn as much as I possibly can, yes," Darby said, trying not to give him what he wanted.

"The answer is yes?" he asked.

"Yes," Darby said remembering Robert's guidance. Wendel was not allowing her to explain anything. She'd already asked more than a dozen times if she could explain, and he continually denied her that opportunity. Now he was pushing to prove her grandiose ideology.

"And you'd agree that if an airline receives credible information that a pilot may be unfit to fly, it has a duty to investigate that further, correct?"

"Define credible. If there was a *credible* concern then I would agree," Darby said.

She agreed that an immediate and prompt response to investigate was required if there was a concern, that the airline would have a duty to investigate, and that nothing in this industry was more important than safety. This was wordsmithing of another kind. She wanted to explain her responses were only if the report was credible, but Wendel refused. Then he shifted gears to her concerns that Global had a negative safety culture.

"Does everything that an airline does, in your view, have an impact on safety culture?"

"I'm going to say yes. And may I explain?"

"Not right now," Wendel said with a smile.

Fuck you, Darby thought returning his smile.

He then handed her a document and asked her if it was the grievance she had submitted. Darby answered. Wendel made a snarky comment and Robert called him out. Then the attorneys engaged in another spirited debate between themselves. Judge Geraghty finally broke into Robert and Wendel's now full-fledged argument.

"Do the parties need a break to regain their composure?" Geraghty asked.

"My composure is perfect right now. I do not need a break," Wendel said. "Thank you."

"Is there a question?" Judge Geraghty asked him.

"It's a very simple one," Wendel said.

Then friggen ask it, Darby thought.

"You disagree with his conclusions, correct?" he asked, referencing Dr. Wood.

"The conclusion that a woman couldn't possibly go to school, take care of children, and fly, so she must be manic?" Darby asked with all the weight it deserved for the court. "Yes, I disagree with that."

"Your honor, it's approaching eleven thirty," Wendel began. "I've got questioning that could take us through the next hour plus, do you mind if we take an early lunch?"

CHAPTER 38

LUNCH

THE SECURITY TRANSPORT service from the courtroom to the main lobby and cafeteria was in full swing. Darby held back for the last elevator and then asked the escort if she could go see Dr. Banks, explaining to her what had happened and that she had never even met the man.

"He gave me my First-Class Medical Certificate," Darby said, "despite Global's shenanigans, and I'd like to thank him."

The woman hesitated a moment, and then said, "Of course. But please don't go anyplace else and meet me back here at 1230."

Dr. Michael Banks was the Western Division FAA Aeromedical Director. Her medical examiner's boss. Banks had issued her medical certificate sight unseen based upon the Mayo Clinic's report and her AME's assessment. Someone from the FAA had warned her AME to not get backed into a corner, so despite his giving her the examination, he denied it. But felt really bad and reached out to Banks.

Global did not like that decision so they called Dr. Newton Witter, the deputy federal flight surgeon, to challenge her medical. Witter had at one time been Global's in-house doctor. He was now the top guy at the FAA medical department and ordered Dr. Banks to conduct another full evaluation. Meaning—he had to investigate himself. Banks came to the same conclusion as the first time, and she retained her medical certificate.

Darby walked through the door, and down an aisleway between a dozen cubicles off to her left, with office doors on the right.

"Excuse me," she said to the first human she found. "Is Dr. Banks in? My name is Darby Bradshaw and he helped me out of a bind. I just wanted to thank him."

"Yes. Give me a minute," the woman said. She quickly navigated the cubicle area and walked across the aisle and knocked on his door. She stepped inside, and then moments later she came out followed by Dr. Banks.

"Darby!" he said, extending his hand. She took it and he covered it with his other hand and shook. "It's so nice to meet you. I've got someone you have to meet. Your biggest fan."

He walked a few feet down the aisle, said something over the counter and a head popped up. Followed by, "Oh my God." The woman rushed around her cube and ran to where they stood. She shook Darby's hand and said, "I'm so glad to finally meet you."

"Colleen," Darby said. "The pleasure is mine. You helped me through this more than you know with your kindness."

"You did this," Colleen said. "You just keep fighting the good fight."

"Thank you," Darby said. "We're in trial on the top floor of your building."

"I wish I could be there for you," Dr. Banks said. "But we'll just leave it at that. Do you have a few minutes to talk?"

"Of course," Darby said. She hugged Colleen, and then followed Banks into his office.

Colleen had scanned all of the documents into the computer that Darby provided. She conveyed her feelings to Darby of her dismay at what Dr. Wood and Global were doing. Her support at one of the darkest moments of Darby' life was something that kept her going. She gave Darby hope.

"Please, take a seat," Dr. Banks said, extending his hand toward a chair. He closed the door to his office and sat behind his desk.

"It's so nice to meet you," Darby said. "I cannot thank you enough for what you did."

"It was the right thing to do. My boss called me and said, '*Why did you give her that medical*' and I told him that it was the right thing. Then he told me I needed to read all the documents and see if I came to the same conclusion."

"Global wasn't happy," Darby said. "They had called Dr. Witter to have it undone."

"Well, he allowed me to make the final decision," Dr. Banks said. "You know, I would love for you to meet my wife one day. She's a highly accomplished woman. You two would hit it off. I'm also thinking you should get your PhD."

Darby laughed. "That would really make me manic now, wouldn't it?" She then told him about Dr. Wood's testimony, and he shook his head without comment.

Dr. Banks then leaned forward, lowering his voice he said, "Maybe it's just because I read spy thrillers, but people are killed for a lot less than you've done. You need to be careful."

CHAPTER 39

BACK ON THE stand, Darby thought about what Dr. Banks had told her—*be careful people are killed for far less*. The irony of that statement, coming from the FAA medical department, was not lost. *You're only paranoid if they're really not out to get you*, Darby thought, when Wendel asked the next question.

"Excuse me?" Darby said. "Could you repeat the question?"

"You're not denying, in this case, that Dr. Wood reached the conclusions he reached, based on his own ideas, right or wrong, correct?" Wendel asked.

"Say that one more time?"

"Contending here that Dr. Wood was coerced, was being untruthful when he reached the determination that he believed that you suffer from bipolar. You're just saying that you disagree with it, correct?"

"Are you asking me if I believe he did this with intent to do harm, or was he just incompetent?" Darby asked.

"Do you believe that Dr. Wood was incompetent?"

"No, I do not believe he's incompetent."

"Do you believe that Dr. Wood was being untruthful when he reached the decision that he thought that you suffered from bipolar?"

"For somebody of his experience level and his knowledge, to

prepare that report and make the analysis on, let's say, speech pattern of talking fast, without ever knowing what my speech pattern was before we met, and never following up or asking… And because he spent hours with executives from the company in a covert hotel meeting, only to be concerned with my calling the CEO by his first name, or my assertion that we don't have a chain of command requirement, of which all executives have testified in depositions that Global doesn't have one, yet Wood believes we do so therefore *I'm* lying. Yes, there were some grave errors in his analysis."

"Do you remember the question?" Wendel asked. "My question was, to you?"

"Yes," Darby said. "Do I believe it was false or he was qualified?"

"No, no, that's not the question!" Wendel snapped. The question is, do you believe that Dr. Wood was untruthful when he reached the conclusion that you suffer from bipolar?"

"That's what I meant when I said false. Isn't false and untruthful the same?"

"It's kind of a yes, or no?" Wendel said.

Fuck you and the chariot you rode in on, Darby thought with a smile.

"To answer your question, I am perplexed," she said. "Because, after listening to him, and watching him, he sounded like he was sincere. He almost sounded like he honestly believed what he did. He is a man of assumed competency, and he's spent many years evaluating pilots, that he should know better. But the fact the company paid him $74,000 and he made such gross errors, and it's not only my complaint but half a dozen others that the Illinois Prosecution Board is investigating. Yes, I believe that this was with intent to do harm and not an evaluation."

"The Tribunal will disregard any comment about a prosecution board," Geraghty said. "There's been no finding and I won't consider a mere allegation to a medical disciplinary board."

"I'm also trying to understand that response," Wendel said. "Is it your testimony that Dr. Wood had an intent to do harm to you?"

"I believe Global paid him for one goal only," Darby said.

"You're saying that you believe that Dr. Wood had the intent to harm you, that's your testimony, yes or no?"

"No… I'm not saying he had an *intent* to harm me," Darby said. She believed his motivation was the money Global was paying him. He didn't give a rat's ass about her. He didn't care about harming people, either way. It was all about the money.

"Okay. And do you believe that Dr. Wood was being dishonest in his conclusion, as a psychiatrist, that he believed that you suffered from a bipolar disorder and were unfit to fly?"

"I believe so, yes," Darby said.

"Okay. And you believe he acted in bad faith in reaching that determination?"

"Absolutely," Darby said.

"And what knowledge do you have to support the accusation that Dr. Wood acted in bad faith and was dishonest in reaching the conclusion that he thought you were unfit to fly?" Wendel asked.

Darby glanced at Robert with raised eyebrows, and he gave her the nod to have at it.

"First off," Darby began, "when I went through his medical report and looked at all his items and how he analyzed them, there is no way that an individual could have a 25-year manic episode *without* performance issues in her life. His inability to assess speech patterns, assert paleological thinking, nothing really worked for him. His writing was incoherent, random and he attempted to make mountains out of pimples.

"On top of that, when I met with Dr. Sorenson from the Mayo

Clinic, he introduced himself and made a pleasant comment about my achievements. I said, *'Didn't you read Dr. Wood's report?'* And his reply was, *'We all did, and we know the difference between a political corporate action versus a medical diagnosis.'* Then, I subsequently found an email in Dr. Wood's discovery, that Dr. Sorenson had written the same thing to Dr. Wood, about this being a political corporate action. That never found its way into my medical report.

"Then the e-mail from the FAA to my AME saying, *'Global is the baddies'* and that this was, *'A political timebomb between the Mayo Clinic and Dr. Wood,'* all added credence that Wood was fighting the Mayo Clinic doctors, that this was a political issue, not only with Global, and it had nothing to do with my mental health.

"Global's over-involvement in the evaluation process and the effort to create a diagnosis that would remove me from duty, was not a biased assessment. Global violated the contract a dozen times during the process with their interference.

"Then Global bought off Dr. Gelder, the first doctor I had selected. They told him he couldn't work with me because of a conflict of interest. Logic would dictate if Global trusted Gelder's opinion enough to put him on a retainer, and that forensic psychiatrist tells them, *'But I read Darby's report and talked to her, and she's not bipolar,'* that Global would end it. Yet they didn't listen to his assessment and told him if he wanted to work for them, he had to drop me.

"Now let's look at the Mayo Clinic. Ten doctors review Dr. Wood's report. I met with four. I have many tests, retook the MMPI, they even did blood work to see if there's any physical issues. After all that, even though they cleared me, Global refused my return to flying.

"Then Global violates the contract again and gives this entire packet to the FAA. They force the FAA regional director who gave me my medical to do it again, and the FAA medical appeals board reviews it and ultimately says I'm not bipolar. Global still won't let me return. If you want to state they were following the contract, then I would challenge the many ways they violated it in an effort to have me fail the process.

"And even though the contract says that the Neutral Medical Examiner is to be selected by a mutual agreement between Dr. Wood and the Mayo, no other involvement, I found an e-mail from attorney Wolfe telling Dr. Wood, *'This is your call, this is your decision, you get to decide if you want Dr. Hanover or not.'* But it was not his decision. It turned out that Dr. Wood also knew Dr. Hanover, even though he stated that he did not.

"And then after Dr. Hanover cleared me, they still told him to do it again, this time with no expense spared. They said, *'No expense spared, and we will fly anyone out to see you, anyone you want.'* And so yes, after all these things, I absolutely believe that this was an overt act to not only remove me from duty, but to destroy me. A bipolar diagnosis would remove me from my career and completely discredit me for anything and everything I would ever do in aviation in the future. That is nothing short of criminal. Did *that* answer your question?"

CHAPTER 40

DARBY WAS QUIET on the drive home. Tom was their chauffeur for the day, and he and Robert disccussed the trial on the way to Robert's hotel. She was too tired to talk about anything, but her mind worked overtime.

"You did great today," Tom said, after he dropped Robert off. Darby glanced his way and said, "Thanks." She wasn't sure that doing good would win this. There was something going on, but she couldn't figure out what and it was driving her nuts.

"Is Chinese okay tonight?" Tom asked.

"Perfect," Darby said, having missed lunch again.

"Good, I already ordered it, and we should beat it home by five minutes."

"I knew there was a reason I loved you," Darby said.

"You mean not for my effervescent personality and witty charm?" He said, stopping at the light. He looked left and made a right turn.

"Yeah, that, too," Darby said and smiled. "You know… what's bothering me with all this is…" She hesitated for a moment and then said, "This trial is a waste of time. All we're doing is asking what we learned in depositions. Why not just use the depositions and write the brief?"

"I think there is power in the judge hearing it," Tom said. "The written word is nothing. But the emotion, sincerity, and ability to answer questions on the spot is powerful to see."

"I guess you're right." Darby thought of the fool that Dr. Wood made of himself, then said, "I read something in one of Malcom Gladwell's books that talks about that very thing. But sometimes people can be convincing liars."

"Do you think Captain Clark will be that person?"

"I know he will," Darby said, turning in her seat to face him. "But the law is specific, and we have emails that show he was plotting it. That should be proof enough. Clark was surprised we had them during the deposition, and it will be interesting to see how he tries to get out of it."

"Surprised?" Tom said. "Didn't he know Global gave them to you?"

"No. That's something we got from Dr. Wood. They didn't give us any of the important stuff."

"Isn't that illegal?" Tom asked.

"Yeah," Darby said. "I wanted to file charges. Robert reminded me that I would spend a lot of money and it wouldn't matter because we got it and should stay focused on the trial."

"He's a smart man," Tom said, as he pulled into the driveway.

Tom put the car into park and shut it off. He turned toward Darby and took both her hands in his. He kissed one and then the other. Then said, "I'm so sorry you're going through this. I wish I could do something for you and make it all go away."

"You've always been here for me," Darby said. That was more than most people in her life did. She would give her heart, and they would die, leave, or deceive her. But not Tom.

"Don't ever doubt my intentions," Tom said.

"There's no reason I would. But don't doubt my intentions when I say I see dinner pulling in behind us."

Tom glanced back and laughed. "With food involved, I'd never doubt anything."

WITH DINNER OVER, the kitchen cleaned, they soaked in the hot tub with a beer. Then they found their way to bed. Darby traveled through hell this week, but in a mere few hours, Tom had restored her. Now, she lay naked on his chest listening to his heartbeat, as he lightly stroked a finger in circles on her back. Each of them deep in thought.

"Are you awake?" he asked.

"Mmm hmmm," she replied. "Enjoying the moment."

"What would you think if we disappeared and started our lives in another country."

"Is this question fantasy, fiction, or reality?"

"Ah… maybe a little fantasy about the location but wishing it could be a reality."

"That's kind of a hard one with my job," she said. They remained silent for a while, but her mind began imagining another life. She finally said, "I could give up this Global job and we could go to a tropical Island, and I could fly tourists between the Islands. Drink Mai Tais. Wear a bikini instead of sweats."

"I could manage a little bar and learn to play the guitar," Tom said. "We could make love under the stars in a hammock. Would it be unfair to raise kids in that environment?"

"Not if you educated them and allow them to see the rest of the world," Darby said. Then she lifted her body off his chest and looked at him. "Are you serious about this?"

"I am," he said. His eyes were moist. He smiled and closed them. "But I know it wouldn't be fair taking you away from your life and your friends."

"Tom, what's going on?" Darby asked, with concern.

"Nothing," he said. "I'm just feeling bad for all that has happened, and the thought of escaping it all with you sounded like a good way to get away from it."

"That it would," Darby said, placing her head on his chest. *Maybe one day*, she thought as she drifted off to sleep.

CHAPTER 41

WINSTON CHURCHILL SAID, "A lie gets halfway around the world before the truth has a chance to get its pants on." Darby had sat through Rich Clark's deposition, and she knew what he had said under oath at that time. His deposition testimony, while filled with proverbial bullshit, even contradicted the story he wove today. She had no idea what kind of strategy this was.

While Darby stared dumbfounded listening to the questions from Wendel and new answers from Clark, Robert was hurriedly writing. Clark had opened by sharing stories of his love of aviation and how he'd pumped fuel to start his career. He spoke for about thirty minutes in response to Geraghty's question regarding his aviation background. He laid it on heavy for the judge, but like mayonnaise, there is a point when you make it too thick and it's just gross.

Darby glanced back at attorney Dickerson, the candy eating lady with scraggly hair and ugly shoes, and she was staring her way. She did not have the heart to tell her that her Gucci purse didn't help her image. Dickerson and Darby had sparred during discovery as she was nothing but a corporate hack that had looked Darby up and down with disdain. Now she smiled smugly at Darby. Darby returned the smile with a wink, and then pulled her attention back to Clark.

"And we have a robust reporting culture," Rich Clark stated. "Our ASAP program now has, for the year 2018, just over 25,000 reports that were brought forward from our pilot group."

He is such an idiot, Darby thought. Clark had no idea what a reporting culture meant in response to safety management systems. A reporting culture was when the pilot group could bring forward safety concerns and failures within the system or by management, not themselves.

Darby opened her notebook to Clark's tab and took notes. Then she wondered how she would dispose of him. She turned to Dr. Wood's picture for inspiration. She had tied Wood to a bed, arms spread wide. Bars on the windows. A cleaning man smiling with a broom in hand stood to the side. Sheer terror on the doctor's face. She had always enjoyed drawing, but typically it was flowers, butterflies, and rainbows. This was new, and it was therapy.

✈

DARBY AND ROBERT had caught the elevator with the Global group, so they could have a few minutes downstairs before Robert sequestered himself at a table alone. The elevator was full, and it hesitated before it began moving. God forbid she would be stuck with these people.

Then someone said, "I think we maxed out the weight."

Dickerson said, "It's so hard to lose weight sitting at a desk all day."

Robert grinned but restrained from commenting. The voices in Darby's head said that perhaps it was the continual motion of her stuffing candy into her mouth all day, which might be the real problem. The only deposition Dickerson had not eaten her weight in chocolate was Walter Croft's. Linda had advised her that sometimes those responses were better unsaid.

Then Dodson said, "I know about sitting. It's hard to lose weight while flying too."

Sorry Linda, Darby thought, and said, "Are you sure your problem isn't all those girly drinks with umbrellas while on vacation?" He smiled at her, a real smile. *Hmmm...*she thought. Who would have guessed? Dickerson, however, gave her a sideways scowl.

Prior to lunch Robert had assured Darby that she had nothing to worry about with Clark shifting his testimony. As a matter of fact, shifting rationale is good enough to win the case, so his conflicting testimony would work in their favor. He had said, *'Bring some popcorn, there'll be a show after lunch.'* Then he went to a table to work by himself while he ate.

CHAPTER 42

RICH CLARK EXUDED the ultimate professionalism. During his direct examination he was extremely polished as Wendel questioned him. He sat proudly, spoke confidently, and with exquisite inflection. But one thing about Rich Clark, you did not challenge or interrupt him. They had learned a lot about Clark during his deposition. Today, Robert had already lit his fuse by doing both, and he was smoldering.

"The FAA requires the implementation of an SMS program by 121 carriers, correct?" Rober asked.

"Correct," Clark responded.

"And once implemented, the carrier is required, by law, to comply with its SMS program, correct?"

"It's designed—"

"I'm asking you a yes or no question," Robert said cutting him off again. "So, you can, answer yes or no."

"*You* can repeat the question then," Clark said. His disposition had shifted both verbally and physically. He was becoming what Kathryn's daughters called a hot mess.

"And so, in January 2016, the FAA required Global to comply with that program, correct?" Robert asked.

"We did not have certification at that point."

"My question is, and I'm asking for a yes or no response, the FAA required Global to comply with the SMS program it had in place in 2015-2016, correct?"

"With the SMS program it had in place, yes."

Robert asked Clark if he had been deposed on December 18th, 2018, and he agreed that he had. Clark also agreed that his testimony was under oath and truthful, and that he had been advised that the transcript could be used in court, and that Wendel had represented him.

"Okay. Now, you say Dr. Marsh made a recommendation that Ms. Bradshaw be referred for a Section 8 Mental Health Evaluation?"

"Correct."

"And did Dr. Wood, also, have some input?" Robert asked.

"Marsh and Wood talked on the phone and the recommendation came from Dr. Marsh."

"And would you agree that Dr. Wood based his recommendation, in part, on memory issues that had been brought up with respect to Ms. Bradshaw?"

"I don't recall his exact language on the phone," Clark said.

"Well, do you recall the issue of deficiencies in Ms. Bradshaw's memory, being referenced by either Dr. Wood or Dr. Marsh?"

"I'm not sure if I recall memory or cognitive issues."

"Okay. Well, how did the cognitive issues relate to what Ms. Abbott had reported?" Robert asked.

"I'm not sure that they did. What I recall was the concern over the attitude that someone was out to harm her," Clark said.

"Well, didn't the reference to cognitive issues relate to information provided to the doctors that Ms. Bradshaw had violated social media and uniform use policy?"

"No. Those were not connected, at all," Clark said.

Dr. Wood had testified that the memory issues were the company's greatest concern. She glanced back at Dodson, who wasn't paying attention. Dickerson glared.

"Did you form an opinion as to whether Dr. Marsh's decision was based on the set of circumstances that led up to Ms. Abbott speaking with First Officer Bradshaw?"

"No, I did not," Clark said.

"Isn't it true that Dr. Marsh identified that with respect to his recommendation, the biggest concern was that Flight Operations, was Ms. Bradshaw's reference to Flight Operations being out to harm her in some way?"

"I don't recall him saying that," Clark said.

"If you could look at your deposition testimony at page 29?" Robert said.

Robert read Mr. Clark's deposition testimony. "And your answer is," Robert said, "'*Well, the biggest concern, really, was the concern that Flight Operations was actually out to, in some way, harm First Officer Bradshaw.*' Now, looking at the top of page 30, starting at line 20 you state, '*Answer: He took her input and reviewed the set of circumstances that led up to Ms. Abbott speaking with First Officer Bradshaw.*' Did you provide that testimony?"

"I did, and I may have mis-spoken there, or it's not—"

"Well, I didn't ask you that," Robert said interrupting him. "I asked you did you provide that testimony?"

"I believe I did," Clark said.

"And now you consider that to be factually inaccurate?"

"I don't think—"

"I'm asking you yes or no, do you consider that testimony now, today, to be factually inaccurate?" Robert pushed.

"Objection!" Wendel said. "That's beyond the appropriate interruption and badgering. That type of question is the type of question that the witness needs to be entitled to answer, as opposed to a simple yes or no question. I understand that counsel is trying to elicit just yes or no, and leave things for redirect, but the type of question that he asked about whether a witness is being accurate in deposition testimony versus the questions that are being asked now are those that cannot be answered yes or no. He should be allowed to explain."

"Overruled," Judge Geraghty said.

"Now, if I could direct your attention to starting at line 11," Robert said. *'Question… what facts did he identify for recommendation? Answer, 'well, the biggest concern really was the concern that Flight Operations was actually out, in some way, to harm First Officer Bradshaw.'* Did you provide that testimony during your deposition?"

"Yes, I did."

"Do you now consider that testimony to be factually inaccurate?" Robert asked.

"No."

"And I'm going to refer you to line 1. Your question, *'But you had previously considered referring Ms. Bradshaw for a Section 8 referral?'* your answer, *'Answer: I wouldn't say that I had considered referring her for a Section 8.'* "Did you provide that testimony during your deposition?"

"Yes," Clark said, his anger boiling.

"And would you consider that, today, to be factually accurate?"

"I still consider that accurate, yes!" he snapped.

Rich Clark was digging his own grave as Robert handed him the shovel. Everything he was asserting to be honest in his deposition, opposed what he testified today. He'd gone from sitting upright with his chest puffed out, to slumping, red-faced, and his now narrowed eyes, throwing daggers, continually flashed at his counsel. Darby wasn't sure if they conveyed, *get me the hell out of this*, or *what the hell did you get me into?* Robert pushed and would only allow yes and no answers and that continued to infuriate Clark.

"Is that your testimony during your deposition?" Robert asked again.

"Yes, it is."

"Is that factually accurate testimony?"

Clark paused a second and then said, "Yes."

That testimony also conflicted with what he'd said that morning. Darby folded her arms and smiled, and that, too, inflamed Clark. Robert continued for an hour questioning him on her alleged social media violations and what he had said to Global's Dr. Marsh and Dr. Wood at their multiple meetings. All his deposition testimony contradicted his trial testimony this morning.

"Did you provide this testimony during your deposition?" Robert asked again.

"Yes, I did."

"And is this testimony factually accurate?"

"I don't believe it is 100 percent accurate," Clark said. He was now coming to the party. Supporting assertions opposite to what he said in front of the judge would not serve him well.

"More specifically in terms of your decision, did Ms. Abbott's communication to the effect that Ms. Bradshaw felt she had a target on her back, did that contribute to your decision to issue the Section 8?"

"No."

Robert then asked Clark if that was typical for the Director of Health Services to recommend the pilot to a Section 8, and Clark told him that it was.

"If I could direct your attention to page 28 of this deposition,"

Robert said. "And then direct you to line 19, where it reads— 'Question: Is that typically how a Section 8 Mental Health Evaluation gets initiated, that the DHS makes a recommendation? Answer: It's not. It is not typical to have a Mental Health Evaluation, so normally an evaluation comes as a result of what we see in operational performance or training performance.' Did you give that testimony?"

"Yes, I did."

"Okay. And do you consider that testimony to be factually inaccurate?"

"No, I do not."

Wendel objected, and then called for a 15-minute break.

CHAPTER 43

DARBY RUSHED TO the restroom. She finished her business and stepped out of the stall and up to the counter to wash her hands. This was better than she could have ever imagined. Rich Clark was perjuring himself over and over. This was not an omission or forgetfulness. This testimony was a completely different story. If she was lucky, he would go to jail.

Darby had just added a touch of lipstick and then fluffed her hair when attorney Ms. Narcea walked out of a stall.

"Do you plan to keep working after you have the baby?" Darby asked.

"Of course," she said sticking her hands under the faucet. "Why wouldn't I?"

"Well, you better be careful to stay away from Dr. Wood. Or you, too, could be diagnosed as manic."

Darby thought she was funny, but Narcea rolled her eyes.

"Good luck with the rest of your witnesses," Darby said. "You're probably going to need it." And she walked out of the restroom.

Returning to her seat Robert, was busy reading testimony, so Darby opened her notebook to Clark's tab. She began doodling bars over his sketch, until he was fully caged. She was just adding the touch of a smoking gun at his feet when the group of attorneys strutted in, Wendel avoiding eye contact with her. They acted as if they were on top of the world, instead of ten feet under as the result of their incompetence.

Clark returned to the stand, and Darby winked at him. He glared, and turned another shade of red. If he didn't hate her before, he did now. But this was the most fun she'd had at trial all week. She only wished she had listened to Robert and brought the popcorn.

CHAPTER 44

ROBERT BEGAN WHERE he had left off, proving Clark's inconsistent testimony was a clear element of the law—shifting rationale.

"Did you have many conversations with Dr. Marsh after March 17th?" Robert asked.

"No."

"Did you have any conversations with him concerning Ms. Bradshaw?" Robert asked.

"I don't recall."

"If I could refer you to your testimony starting at the bottom of page 34, line 22." Robert was going to help his recollection one more time with sworn testimony that he had made only three months earlier.

"Did you provide that testimony during your deposition?"

"I did," Clark said.

"And was this, *as well*, inaccurate, Sir?" Robert asked.

"I honestly do not recall him asking me that," Clark said.

"Have you had any illness between the time of the deposition and today?" Robert said.

Darby had just taken a drink of her water and she practically choked on it.

"No," he said glaring at Darby.

She wiped the water from her face, while trying to hide her laughter, as Robert questioned him about the instructor not giving the required oral but inputting grades, and he never investigated it. He agreed that he never knew of, or saw *any* social media violations, but just heard about them regarding Darby. Then they dug deep into the performance and compliance issues that Clark had stated were significant.

"Did you tell Captain Wyatt that Ms. Bradshaw had raised FAA compliance issues of significance?"

"He was in the meeting with her on the 28th. He already knew that," Clark spat.

Robert discussed Global's efforts to force pilots to fly fatigued, known as pilot pushing. Clark admitted that to be a problem. He said ALPO should be a responsible partner with respect to safety and compliance issues. Robert then handed him a copy of the FAA report showing Global was in violation of duty-time regulations.

"When did you first see this report?" Report Robert asked.

"I believe in preparation for this hearing."

"Okay. And if you can turn to page 14 and I'm going to refer you towards the top. It reads, *'Corrective Action AIR No. 2016SO650014 was initiated in accordance with FAA compliance philosophy.'* Did you have any knowledge of this AIR Corrective Action prior to this year?"

"I did not."

How the hell could he not have knowledge if he was running Flight Operations? He had been the vice president under Wyatt, and when Wyatt retired, he became the senior vice president. *How could he not know?* Darby wondered.

"I'd object to this entire exercise," Wendel said. "Because what Mr. Allen is doing is unfair to this witness. I've objected at the beginning. And over my *strong* objection you allowed it to continue, but I'm going to make the statement on the record, again, that when a party is trying to use deposition testimony and not allowing the witness to explain the answer and just answer yes or no, and only using partial information in the deposition, they are misleading.

"They're creating a record, a public record, that is inaccurate and it's simply not right! It's not right to the witness. It's not right to anyone. It was not done on direct in that way, at all, and it shouldn't be done here. And the witness is not being allowed to explain why there's differences between the testimony here and not allowed to provide any information. And there's so many of these, and it is 4 o'clock p.m., that we are not going to be able to get through that on redirect in an appropriate way."

If you would shut the fuck up, we could, Darby thought as Wendel continued to rant.

"And I just think the ruling, I take exception to the initial ruling on it, and I make the same objection that I made originally," Wendel said, aggressively.

"Your objection is noted," Geraghty said. "You can cure that on redirect. If you recall, when you were asking questions in examination of Complainant, I applied the same criteria to her as I'm going to apply to this witness. And what's good for the goose is good for the gander."

You go judge, Darby thought for the second time. Maybe this was a fair process after all.

Robert continued to ask questions and Wendel objected. Robert finally explained if they could clarify that for the record, that Clark did not believe Darby made any statements in bad faith, he would end this line of questioning.

"Let me just glance at my client to make sure," Wendel said, and looked at Clark who nodded. Then he said for the record, "Yeah, that's no problem."

"Okay. So established," Judge Geraghty said, "All right. Can we break now?"

"Yeah, this would be a good time," Robert concurred.

"All right. And we're going to stay on the record for this. It is now 4:30 o'clock p.m. I have concerns about whether or not we're going to finish with this witness today. Are we?"

"I think almost certainly not," Robert said.

"You've got to be kidding me!" Wendel spat. "Global is an airline and trying to operate as an airline, they can't have the head of their Flight Operations here indefinitely answering questions in this case. Captain Clark has been here for days. He's sat here through two interminable questions of pilots that were completely irrelevant and, also a very, very lengthy direct examination and very lengthy redirect examination. Counsel needs to ask the questions and be done with this witness today. Otherwise, it's not a fair process for the airline."

Not fair for the airline? Darby thought. Now that was a first.

"Any other reason?" Judge Geraghty calmly asked. "You're the one that called him."

"Well…" Wendel said but had no other response. Darby fought a laugh.

"You had other witnesses who were lined up," Judge Geraghty said. "Do you want to see if I can continue past 5 o'clock p.m.?"

"I think that Mr. Allen is doing this in bad faith, in order to purposely harm Global Air Lines. I believe that!"

"The Tribunal has no evidence to indicate that," Judge Geraghty said. "It has been a lengthy hearing, I will grant you that, but sometimes that's what happens. We can continue with the cross. What my thoughts are, here's my concern, is we still have this witness on the stand, we've still got to close up and pack all this stuff and get out of this facility, so I have some serious concerns about are we going to finish this today."

"Well, Captain Clark is not going to be able to come out here for quite a long time, if we are going to continue his testimony, so we're not going to be able to…"

"April 29th to May 1st is when it's going to be," Judge Geraghty said.

"Well, Captain Clark is not available on those days," Wendel snapped.

Wendel was pushing the envelope and every one of the judge's buttons. You'd never know by looking at him, but there was no way someone could take Wendel's accusations and not form an ill opinion of them.

"Well, that's the decision you have as to whether or not I will accept his testimony since it's incomplete" Judge Geraghty said. "That's a decision that you will have to make."

CHAPTER 45

KATHRYN HANDED DARBY a glass of wine and a beer to Tom, seconds after they walked into the living room. "Robert, what can I get you?" she asked.

"Do you have Basil Haden?"

"You got it," Kathryn said and headed toward the bar.

Darby handed her wine to Linda and said, "I'll have what he's having."

Once the drinks were in hand, they all sequestered in the living room. A platter of cheese, crackers, and salami sat on the table before them. A bowl of grapes and strawberries lay beside it. Laughter filled the room at the destruction of Rich Clark, which ended the week on a high for Darby. Linda's husband, Niman, Tom, John and Kathryn had all missed the show.

Robert described the blow-by-blow play that could only come from an attorney's perspective. He recanted Rich Clark's testimony and then said, "Absolutely everything he stated was opposite to his testimony. I finally asked him if he'd been sick."

"You didn't," Niman said.

"I did. It just came out," Robert said.

"Then water came out my nose," Darby said, "and I'm not sure what was funnier, Robert saying that, or Clark's expression when he did. He wanted to jump off the stand and pummel us."

The judge was a fair man. She had suspected if Clark had claimed his brother died, Wyatt retired, and his promotion was overwhelming, that Judge Geraghty would have felt empathy. But the truth was, Clark's ego was bigger than his brains and he'd never admit he couldn't handle things. Besides, he could not think that quickly.

"I'm dumbfounded as to how Wendel could allow that testimony to occur," Robert said. "He was at the deposition and heard our questions and the responses. It's embarrassing."

"And Wendel even complained that using the deposition wasn't fair," Darby said. "I thought that was the purpose of it."

"I question, again, if Wendel's been to trial before," Robert said stacking cheese on a cracker.

"I think he shit his pants when Robert said he wasn't going to be done today," Darby said. "He literally blew a gasket."

"He told the judge that Clark wasn't available," Jackie said. "How'd he know his schedule?"

"He didn't," Darby said. "Wendel's full of crap."

"So now what?" John asked Robert.

"The hearing is recessed until April 25th, at 9 a.m. East Coast time. Then they scheduled their final witnesses three days later."

"That's 6 a.m. in Seattle," Jackie said. "That's crazy. I won't be able to get a sitter."

"Early works for me," Kathryn said and turned toward Jackie. "I'll take notes for you."

"What's worse than the ungodly hour," Darby said, "is that they're not bringing their other witnesses back until Monday, so Robert has to sit in town over the weekend."

"I'll keep myself busy," Robert said with a grin, standing to refill his glass.

Darby knew that Global scheduled this three-day separation on purpose to cost her, but little did they know that Robert Allen was a good person, and her expenses would not exceed his hotel accommodations and the time he worked on her case. He wasn't a typical attorney focused on billable hours. More than that, Dodson had even agreed to pay protect her for her ten-day trip, so she could pick up additional hours after trial.

"What's perplexing to me," Linda said, "is how much time Wendel wastes objecting, and making a big deal out of nothing."

"Exactly," Jackie said. "It's as if he wastes time arguing, and then complains about how much time the trial takes."

"None of this makes sense," Niman said. "What's their gain?"

"We've all been questioning that," John said.

"I've never seen anything like it," Robert said returning to his seat. "I've never dealt with a company that pursues trial with less of a defense than Global has."

Darby sipped her drink, listening to the banter. What the hell was she missing? Why were they wasting so much time and treasure? She stared into her gold liquid and decided she should start meditating to clear her brain and stop thinking so hard, or she would never figure this out.

"Due to two early flights tomorrow," Kathryn said, referring to Tom and Robert, "I'm going to distract you all with an early dinner if you'd like to join me at the table?"

Chapter 46

DARBY AWOKE WITH a start and reached across to an empty bed. Tom had snuck out early. She glanced at the clock and then slowly sat up brushing hair from her face. She pulled on her robe and went downstairs to the kitchen and made a cup of coffee. She took one sip then headed back up the stairs and sat on the end of her bed.

The week had wiped her out, and perhaps the reason she had not yet figured out what the hell Global was up to with this fucking trial. She stared at her desk, specifically the folder, thinking about what Dan had told her. She stood slowly and moved to her desk. Exchanging her cup of coffee for the folder, she sat.

She removed the patent information that Dan had told her about regarding the uninterruptible autopilot. Darby had looked it up—number US 7,142.971 B2 and printed the documents. He was correct. Drake Industries had applied for the patent on November 8, 2006, with Boeing. She began to read it.

The methods and systems of the present invention for automatically controlling a path of travel of a vehicle and, in one embodiment, for engaging an uninterruptible autopilot mode provide techniques that prevent unauthorized persons from accessing the controls of a vehicle.

The methods and systems therefore increase the likelihood that a vehicle may be safely operated to safety because unauthorized persons are not capable of gaining any type of control over the operations of the vehicle. To provide the increased safety, the techniques of the present invention permit irrevocable and uninterrupted automated control of the vehicle, such that once the automated control system is engaged, it cannot be disengaged by anyone onboard the vehicle.

What the hell? Darby thought. Granted, this could take control from terrorists, but it would also take control from the pilots. The rationale was that unauthorized terrorist onboard could not force pilots to fly the plane. But what they did not say, was this technology could fly the planes for the terrorists who were not on the aircraft. It also meant that pilots would be unnecessary. She continued to read.

The method and systems of the present invention, therefore, provide techniques for increasing the safety of vehicles over the conventional safety techniques that are revocable and/or alterable. The method and system for automatically controlling a path of travel of a vehicle may include engaging an automatic control system of the vehicle.

A chill went through her body. She set the document on the desk and reached for her coffee. She sipped, thinking about what this meant. She set her cup down and continued, and when finished reading the last paragraph, she said, "What the hell?"

She opened her laptop and began searching other patents. "I'll be damned," she said. Pushing back from her desk, she reached for her phone and called Kathryn.

"Kat, are you busy?" Darby asked when she answered.

"Nothing I can't drop for you. What's going on?"

"We need to talk. I'll be there in an hour."

After ending the call, Darby ran to her bathroom and turned the shower to hot. She dropped her robe to the floor and stepped into the flow of water. Tilting her face to the warmth felt like heaven. She reached for the shampoo and thought about the trial as she rubbed suds into her hair. She was thinking about the conversation the night before, as she rinsed. The craziness of the trial and how it was a total waste of time amazed her. They'd beaten the week to death last night and then Kathryn had called them for dinner.

Holy shit, she thought, *could it be that simple?* Darby turned off the water and wrapped herself in a towel. "How could I have been so blindsided by this?"

She had forgotten a lesson her dad had taught her early in life—*stop trying so hard, sometimes it's the simplest solution that solves the problem.*

CHAPTER 47

THE FRONT DOOR opened before Darby knocked. Kathryn stepped aside and she rushed in. She hung her coat and purse on the rack. The ponytail she had pulled her hair into was still wet.

"Thank you for dropping your life for me," Darby said heading toward the kitchen, smelling something wonderful.

"I've got a pot of coffee made and warmed up some blueberry muffins."

Darby set the folder on the table and opened a cupboard. Reaching for a cup she said, "I know why Global took me to trial." Then reached for a coffee pot.

"Is that what this is about?" Kathryn asked as she removed the hot cream from the microwave and added it to Darby's cup.

"No," Darby said ripping open two packages of Stevia. "But it's all connected. I think."

They sat at the table and Darby reached for a muffin. She took a bite and moaned in delight and then said with her mouth full, "I have to show you something."

She set the muffin on a plate and opened the folder. "This is a 14-page patent, filed on November 8, 2006, for the uninterruptible autopilot. They say that it's to prevent hijacking. The problem is that it enables full control from the ground and could also lockout the pilots."

"Or the terrorist," Kathryn added.

"Yeah, that's what they say," Darby said. "But they've spent millions keeping them off the planes. So, are they now saying, that those security measures are no longer working?"

"Good point. They've been working since 2001."

"Exactly. But Homeland Security is supporting the patent, despite all their protections in place." Darby took another bite of muffin and said, "Look here," turning to the last page.

"On December 4, 2006, almost a month after the application, they stated, *'Boeing is, of course, not the first autopilot technology in existence, but this one has been designed with counterterrorism first and foremost in mind. Not only is it "uninterruptible" — so that even a tortured pilot cannot turn it off,'*" Darby read, emphasizing tortured.

"*'But it can be activated remotely via radio or satellite by government agencies. The system might even include sensors on the cockpit door that activate the autopilot if a certain amount of force is used against it. There is a need for a technique that ensures the continuation of the desired path of travel of a vehicle by removing any type of human decision process that may be influenced by the circumstances of the situation, including threats of further violence on-board the vehicle," the patent application explains. To make it fully independent, the system also has its own power supply, independent of the aircraft's circuit breakers.'*"

"The *tortured* pilot," Kathryn said, "That's a little dramatic."

"The one thing terrorists don't do in flight is torture the pilots. They kill them. But, if someone hacks into this thing, then the pilots can't turn it off."

"I'm surprised I haven't heard of this," Kathryn said. "Why would you? You're just the FAA."

Kathryn placed a hand to her forehead and closed her eyes.

"I was joking," Darby said. "I know you don't have any control."

Kathryn opened her eyes and dropped her hand to the table. She drummed her fingers and stared at Darby. "It's not you."

"What?" Darby said.

"John told me that Airbus has already successfully concluded autonomous taxi, take-off and landing tests, of what they call the ATTOL project."

"That was supposed to be two years out," Darby said.

"They're a year ahead of schedule," Kathryn said.

"They are getting rid of pilots," Darby said.

"It's worse than you can imagine," Kathryn said. "They're using machine learning algorithms and saying the technology is to support pilots, so you can focus on strategic decision-making and mission management."

Oh Gawd, Darby thought. Mission management sounded like a Rich Clark phrase. She picked at a blueberry in her muffin and then looked up.

"This kind of makes sense," Darby said. "It's all connected. But this patent is with Drake Industries and connected to *Boeing*. The ATTOL system is Airbus."

"It is," Kathryn agreed. "But Drake Industries could be involved in both."

"Then why kill Boeing's MAX?" Darby said. "Hanley also told me that this was not the first patent. He had no other number, and said it was some Black Hawk mission from the military. I know that the military has been flying drones for years. But I did a little digging anyway. I found something from September 17, 2001."

"That was just one week *after* 911," Kathryn said. "That type of technology does not come overnight. They'd been working on it."

"Not some U.S. military project on this one," Darby said. "This patent is by a 'Chinese' company with the name written in kanji."

She had no idea how a Chinese company could make a U.S. patent, but apparently they could because they did. What she also knew was that the knockoff parts that went into the MAX were supposedly from China. She had no doubt that Drake was part of that.

"Hànzì is from Mandarin," Kathryn said. "Kanji is Japanese."

"How do you know this stuff?" Darby said.

Kathryn shrugged, then asked, "Is it the same patent?"

"I just printed the abstract," Darby said, pulling the document from the folder. "It's titled, *Anti-deviation adaptive pilot using airplane-carried pre-inhibition system based on electronic GPS map to prevent suicide hijack event.*"

"They are both asserting hijacking," Kathryn said.

"Controlling people by fear," Darby said. "The abstract says, '*An anti-deviation adaptive pilot using an airplane-carried pre-inhibition system having GPS electronic map to prevent suicide hijack event features that the data about driver identity and state, real-time driving state, real-time GPS data, fly height, pre-firmed electronic map library, automatic approach library, and the targets to be inhibited to fly over them are processed by computer system to judge if the airplane is legally or illegally operated and to take relative protecting measures.*'"

"That's a mouthful that makes no sense," Kathryn said, taking the document from Darby and reading it. Then she said, "Okay. How does all this tie to Global and the trial?"

"Distraction," Darby said, standing to get another cup of coffee.

"What do you mean?"

"Last night you told us that you were going to distract us with dinner," Darby said, turning Kat's direction. "Then this morning in the shower I was thinking about everything. And what has Wendel been doing? Wasting time. They cannot win. But if they did win, what do they win? Nothing. This trial is all smoke and mirrors."

"They're distracting *you*," Kathryn said. "Taking your time. Keeping *you* busy."

"I'm their proverbial pain in the ass. I'm calling them out on their shit." Darby reached for the pot and filled her cup. She returned to the table and freshened Kathryn's cup.

"What are you going to do?" Kathryn asked.

"I'm going to be their worst nightmare," Darby said, returning the pot to the hot plate. "There has to be double jeopardy protection for crazy."

"Perhaps," Kathryn said with a slow smile. "But being sane one day doesn't necessarily mean they didn't drive you crazy the next."

"Good point. On another note, did you get the restraining order against Bill?"

"I did. And for the girls too." Kathryn stood and went to her purse. She opened it and removed a slip of paper and handed it to Darby. "Call this number, you need one as well."

"When are they getting out?" Darby asked.

"Yesterday," Kathryn said.

CHAPTER 48

TOM WALKED OFF the plane and headed through the terminal. He paused and sent a text message. Within a few minutes he received a response. He looked at his watch and glanced left and right, noticing a Starbucks. This was going to be a long night and he needed his wits.

Within minutes he was standing in line and responding to the next series of text messages. He glanced at his watch again, then stepped out of line carrying only his overnight bag.

Tom found the parking garage and rode the elevator to the third floor. He looked at the text message again and assessed the numbering system for the parking stalls. When he found the row, he walked to the number indicated. A black suburban filled the stall, the car idling.

Tinted windows blocked the vision of who sat inside. He opened the door and climbed in as directed. The car was empty. The black partition, blocking the driver from sight and sound, was up. As soon as he sat, the doors locked, and the driver backed out slowly. The car drove around to the back of the garage and stopped. The right front door unlocked, opened, and his boss climbed inside. They drove in silence and darkness out of the garage.

"I'm sorry that I argued with you," Tom said, after the partition lowered four inches. He wasn't sure if there was any way out of this. But he was not above groveling.

"Not many do that," the man said, "and live to apologize."

They sat in silence again and then Tom said, "When did you arrive?" vying for a safe subject beyond the weather.

"Yesterday." The man fumbled with something in the front seat.

Tom's heart raced. *Oh fuck. This is going to be it*, he thought. He closed his eyes and said a silent prayer for Darby, when he heard the match strike. He opened his eyes and breathed deeply. Then he coughed as cigar smoke drifted into the back seat.

After another minutes of silence passed, the man said, "I've missed this, probably more than women." Then he laughed and lowered the front window enough to allow the smoke to escape that direction. "But that's not why we're here."

Tom did not think it was. "What can I do for you Sir?"

"That's the million-dollar question isn't it," he said. He took a draw on his cigar and said, "If I were to fire you tomorrow, would you stay with Darby?"

"Yes." Tom wanted to tell him that he loved her. But he wasn't sure if that would help or hurt Darby. He was to protect her, to keep her alive and report what he heard. So, he thought. He wasn't so sure anymore, and suspected he was just a spy. For what, he had no idea.

"Nobody tells me no," the man said.

When Tom said, "I...," the man's hand went up and Tom fell quiet.

"I do admire your dedication. There's not a hell of a lot of that in the world today."

"No there's not," Tom said more under his breath than in reply.

"I have one final ask."

"What is it?"

"Does it matter?" he asked.

"No," Tom said, "It doesn't matter."

Tom listened. Then the partition went up. They drove for another fifteen minutes before the car stopped. The locks opened and he exited on the side of a dark street. Stepping aside, the car drove off. He had a two-year limit to fulfill this task. Why the flexibility?

Now he just needed to figure out where the hell he was, get a room for the night, and catch the first flight home. He would return to his life with Darby and make her the happiest woman he could. For two years at least, or until she threw him out.

CHAPTER 49

IS THIS A fucking April's Fool's joke? Darby thought. Will they never stop their evil ways? Leaning back, she stared at the email. Her greatest fear was when this was over, if they would continue their bullshit through the end of her career. She was about to respond, and then decided that this was war, and actions spoke louder than words. Besides, you should never email drunk or mad. Instead, she logged onto Global's website and began to work on the solution.

Her phone rang and she smiled at the name on the screen. "Jessica, how are you?"

Jessica was one of Kathryn's twin daughters. She and her sister Jennifer were in California, away at their first year of college.

"Hey Aunt Darby, how was trial?"

"A time suck, but had its moments of humor," Darby said. "Are you sure you don't want to go into law?"

"I would hope you'd be done before I graduated," Jessica said. "Therefore, I couldn't do you any good."

"I'm not so sure if we will be done by the way it's been going. But I'm not talking about needing help with this trial." Darby stepped away from her computer and sat on the bed. "I might need a criminal defense attorney."

"For what?"

"Murder," Darby said. "But enough about me, how's school going?"

Jessica laughed. "I don't want to worry mom, but I think I saw Dad," she said. "I acted like I wasn't paying attention, but I'm sure it was him. He was parked across the street from campus pretending to read a paper."

Darby's blood ran cold. "Oh Honey. Do not go anywhere near him and don't go anywhere alone. Your mom got a restraining order and he is not supposed to come within 100 yards of you or your sister."

"Remember that book you gave me and Jen, *The Gift of Fear*," Jessica said. "Well, it said that restraining orders don't keep the crazies away. I'm kind of scared."

"Sweetie," Darby said, sitting upright. "Your Dad *is* crazy, but for a cause. He was trying to control the industry. He would never hurt you girls." Something that she did not fully believe.

"I don't think he cares enough about us to hurt us," Jessica said. "But he might try to do something to us to get to Mom, that's what I'm scared about."

It's hard enough growing up as a teenage girl, but to have your dad be a known and convicted murderer and sent to prison, then out and stalking you, with the belief he could kill his own kids, nothing could explain those feelings.

"You need to alert campus security."

"I already did," Jessica said. "Would you mind telling Mom? I'm going to have a hard enough time telling Jennifer about this. And I'm not sure who'll take it worse."

"I've got it on this end," Darby said. "I could send Tom to be your bodyguard. I'm heading out on an eight-day trip tomorrow and won't need him until I get home."

"I'd love it. But I can't be responsible for my crazy ass horndog friends," Jessica said.

Darby laughed. "I love you, kiddo. Give a hug to your sister and be safe. I'll talk to your mom today and calm her down before she calls."

They said their goodbyes and Darby returned to her computer. She finished manipulating her schedule. Then she wrote to her union regarding her pending grievance hearing. She removed her suitcase from the closet to her bed, and threw in the essentials, and four uniform shirts. She set it aside to add her toiletries the following morning. She then dialed Kathryn's number.

Kathryn answered and Darby said, "Promise you won't freak out."

"About what?"

"Promise first," Darby said.

This was not the first time they had had this conversation and Kathryn learned that she could not fight it and would never get the answer she wanted without a promise. She promised.

"I just got off the phone with Jessica. She saw Bill."

"Oh my God," Kathryn said. "I need to bring them home. They're not safe down there."

"No, you don't," Darby said and told Kathryn about their discussion. "They're smart and won't be alone anywhere on the campus. Security already knows. You can't protect them while you're at work."

"I'll see if John can get extra security," Kathryn said. "Can we send Tom?"

"That's what I thought," Darby said heading downstairs. "Jessica advised against it."

"Why?" Kathryn asked.

"Don't ask," Darby said, opening the fridge and grabbing two beers. "I'd wait and call her later tonight, she's telling Jennifer."

"Thank you," Kathryn said.

"Of course," Darby said. "And Kat, Tom will keep an eye on them."

They said goodbye and Darby wandered outside with the beers. Tom was already sitting in the hot tub, his first bottle empty.

"You're a life saver," he said wiggling the empty. "Are you all packed?"

"I am." Darby handed him both bottles, then pulled her shirt over her head. "But those assholes at Global did not pay protect me for my trip on the 25th for trial. Dodson said that I could drop it but without pay." She unbuttoned her jeans and stepped out of them.

"I heard him agree that he would pay you for it. Are you going to fight it?"

"Nah. I've already traded it for another trip," Darby said, stepping out of her panties. "It's not as long but gives me a chance to snatch another trip before trial. And something else might pop up. It's not perfect, but I mitigated the damages." She removed her bra, tossed it to a chair, and climbed into the tub.

Tom handed her a beer and said, "You're taking this with …uh stride. What's up?"

"I'm not giving them the satisfaction of pissing me off," Darby said. "Besides, this will set me up for a green slip to go out on the 29th after trial with double pay."

He pulled her close and kissed her. "I'm going to miss you. Would you care if I followed you around on your trip?"

"About that," Darby said. "Bill showed up at Stanford."

"Should I hang out in California for the week," he asked pulling her onto his lap.

"Would you mind?" Darby asked.

"Not at all," Tom said.

"Thank you," Darby kissed him on the cheek. Then she pulled back and said, "Just don't let any college girls see you. You wouldn't be safe."

CHAPTER 50

DARBY FILLED UP her schedule and would still arrive home before trial. She wasn't home free yet, and there was only one commuter flight that could get her there in time for a 6 a.m. start time the next morning. She would be exhausted, but she'd be damned if she would miss trial. The guys she was flying with allowed her to be third pilot on the return so she could rush off the plane after landing, which could be the deciding factor of making her commuter flight or not.

They had already read the descent and approach checklist and Darby had called in their arrival to Operations. Now she was simply looking for traffic and listening to clearances.

"Ding, ding," the flight attendant call system rang, and the light illuminated flashing.

"Darby, can you get that," the captain said.

"On it." She was already switching her radio. "This is the flight deck."

"We have a suspicious passenger," the lead flight attendant said. "He's an older guy traveling with a young Asian girl. She's been super nervous the entire flight. He wouldn't let her go to the bathroom alone. Can you call it in?"

"Of course," Darby said, and then she asked for their seat numbers, and some seat specifics. After she disconnected, she said to the crew, "Did you hear that?"

"We did," the captain said.

"Why would they wait the entire flight to let us know?" the first officer asked.

"Don't ask," Darby said while dialing in the flight operations radio frequency. When they answered she said, "Operations, Global 42."

"Global 42, go ahead."

"Ops, our flight attendants just notified us we have a suspicious white male approximately 50 years of age, traveling with a minor Asian girl. He escorts her to the lavatory, and she appears nervous. They have seats 5 A and B. Could you have security meet the aircraft?"

"Absolutely. Thanks for calling it in," the station operator said.

Shortly thereafter, they landed without incident and Darby checked her watch again. She could make it if their gate was open. They taxied around the corner and luck was on her side. They pulled in, shut down the engines, and Darby gathered her things.

Unfortunately, the station was not using the forward door, and everyone was exiting through number two. Therefore, she had to navigate the first-class section, excusing herself to the highest paying passengers, to work her way out. By the time she finally got off the plane, security had already pulled the suspicious passenger and the young lady to the side. He was raging and waving a hand. Darby ignored his glare, gave him a quick nod, and rushed to the first monitor she could find to check her gate.

Shit, she thought. She had to get to another terminal in fifteen minutes, and that would give her ten minutes before they closed the door. Darby ran. She ran through the tunnel dragging her bag behind and took the escalator upward. She got to the street and ran down the sidewalk to the crosswalk and then flew across the street with a red light, holding up a hand and waving thanks to those who opted to stop versus hitting her.

Once across the street, she cut around the parking garage. Looking both ways she ran across the other street, this time making the walk signal. Once inside, she turned left, and took the moving escalator up, running steps two at a time and carrying her bags.

Off the escalator she ran to security praying that she would not be selected for further screening. She handed her passport to the agent and scanned her ID.

"Sorry," he said. "Random check."

Fuck. Fuck. Fuck. Darby thought.

"Go to the front of that line," he said. "You don't have to take anything out."

"Thanks," Darby said and headed that direction. She excused herself as she cut through passengers. She made it to the front of the line, threw her bag and purse on the conveyor, then removed her shoes hopping from foot to foot, and tossed them on the conveyor. She pulled her belt out of the loop, and stuffed it into her hat with her passport, ID, and everything from her pockets.

Once on the other side, she stuffed everything back into her pockets, put her belt into her purse, stuck her hat on her head as she slipped into her shoes, grabbed her stuff and ran.

Darby made it to the gate with three minutes to spare, but the jumpseat was taken and the flight was full. She fought tears when a hand touched her shoulder.

"College girls *are* dangerous," Tom said with a smile, holding out two tickets. "Come on, we have a flight to catch." He took Darby's suitcase and guided her toward the door.

"I thought you went home last night," Darby said.

"There was no better excuse to stay the night than to meet my girl," Tom said. "Besides, it gave Bill and I time to have a little talk. I don't think he'll be back."

"Are you kidding me?" Darby said. She was close to tears for another reason now.

"Welcome," the Alaska Airlines agent said. "Ms. Bradshaw and Mr. Smith. Your seats are 2 A and B. Enjoy your flight."

They walked onto the plane and the boarding door closed behind them. Within twenty minutes Darby was out of her uniform shirt and had a bourbon in hand. Twenty minutes after that she was sound asleep on Tom's shoulder.

CHAPTER 51

DARBY AWOKE TO the ringing of her phone. She glanced at the clock and grumbled. "Oh God," she said, then answered it. She answered only because the call was coming in from a Global Air Lines company line.

"Good morning," she said, trying to clear her throat.

"Is Ms. Bradshaw in?"

"Yes," Darby said. "It's me."

"Darby, this is assistant chief pilot Graham calling from Oklahoma City. Do you have a minute?"

"Do you know what time it is?" Darby asked. The assistant chief pilots were first officers who were climbers. Most weren't that bright.

"It's 0700. Sorry to call you so early, but I've got a flight to catch in an hour."

"Try five," Darby said.

"Oh… yeah, you're in Seattle, aren't you? Sorry."

Darby did not believe that statement dignified a response, especially without coffee. Therefore, she remained quiet and tried to shake the cobwebs from her head. She sat up and wondered where Tom was. Then she remembered he had left so she could get some sleep.

"I'm calling you about you reporting that passenger to Los Angeles operations," Graham said. "Those calls are supposed to go through dispatch."

"Where's that written?"

"It's not."

"Okay then," Darby said rolling her eyes. "I didn't have time to call dispatch. We were too close to the landing to tag team with Oak City when LA could handle it. What's the issue?"

"The issue is we want dispatch to deal with the decisions as what to do," Graham said, "in the event it deals with a high-value customer."

"You're saying high-value passengers are exempt from sex trafficking?"

"That's not what I'm saying. But they might be innocent."

"If he was innocent there should be no anger," Darby said. "If it *was* his daughter, he'd be thankful someone was looking out for our children, because next time it could be his."

"But it was his adopted daughter," Graham said, "He was pissed."

Darby highly doubted that it was a legitimate adoption, and she felt sick to her stomach. If that young lady was part of a sex trafficking process, and they let him go because he spent a lot of money at Global, she would… she didn't know what she'd do. All she knew was that she wanted to scream.

"If your daughter was being taken to a foreign country against her will, would you want to waste time to call dispatch in another city, or just grab the asshole when the plane landed?"

This time silence was on his end. She glanced at the clock again and then realized what day it was and why Tom had allowed her to sleep. She had 50 minutes to get to the courthouse.

"Thanks for waking me up," Darby said. "If there is nothing else, can we talk about it later?"

He agreed that was a good plan and said goodbye. Darby rolled her eyes, wondering if he'd heard what she'd said.

CHAPTER 52

DARBY PICKED UP Tom and then Robert, and they met Kathryn and Linda in the courthouse lobby. They were in the elevator on their way to the top floor when the judge's assistant, who happened to be their escort, said, "Global never tested the video system. I have been writing to them for weeks, and they've been either telling me they didn't have time, or there would be no issue."

"Are you saying this might not work?" Darby said, stifling a yawn.

"There shouldn't be a problem," she said. "They're just arrogant and ignored all my emails. I've told Judge Geraghty about it."

"I've done video meetings here," Kathryn said. "Not an issue."

Tom took Darby's hand and squeezed just as the doors opened.

They all walked down the hall, but this time adjourned into a conference room next to the courtroom. They sat around a long wooden conference table with a speaker phone system in the center. Judge Geraghty walked in, and they stood and said good morning. Precisely at 6 a.m. Geraghty's assistant called Global's contact number and connected to the speaker phone.

"Your honor, this is Wendel Kowalski. We seem to be having a problem with the video. We have no idea what's happening, but we can't get in."

"Sir, you *will* get this sorted out," Geraghty said. "We have a couple things to try," Wendel said. "I'll call you back."

While they waited, Kathryn and Darby began discussing the ASAP system, and Darby commented how surprised she was that Global had 25,000 reports in that previous year.

"That system is not doing what it's supposed to be doing," Judge Geraghty said. "The ASAPs are at an all-time high and the fixes are at an all-time low."

Then the speaker phone system rang, and Judge Geraghty stood and pressed a button. "Yes," he said.

"Sir, we cannot get this thing working," Wendel said. "Would it be possible to call your cell and do video chat?"

"I am not giving you my cell number!" Judge Geraghty boomed.

"We are as upset as you are about this," Wendel said, "But it's not our fault."

"You've had weeks to sort this out," Geraghty said.

"We tried to do a test with your assistant," he said. "But she just wasn't available, and it was difficult to work with her."

Wendel had no idea that she was sitting in the room and had printed all the emails identifying her effort to get Global to test the system to no avail. It was probably a good thing for him that he did not see the knowing exchange between Geraghty and his assistant.

"Sir, I would not go down that path," Geraghty warned.

"I'm sorry, we're just all disappointed here. I've got technical support and we're going to try one more thing."

"I'll be waiting," Geraghty said. He ended the call and left the room.

Darby took the time to use the restroom and as she walked

down the hall she heard the judge saying, "And they asked for my cell number."

Darby smiled. Global was not scoring points this morning. She returned shortly thereafter, as did the judge. They were all sitting around the table again when the next call arrived. The judge stood and reached down and pressed a button and answered. He was standing above the speaker when he said, "Hello."

"Your honor," Wendel began. "This is so very disappointing for us. But we figured out what is happening and why we can't get in. Your security system in the FAA building is too robust to allow us access."

Darby slid her legal pad to the center of the table and turned it sideways to orientate it for the judge to read and began writing—*Global had a trial in this courtroom. The Securing trial. Video.*

Geraghty's face reddened and he said, "Sir, I can order Mr. Clark to Seattle tomorrow if I choose. But I'm going to let both counsels determine how to deal with this. I'll have Mr. Allen call you and then we'll decide how to proceed." He ended the call and said to Robert, "Whatever you decide, it's your choice. You can reschedule. Force him to come to Seattle. Whatever you decided, I will order it."

"May I use one of the briefing rooms?" Robert asked.

"Of course," Judge Geraghty said. "We'll reconvene in thirty minutes."

Darby and Robert went to the briefing room and Robert closed the door.

"He's pissed," Robert said. "But here's what I'm thinking. We have everything we need from Clark's direct testimony. We have his deposition. And he doesn't want to come to Seattle."

"You're thinking a little negotiation is in order?" Darby asked.

"I am."

"But I really want to haul his ass back up here. Only because it will piss him off."

"We don't want to risk him devising some new plan," Robert said. "We've got him now and I don't believe the judge is happy with him or Global."

"Okay. Let's see what they say."

Robert sent Wendel a text. When Robert's phone rang, he answered it on speaker.

"How do you want to work this out?" Wendel asked.

"We have only one offer. Clark's deposition and trial testimony are admitted in full, and you waive your right to cross examination, or we bring him to Seattle on Monday."

"Uhhh, well… um," Wendel stuttered. "Let me call you back."

Robert ended the call. "This is truly the best way to handle this."

"They lied to the judge today," Darby said. "I doubt Clark has ever been more humiliated than when you questioned him. He doesn't want to come back. He'll agree to anything."

It wasn't more than five minutes and Robert's phone rang.

"You have an agreement," Wendel said.

"Okay, I'll go tell the judge," Robert said. "We'll call you back."

Robert and Darby returned to the courtroom and Robert explained the agreement to Judge Geraghty. Geraghty sat for a minute working through whatever emotions he was dealing with.

"I… Oh…Okay," Geraghty finally said. "I told you, that you could decide, so that's what it is. But I had some questions for him, that I hope will get answered."

The judge always had the best questions and if she hadn't been so jetlagged and fatigued, she might have told Robert to haul Clark's ass to Seattle with a clear brain. But Robert was right—Clark's damage was done. Then she thought about Walker's testimony. He had also called into the courtroom via Zoom without issue.

CHAPTER 53

MONDAY MORNING ARRIVED like a delayed flight that was long overdue. They were in the final stretch and on the way home. Darby doodled in her notebook as Dr. Marsh explained his role as the Director of Health Services for Global. But unlike his deposition, today he was calm and professional. His medication clearly helped. They even dressed him up.

Dr. Marsh served as the Director of Health Services, or DHS, for Global. He was the representative for the company on Aeromedical Certification issues. His duties included fitness for duty evaluations from the medical standpoint if the pilot didn't meet Medical Standards.

Wendel asked Dr. Marsh questions regarding his contact with the FAA. Judge Geraghty, however, was showing displeasure with each question because he learned that Global had been keeping mental health concerns from the FAA during the process.

"Am I understanding your testimony that you had concern that Captain Bradshaw had not identified all of this information to the FAA?" Wendel asked.

"Objection, leading," Robert said.

Wendel said, "It is leading, but—"

"It's your witness, so rephrase," Judge Geraghty said.

"Did that help you form an opinion as to how the FAA may have ... or what information the FAA may have gotten from Ms. Bradshaw?"

"Objection calls for speculation," Robert said.

"Sustained," Judge Geraghty said. "I mean I'm already hearing testimony essentially this process is keeping the FAA in the dark."

"Right," Wendel said.

"So, it doesn't surprise this Tribunal, anyhow, that a first-class medical gets issued in the absence of the information. The bigger question I have is how this process promotes the highest level of safety, if in fact you have an airman who has a mental health evaluation, and we are affirmatively keeping this information from the FAA."

"Yeah. We should lobby Congress," Wendel said. "I mean what else can I say. But I mean... I don't mean to be cheeky. I mean, I think you need to hear from the Labor Relations people, including maybe ALPO, about why the provisions are in there, because I think it goes ... to use a phrase that you used in the past ... I think it may be out of the lane of this process, and that's why I was being a little bit flip with my statement. But I agree, overall, you know, we're all human beings here, listening to the same testimony, and I understand your view."

This is getting sporty, Darby thought and shifted her attention back to the judge.

"And I clearly understand that I'm not the super HR involved in this," Judge Geraghty said, "but there's something troubling when a process allows private entities to affirmatively withhold information that directly goes to the heart of the Federal Aviation Act."

Wendel said, "Right. And of course—"

"Now, it's not my lane to deal with that, I got that," Geraghty said interrupting him. "That doesn't mean I like that. Go ahead."

"Yeah, we hear it. And I would say that... if it gives you any comfort, maybe we should have this conversation off the record," Wendel said.

"No!" Judge Geraghty boomed.

"I'll stop," Wendel replied.

About fifteen minutes too late, Darby thought. Wendel ran on for another three hours with questions for Marsh to describe the mental health process, how he became involved, what he believed his role was with Darby and their interactions. Then it was Robert's turn.

CHAPTER 54

DR. MARSH CROSS EXAMINATION

ONE OF ROBERT'S goals with Dr. Marsh was to show there was no reason to have sent Darby to Chicago, for any other purpose other than Dr. Wood was a bought and paid for hitman. Marsh testified that he knew Darby lived in Seattle and was based in Los Angeles, and that there were psychiatrists in both those cities. He had looked at a list with a half-dozen qualified doctors and made no effort to contact any of them.

Dr. Marsh testified that it was important to *not* proceed with any referral until he obtained the pilot's side of the story, and yet the decision to ground her had occurred before he met with Darby. He also stated that Darby had no recorded history of mental issues, no substance abuse, and she was not taking medication. Dr. Marsh, however, said that one of his reasons for going forward with the mental health review was due to her absence of taking drugs.

"If she *had* been taking some medication, you would have considered that as a mitigating factor?"

"Yeah. Possibly… yes," Dr. Marsh said. "There's a possibility. Is it possible she was having an adverse reaction to medication or side effect, an adverse interaction with another medication or supplement."

"So, the fact that she wasn't taking any medication at all weighed against her?"

"Weighed against her in what..." Dr. Marsh said and scratched the back of his head.

"In terms of your analysis, in terms of your trying to find some reason why you might not proceed with a psychiatric examination?"

"If I'm understanding the question correctly, she presented to me no history of mental illness or recommendations for treatment or undergoing treatment for that. I took her at her word. Again, if she did say it was something, certainly I would have investigated it there. I can't say that it would have contributed to her behavior and statements, I certainly wouldn't know unless we looked into it. In this case there was no healthcare providers that were treating her for this or recommending treatment."

"Now, would you agree with me that sometimes your evaluations, in your capacity as DHS at Global Air Lines, require you make credibility evaluations?"

"It's possible."

"Well, it's possible or you have?" Robert asked, exasperated.

"All right, yes," Dr. Marsh said.

"Did you discredit any of the information that Ms. Bradshaw gave you on April 27th?"

"No."

"So, you assumed that Ms. Bradshaw was telling you the truth, in terms of what she reported?"

"Yes. As I assumed Ms. Abbott was telling the truth in her written documentation," Dr. Marsh said, more defensive than he'd been all day.

"And more specifically, you made no effort to determine whether Ms. Bradshaw's account of being subjected to retaliation for raising training compliance issues contributed to the emotions that Ms. Abbott reported?"

"Objection. Asked and answered," Wendel said. "We're going to be here for two days with this witness. We keep going over the same questions over and over again."

"I'm specifically asking training compliance," Robert said.

"Yeah. Overruled," Just Geraghty said.

"I know someone else was looking into it. I cannot testify to the safety concerns and things run up there, there's specialists in that. I was brought in to...we have an employee who interfaced with Ms. Bradshaw for three hours and was concerned about her statements and her behavior, and that's what I was doing."

They finally took a half-hour lunch break. Judge Geraghty looked directly at Dr. Marsh and said, "Sir do not discuss your testimony with anyone during the lunch break. You can talk about the weather, Game of Thrones, whatever, but not about that, all right?"

"All right," Dr. Marsh said, bobbing his head. Darby suspected that Dr. Marsh needed a fresh dose of his meds, but she kind of hoped he didn't bring them.

CHAPTER 55

DR. MARSH CROSS EXAMINATION CONTINUES

AFTER THE BREAK Robert continued with his questions and Dr. Marsh grew weary. Robert stuck the billing invoices they'd acquired from Dr. Wood during discovery in front of him. Marsh's eyes appeared to gloss over. He confirmed the invoices were extremely high compared to others. That even a substance abuse evaluation with a psychological test was around $15,000, and that included the cognitive tests. Dr. Wood's bill had not included her testing.

"Did you *any* report prior to the December 7th?" Robert asked.

"No," Dr. Marsh said.

The records identified that Dr. Wood had told Robert Dodson and Joe Wolfe that Darby was bipolar in October, yet Dr. Wood had waited until Christmas Eve to give her notice. A perfect Christmas present to push someone over the edge. When Darby had testified to that fact, Judge Geraghty had questioned her to be sure he'd heard that correctly. He was not pleased.

"Okay. Do you know why Joe Wolfe would have received a report in October, two months before you received a report from Dr. Wood?"

"Not that I recall, no."

"Are you furrowing your brow over that?" Robert asked.

"If he had a conversation with Mr. Wolfe, I was not aware of that," Dr. Marsh said.

Judge Geraghty asked, "Would that be not consistent with the normal process?"

"I believe Dr. Wood did ask, on several occasions, for information. I just didn't know where to get it, and so I think it was like for flight hours and the training programs, and sick leave and things like that," Dr. Marsh said.

"You might be misunderstanding my question," Judge Geraghty said. "My question is would it be not normal for a preliminary report to go directly to the company, as opposed to you as the DHS?"

"The preliminary report should go to me," Dr. Marsh said.

"Okay," Judge Geraghty said, "continue."

Robert questioned Dr. Marsh as to why he forwarded his communications with the neutral doctor to attorney Joe Wolfe, and he'd said it was to keep him in the loop. The letter in reference was Dr. Marsh telling Dr. Hanover to go do the process again, after he had already cleared Darby. She folded her arms and waited patiently to see how he would explain this away.

"Wouldn't it have been sufficient just to tell Mr. Wolf that an NME had been selected?"

"I suppose you're right, but just to explain the nature of the e-mail there, that I was not influencing Dr. Hanover, just introducing the process."

"Did you forward this e-mail to Ms. Bradshaw, as well?"

"I did not."

Robert finished with Dr. Marsh, and Judge Geraghty had some questions. He requested that Dr. Marsh turn to page three in Ms. Abbott's report.

"Now, as I understand your testimony, you, at some point, came into possession of this report immediately prior to that teleconference, is that fair," Judge Geraghty asked.

"That is correct," Dr. Marsh said.

"Okay. And you were basically handed this document to read through it in preparation for this meeting, is that correct?"

"This meeting, today?" Dr. Marsh asked.

"No. The meeting back in March," Judge Geraghty said.

"Yes. So, to clarify, we had a conversation on March 10th, where I heard from Ms. Abbott, and then I said I need something in writing. And this is what I received prior to our conversation on the phone conversation on March 17th."

"Okay. And as I'm going through this, the first page talks about her safety complaints, and then we go to page two that talks about EEO complaints. Does it matter to you, for example in the sub-bullets, *who is the instructor, when did this occur, who is the other pilot* … and how does that relate to any type of medical information?"

"It didn't, in my opinion," Dr. Marsh said.

"All right. The same for the following pages, these list of questions about allegations on who told you not to communicate, unfair treatment, who gave you a copy of the letter of counsel…these series of questions, what's that got to do with a mental health evaluation?"

"Nothing. I was going for the medical standpoint," Dr. Marsh said.

"But would you agree that it does show a list of concerns that the company has, that they want resolved?" Judge Geraghty asked.

"Well, yes, for their EO investigation, and also the safety issues."

"So, we've got diversity, we've got harassment, we have miscellaneous of the green slip policy, the follow-up required. Do you know why they didn't just send you these last two pages, as opposed to giving you this whole litany of questions that they wanted to have resolved independent of any medical issues?"

"I do not know," Dr. Marsh said.

CHAPTER 56

IF DARBY NEVER heard the word 'certainly' again, it would be too soon. Ms. Abbott had been on the stand for no more than fifteen minutes, and she'd already said 'certainly' five times.

"So, tell us about the meeting with Ms. Bradshaw, what happened?" Wendel said.

"Certainly. Again, Ms. Bradshaw came in and just kind of took over, she started talking. It was difficult for me to get a word in edgewise. It was, again, I had to ask for her to literally stop at one point, so that I could introduce myself, remind her why we were here, and explain, again, that I wanted to really look at the EO portions of her concerns and reminded her, again, that I was not a safety expert. So, that, as I understood, was being investigated by a different group of folks in Flight Ops."

There had been a time when Darby thought maybe Ms. Abbott might be a pawn in this game, but she knew otherwise. Abbott was a lying bitch, fabricating everything she had just said, and deserved whatever evil came upon her. *Get a grip*, Darby thought.

"Keep going," Wendel said.

"Certainly. Yeah. She, again, kind of continued to keep talking.

And when I had the ability to ask questions, she would give very lengthy answers. And I found that she was kind of all over the board, it was difficult for me to follow. And I really struggled trying to understand the answer within the questions that I had asked. So, several times I had to ask follow-up questions or ask for additional information, just so I understood that I knew what her concern was or what her response was.

"She seemed a little off put when I would ask for follow-up or to clarify, like I assumed that she wasn't being truthful and that just wasn't it. It was really because she was kind of all over the place. At times she seemed a little bit frazzled. She was tearful and very emotional during our conversation—not the whole time, she wasn't crying the whole time, it wasn't a hysterical crying, but she was very, very emotional. And it was…yeah … it was just a conversation that continued and was very, very difficult to follow."

"You said, '*very, very emotional*,'" Judge Geraghty said. "What does that mean, what does that look like?"

"It looks like tearful and just she described herself as exhausted at times, and it's just her face, just her demeanor was just a look of concern, look of just not kind of knowing what else to do and just very frazzled. So, like I said, she wasn't crying the *whole* time, but she was tearful. She really needed to take a breath at times, where she just couldn't finish what she was saying and needed to just wait for a minute before she could then finish her thoughts."

You lying little bitch, Darby thought, as she drew a picture of single engine high-winged aircraft on page in her notebook in Abbott's section. The funny part of her testimony, as she could find humor in anything, was that during her deposition Abbott had stated she had cried the entire time. Robert had asked if she had called anyone for help. That was Abbott's lightbulb moment, that maybe she should change her story. And she did.

When Wendel finished, they decided to start the cross examination the following morning. Which was a good thing as Robert planned to show no mercy, and that would take time. Besides, if there was justice, Ms. Abbott would lay awake all night worrying about what would come next. But the truth was, her decption probably didn't bother her like it did Dr. Marsh who took anti-anxiety medication for his actions. Darby knew there were some people who didn't care who they hurt for power, postion and money. Ms. Abbott was one of them.

Judge Geraghty turned to Ms. Abbott and said, "Ma'am, because you're still on the witness stand, you cannot speak with anyone about your testimony, okay."

"Certainly," Abbott said.

CHAPTER 57

THE MORNING ARRIVED far too early for Darby. She, Tom, and Robert had all gone out for a quick dinner and a beer, and trash talked Ms. Abbott the night before. Apparently, Robert and Tom thought even less of Abbott than Darby did. To have done what she did for a promotion was pathetic, especially one that wasn't even that impressive.

Robert directed Ms. Abbott's attention to Darby's safety report and asked, "And you read through this document prior to interviewing Ms. Bradshaw on March 8th. Correct?"

"Certainly. I mean, I looked through the entire document. Yes."

"Okay. And you brought it to the meeting on March 8th with Ms. Bradshaw. Correct?"

"I don't know that I brought the document to my meeting," Abbott said.

"Do you recall testifying in your deposition that you actually took notes on this document?" Robert said.

"I did take notes. I don't remember if I brought the entire document or the outline that I made. It may very well have been on this. I'm just saying, I can't remember, again, some of this was completely safety related and not within my scope," Abbott said.

Robert directed her to turn to page 76 of her deposition. He then read where she had testified, that she had taken the safety report to the meeting and had taken notes on it.

"Does that refresh your recollection, that the notes you took were on this Joint Exhibit B, the safety report?" Robert asked.

"It does refresh my memory," Abbott said. "Certainly."

Robert then dissected the two drafts of the report that Ms. Abbott had created, identified as exhibits JX-E 20 and JX-J. As it turned out Abbott's report was in part written by Joe Wolfe, who Darby had never even met, but he wrote questions and filled in responses.

"So, portions of this were written by Joe Wolfe, correct?"

"I can't remember which portions I wrote if he wrote some of the portions. What I'm saying is, he and I came to an agreement in what was going to be in this document."

"And the issues that arise under safety complaints, none of those issues were within the scope of your investigation. Correct?"

"Correct."

"So, you would not have drafted any of those questions under the title 'safety complaints,' correct?"

"Correct. They were pulled from her original complaint and that was the purpose of Mr. Wolfe and I working together, to ensure I understood the buckets of the safety, and the EO-specific complaints."

"My question, though, is if Mr. Wolfe drafted these questions under the heading of safety complaints?"

"If you're talking about who wrote these, he may very well have. What I'm saying to you is, he and I talked together regarding the document that she provided and pulled these out. We had a discussion about these."

Robert confirmed that Darby had discussed, green slips, fatigue, trip buys and social media, which killed her EO excuse. Then he asked her about social media, because on one of the documents were answers from Darby, before Abbott had met with her. Answers that Darby never gave, and questions never asked.

"Did Mr. Wolfe provide you with some answers before you went to speak to Ms. Bradshaw?" Robert asked.

"No. I didn't ask him any questions. They were her concerns, so my focus was being able to talk with her," Abbott explained.

"Okay, please turn to JX-E 006. There's a bullet point, the second to the last bullet point, which reads, '*Are there any other examples of times you have been told not to publicly identify yourself as a Global pilot when publicly opining on the aviation industry [multiple times or not to use Global trademarks on published materials] multiple times?*' Mr. Wolfe provided you these answers even before you went into see Ms. Bradshaw on the 8th, correct?"

"Objection," Wendel said.

"Basis?" Judge Geraghty said.

"Mischaracterizes! There's no foundation for … that they're answers in this document. I don't see any answers in that paragraph," Wendel said.

"Sustained," Geraghty said. "Rephrase. I understand what you're trying to ask but—"

"When you see the term 'multiple times,' do you understand that to mean that Ms. Bradshaw had been instructed multiple times as a Global pilot with respect to publicly opining on the aviation industry?" Robert asked.

"To me, it may have meant she had been asked more than once, and on different occasions, she may very well have been told 'yes' or 'no.' But again, my focus was on what she was bringing up. So, the 'multiple times' wasn't something I really paid much attention to. My goal was to talk with Ms. Bradshaw and figure out what her concerns were."

"I think the question is how did you come to know that it was multiple times," Judge Geraghty said.

"Certainly," Abbott said. "This would be the only thing I would have had prior to talking to Ms. Bradshaw."

"Yeah. But—who put that entry in there, 'multiple times'?" Judge Geraghty asked.

"It was not me. So, if Joe and I were working, if Mr. Wolfe and I were working on this together, it would have been—"

Judge Geraghty said, "So, he would have provided you that information?"

"Correct," Abbott said.

The next bout of confusion was what date Abbott's multiple reports were written, as she had no idea. Robert proved to the judge, however, there were many work products, no clue as to when they were written, and surprise, surprise, Abbott had thrown away all her notes.

"Okay. So, under EO complaints, there's a bold header of 'Allegations against an instructor who later became a line check airman,' bullet point alleges that an *instructor falsified records* by inputting false grades into a computer, *did not observe pilots in simulator, did not provide a debrief,* and indicated that he had the *power to arbitrarily fail a pilot in a training* evolution. The next bullet point is, '*Who is the instructor?*' The next bullet point is, '*When did this occur?*' And here there's another bracketed comment, '*reasonably certain it was 2010*'. Would you agree with me that Mr. Wolfe inserted that observation as well?" Robert asked.

"Yes. He may have," Abbott said staring at the document.

"Well, wait a minute," Judge Geraghty said. "Did anybody else deal with this document besides you and Mr. Wolfe?"

"No," Abbott said.

"Did you have any information at the time?" Judge Geraghty asked.

"No. I did not," Abbott said.

"So, if it wasn't you, then who is it?" Geraghty pushed.

"So, I would suspect that it was Mr. Wolfe," Abbott said, having just pissed off the judge by playing a game of stupidity.

CHAPTER 58

ONE OF GLOBAL'S greatest mistakes was putting forth the instructor who falsified records, of which Darby reported, who later gave her line check, as an EO issue. There was no way they could mold this into a gender complaint.

"But you never spoke to the instructor?" Robert said.

"I did not specifically," Abbott said.

"So, I mean, is it fair to say there was no sense of urgency with respect to the allegations made by Ms. Bradshaw concerning the instructor's comment?"

"That's not fair to say," Ms. Abbott said feigning offense. "I didn't speak with him for a couple of reasons. One, there was also the safety investigation going on. That was critical in the most forefront. Two, I didn't speak to him because I couldn't speak to him directly, just me. So, to ensure that I didn't interfere with any of the safety investigation, sometimes I would take a back seat to what they were doing. But the full intention was to finish the investigation."

"So, you agree it was your policy in terms of proceeding with the harassment and unfair treatment issues that you were going to wait until the safety investigation was completed?"

"Not completely right," Abbott said. "This was information that I could follow up on, I was trying to follow up on many of those."

"Who did you follow up on, on this falsification of training records?" Judge Geraghty said, "And as I understand your testimony, you didn't have access to the training records."

"Correct," Abbott said.

"You didn't interview the instructor?" Geraghty said.

"Correct." Ms. Abbott said. "In speaking with Mr. Wolfe, if we're looking at something that's been falsified, from an EO perspective and an HR perspective, it's a matter of *why* they were falsified. I think, again, it was critical for them, and there were some things the lines were a little bit blurry, quite frankly, because obviously, this would be a safety concern that I think they would also be looking into. But part of my concern is, if this was an instructor who's not treating somebody fairly, then we would want to know about that as well."

"But again," Judge Geraghty said, "You never interviewed the instructor."

"I personally did not," she said.

"Are you aware," Judge Geraghty said, "That falsification in the aviation community goes to lack of qualifications?"

"I'm aware that it's obviously serious," Abbott said. "I don't know specifically."

It wasn't long until Robert began discussing Darby's violation of the alleged chain of command policy when she wrote to the CEO to get a banquet room for a crew Christmas party. While Abbott had nothing to do with flight operations, she clearly expressed her opinion against Darby's inappropriate behavior of writing to the CEO.

"Wait a minute," Judge Geraghty said. "Could one of the factors be, let's suppose that a person has a personal relationship with the CEO but happens to be a line mechanic."

"Right," Abbott said turning his way.

"Would that impact on the appropriateness of reaching out

to someone that they had previous contact or knew, or would you expect that, that had to go to the director of maintenance before it went to the CEO?"

"I would expect that it would go to the person who would be responsible for *paying* for that. So, whoever would give the approval to say, '*Sure, you can have this Christmas Party, and yes, you can use Global funds*' or '*Yes, we will secure the space for you.*' Whoever that person would be, which would likely be that person's immediate leader."

"Are you saying that the CEO wouldn't have the authority to authorize a Christmas party?" Judge Geraghty said.

"Yes. Certainly," she said.

CHAPTER 59

JOE WOLFE DIRECT EXAMINATION

JOE WOLFE STILL refused to look her way, exactly like his deposition. There were people who could harm another, without it phasing them. Then there are others that couldn't as much glance your way due to guilt. Attorney Joe Wolfe was the second type. He also chewed his nails to the nubs and his palms sweat profusely. She opened her notebook and turned to his tab.

"Does labor relations, or you, personally, have a role in determining whether Section 8 mental health evaluation should be implemented?" Wendel asked.

"No," Wolfe said in a calm and professional tone.

"No?" Wendel feigned surprise. "Am I understanding your testimony correctly that your role is to provide counsel on the compliance with the collective bargaining agreement in connection with Section 8, or is there more or less to that?"

"I think that provide compliance is very accurate, an accurate statement."

"Is Section 8 disciplinary or part of the discipline process within the PWA contract?"

"Absolutely not," Wolfe said. "No."

"Why do you say that with such conviction?" Wendel said.

"Well, I mean, Section 8, we view it as, it's a safety function. You know, you start with, where pretty much everything starts in the airline industry. You know, we have a duty to operate with the highest degree of safety in the public interest. And Section 8 is a big part of that. And part of that duty is making sure that our pilots are fit to fly."

Wolfe was well-rehearsed. Darby prayed Robert could break him because he was correct, that's what the process was for—to keep the skies safe. Unfortunately, Global used it as a tool of retaliation, and they did not give an iota about safety.

"Does the collective bargaining agreement have any provision that deals with communication to the FAA?" Wendel asked.

"Yeah. It expressly says in here that the CME, the company medical examiner, will not report his determination to the FAA."

Darby glanced at the judge again, his eyes narrowing ever so slightly. *Keep going down that path Wendel*, she thought. If Wendel didn't understand from Dr. Marsh's testimony that the judge was upset that Global kept this from the FAA, he was more an idiot than she previously thought.

"You presume to have some knowledge on that," Wendel said.

"The DHS, Dr. Marsh in this case, makes his assessment. If he decides that it's going to go to a CME, at that point, the CME does his review and reaches a determination, the pilot still has a first class medical. Nothing has happened. Nobody in that process can take that away. So, that's a negotiated provision that I think serves to benefit both the pilot and the company. The pilot is pulled into this process involuntarily, so there's no need to get them visibility in front of the FAA. And at the same time, from the company's standpoint, it protects the company."

"How does it protect the company?" Wendel asked.

"Well, it protects the process," Wolfe said. "They have the process here."

"Explain," Wendel said, leaning back in his chair and folding his arms.

"We want to get the pilot in and get him through. If the CME reaches a negative determination, there's this tripartite system that we have in place to try to, again, protect the integrity of the process. And having the FAA come into that just really isn't, you know, isn't necessarily a helpful issue. And it doesn't really—"

"Wait a minute," Judge Geraghty said.

"Yeah?" Wendel said, sitting upright.

"Tell me how this promotes the highest level of safety in air commerce for the public. Not the company. Not the pilot. The public," Judge Geraghty demanded of Wolfe.

"Because they're … because they're … they're not allowed to fly in this process," Wolfe said. "We take them down off of …off of the flight…the schedule. They're pay protected, but they can't go fly. So, we've stopped them from flying."

Judge Geraghty's challenge unraveled Joe Wolfe. He no longer held his composure. He couldn't find the words, yet Geraghty waited patiently.

"Now there's only… there's only so much we can do, judge," Wolfe stated plaintively. "We can't go and prevent somebody… Global has provisions where we can stop them from flying commercially. They have policies and procedures that they have to report that to us, but we can't go and control them, that's just a step too far for the company to be able to do that."

"And again, this is where I'm trying to find out is, okay, that you do not provide this information to the FAA," Geraghty said. "You say you can't fly for the public. This person can hop into a Baron, no limitation, go out and have an accident. How does this help the public because you have not provided this information, particularly at the CME level, where you have an adverse finding?"

"Right. Well, we have an adverse finding, but we don't have a *complete* finding at that point. There's still some benefit of a doubt here. Right? It still has to run through the process because, look, doctors can disagree on these things. So, that's where the other two doctors come in to fill out the process," Wolfe said.

"It's your position that, at that point," Judge Geraghty said, "when there's a question, even a medical question, *that* does not need to be relayed to the FAA because, according to the company and the pilot, not the public, there's no safety interest involved here when you have affirmative information that there's a problem potentially with this pilot."

"Judge, I wouldn't say there's no safety interest, but this is what was negotiated between the company and the union. And this is what we have to follow. Now I think that we have severely mitigated any harm by pulling the pilot from Global flying."

"Well, but—" Geraghty began but he was cutoff.

"But, yeah, whether they could go out and fly, that's certainly an ethical and a moral issue on the pilot's part at that point. Because they are definitely on notice, particularly if they have a negative determination, and they've got a DHS and a CME telling them they shouldn't do that."

"Can the company utilize a pilot that is not otherwise qualified to operate the aircraft and has a known or potentially known medical deficiency?" Geraghty asked.

"No. We cannot. We cannot, and we wouldn't," Joe Wolfe said. "Judge, we won't utilize them during this process. That's what I'm saying, we don't fly them. They're not flying while they're in this process."

"They're not flying for *you*," Geraghty snapped.

"For Global, right," Wolfe said.

"So, what I'm hearing is, this contract protects Global and Global's liability. It's not protecting the public."

"This is what was negotiated and for the pilots... and I can tell you, for the pilot's union, they would say, *'There's not a final determination here yet.'* You just... you just have had a suspicion that they're not okay. And just the CME's determination, it still has to run through the process before we'll call it final and binding. At that point, you can tell the FAA and you can tell the world. But until then, we still just don't believe you have a medical."

"Who is 'we' don't believe you have?" Geraghty asked.

"We, the company, the company has come down and said, *'We don't believe that you should have a medical.'* And particularly if the CME has made that decision, then, yeah, we definitely believe it at that point, but it's not finalized. They still have a medical. Now if the pilot were to go and try to renew their medical during this process, that's a whole different animal. At that point, now, you're on your Form 8500. You have to disclose certain things."

"Who does?" Geraghty asked.

"The pilot does," Wolfe said. "The pilot is obligated to disclose that."

"The company has affirmative information that there's potentially a serious medical deficiency," Geraghty said. "Are you saying that the company is under no obligation to report that to the FAA?"

"That's what I'm saying, Judge. There's a contractual obligation to *not* report it."

"All right. Continue," Judge Geraghty said.

Chapter 60

THE ART OF a live-stage improvisational performance is to play to your audience. If what you're doing is falling flat, or aggravating them, it's best you change directions. Wendel was too ignorant to see where this line of questioning was taking him, so he continued.

"In fact, how long has Section 8 been in this contract and this form to your knowledge?"

"This provision has been in since 2000. The tripartite medical challenge process has been in since, you know, I think it goes back to maybe the '70s or '80s. I'm not sure exactly how far back it goes but it's been around a while."

"Does the FAA have to review collective bargaining agreements? Does the FAA have an opportunity to see what's in it?" Wendel asked.

"No. The FAA does not see them."

"Do you know whether the FAA is aware of these policies and programs?"

"I'm certain the FAA is aware of ours," Wolfe said.

"How are you so certain?" Wendel asked.

Oh, you guys are not only idiots, but you are fucking idiots, Darby thought, trying to avoid smiling.

"Well, I can tell you that right now the Federal Air Surgeon use to perform the role at Global that Dr. Marsh performs," Wolfe said.

"Who is that?" Wendel asked with feigned curiosity.

"That's Dr. Newton Witter."

"The company's former flight surgeon is now responsible for the FAA—" Geraghty said.

"He's our former flight surgeon but he performed medical reviews on behalf of Global in the late '90s. And this issue, these issues have come up periodically. I mean, Global was in, you know, litigation in the '90s over different things. This is … you know, and it's gone on and on. And of course, in this case, the FAA was made aware of what was going."

Back in the late 80's or early 90's a pilot identified millions in Global pension fraud. The company went after his medical in a comparable manner to what they did to Darby. Dr. Witter had been the hitman just as Dr. Wood had been hers. The judge in that case had ordered Dr. Witter to never work for Global again, therefore, he became the Deputy Federal Flight surgeon for the FAA. A person would have to understand the incestual relationship with Global and the FAA to see the logic there.

"If I understood your testimony correctly, you testified that you became aware that, at some point in 2017, Ms. Bradshaw had obtained her certificate from the FAA," Wendel said.

"Correct."

"And were you surprised by that in any way, or did you find that to be completely normal?" Wendel asked.

"It was a surprise, because again, she had just received a determination from the CME of bipolar disorder," Wolfe said, with deep concern.

"And wait a minute," Judge Geraghty said. "And so, what? You've hid it from them… hid it from the FAA so far so what's the difference?"

"Well, because the difference is a pilot has to disclose that information," Wolfe said.

"So, you're relying on 6153, on the pilot," Judge Geraghty said. "What about 121.383 for the operator?"

"I'm not familiar with that one, Judge," Wolfe said.

"So, you don't believe that the company has any obligation to report when there's a diagnosis, a disqualifying diagnosis—" Geraghty began.

"According to this contract—" Wolfe said cutting him off.

"I'm talking about the FAA, the regulations!" Judge Geraghty snapped.

"That's yes. Because it's still ongoing and has not been finalized. So, the company would not, at that point, have an obligation until the process has run its course," Wolfe said.

"But that same rationale does not apply to the pilot?" Geraghty asked.

"I think the pilot has to disclose on that form that they have that diagnosis and give the FAA the opportunity to explore that," Wendel said.

"And what makes you think that... what gives you a basis to believe that they didn't disclose and the FAA decided to issue it anyhow?" Judge Geraghty said.

"That's the point, Judge. Nobody knew the answer to that question. That's why Dr. Marsh felt like he needed to find out what was going on," Wolfe explained.

"Do you understand the optics that I'm seeing here is that it's okay when it's beneficial for the company *not* to disclose information to the FAA, but when it's not beneficial to the company, it *was* disclosed to the FAA," Judge Geraghty said.

"Well, I think the difference is, is that the pilot was under no obligation to go get a medical at that point. There is nothing to say, *'Yeah. I have to go renew my medical because'*—"

"Where does it say that?" Judge Geraghty asked.

"Well, it doesn't say it anywhere but she's not able to operate an airplane for Global," Wolfe said again.

"With a first class medical, can't you operate as a GA pilot?" Judge Geraghty asked.

"I would assume you can," Wolfe said.

"Okay," Judge Geraghty said. "You need to have a medical. You need to have at least a basic medical. And if there's something disqualifying, you have to have a special issuance. So, explain to me this inconsistency."

"I mean, what's on the forms for the FAA when the pilot goes in and gets a medical, they are voluntarily going and doing that. They're saying, *'I'm here and I'm going to go do this, and I'm going to be honest and upfront on all of these forms.'* And that's fine. If all of that is disclosed, the FAA gets to look at it and makes its decision.

"The company, on the other hand has no obligation until we go all the way through this process. We were trying to follow the process and get to the end of it. And if we could have gotten to the end of it, then, at that point, then we have an obligation. That's when our obligation is triggered. Now that's the best that I can explain it," Wolfe said.

Judge Geraghty asked Wolfe if he understood the consequences to a pilot if they lied on their medical application. Wolfe said that the pilot could permanently lose their license and liberty, and that it was criminal. Geraghty told him that wasn't quite true and that beyond some exceptions, it was a one-year revocation. Wolfe then turned two shades redder.

CHAPTER 61

JUDGE GERAGHTY'S TURN WITH WOLFE

ARGUING WITH A federal judge was not the brightest strategy. *Big, big mistake*, Darby thought as she sketched Joe Wolfe sitting on the stand. It was now the judge's turn to question Wolfe, as if most of the direct examination wasn't by him anyway.

"Okay. And then there's a section in there that says, *'Safety Complaints.'* Do you see that with a bunch of bullet points?" Geraghty asked.

"Right," Wolfe said staring at the document.

When Geraghty asked Wolfe why he'd provided safety information to Ms. Abbott, his rationale was they wanted her to be aware of what else was out there. But he made the big mistake of saying 'we' during his explanation and Darby watched the judge's expression change.

"Just a minute. You said, 'we' had broken down, who is *'we'*?" Judge Geraghty asked.

"The combination of Captain Clark, corporate attorney Martha Jones, and in that meeting, when we went through and parsed out the document, we had broken it down into safety... a safety bucket, an EO bucket and then a miscellaneous bucket. So, we just—"

"Again, so I'm understanding your testimony," Geraghty said interrupting him, "the three of you broke these down and did these bullets?"

"*We* didn't do these bullets. I think I probably wrote it up, these bullets, and then sent them out to... I remember sending them out to Ann and Martha."

"Well, what happened to Captain Clark?" Geraghty asked.

"I don't know that, at that point. Captain Clark was being included... this was really just executing what he had drafted and directed to happen," Wolfe said.

Judge Geraghty continued with his questions regarding details of Darby's medical and certificate issuance. He wanted to know if Global had turned over her medical reports and psych evaluation to the FAA. Wolfe was unaware if they had. Then Wendel requested if he could ask a clarifying question.

"Do you know if any of that information was requested by the FAA?" Wendel asked.

"I don't. I don't know," Wolfe said.

"How would they know?" Judge Geraghty said with sarcasm missed by Wendel. "You've kept them in the dark the entire time."

CHAPTER **62**

WENDEL OFFICIALLY PLACED Joe Wolfe on the least-liked witness list, right up there with Clark, Dr. Wood, and Abbott. She wasn't sure what Robert could do to pull him down any farther. Glancing at the clock she yawned. This was going to be a long night. They had never run this late before, but motivation to end this trial was high on all sides.

Robert asked him if he'd ever been involved in a Section 8 process that cost as much as this one, and he had not. Then he asked Wolfe about the Chicago hotel room meeting with Dodson and Wolfe and asked about SMS.

"And during that meeting, face-to-face in Chicago, Dr. Wood asked the two of you, you and Captain Dodson, for an explanation of SMS. Correct?"

"He wasn't asking for an explanation of SMS. He just noted that, that was something that was very concerning for Darby. And he asked us what we knew about SMS."

"Well, what did you tell him as to what you knew?" Robert asked.

"I told Dr. Wood... I told him I am not a subject matter expert on SMS, but I will find out for you where Global's SMS program is, what we're doing to implement SMS, and I'll give you whatever information you want about it. I'll make sure that happens."

"Well, how about Captain Dodson? What information did he offer on SMS?"

"I believe it was much the same," Wolfe said. "I don't believe that Captain Dodson was a subject matter expert but, again, along with me, we would work together to get him as much information as he felt like he needed regarding Global's SMS program."

Darby smiled. Dodson had not a clue, despite that SMS was a federal regulation requiring all employees to be SMS trained. The funny, but sad, part of all this was the FAA administrator who had enacted SMS as a regulation, sat on Global's Board of Directors. Yet not one manager up to and including the CEO knew anything about it or what it was.

"Do you recall what the doctor thought he needed about SMS?" Judge Geraghty asked.

"I think he was, at that point, Judge," Wolfe said, "he was just more interested in wanting to learn about what it was. It was something that significantly bothered her. And so, he had pulled that out of one of the documents that he had read."

Robert asked Wolfe many of the same questions he had asked Abbott about progressive discipline, who was at the meetings, who selected Dr. Wood, but also Wolfe's overall involvement. None of their stories matched up and Darby noted that Judge Geraghty took many notes. In no time it was 5 p.m. and they took a fifteen-minute break.

Darby spent five minutes in the restroom and then worked on her drawing of Wolfe. She finished the last touch to her artwork just as the group returned.

Once back on the record Robert asked Wolfe about sick leave. He explained that it wasn't an accrual at Global, that Global did it on a year-to-year basis. So, it maxed out, depending on seniority, the pilots could have up to 270 hours.

"When can one use sick leave at Global?" Judge Geraghty asked.

"When you're sick."

"So, there's a medical deficiency," Judge Geraghty said.

"Exactly. Well, when you're unable to execute your first class medical and able to fly."

Robert stuck multiple email exhibits under Wolfe's nose, of which Clark had written that stated he'd planned to enact a Section 8 on Darby. Wolfe danced around them but had no idea what they were planning. Then Robert read his deposition that contradicted his current testimony. Wolfe wasn't sure which way was up.

"Is it your testimony today that you had knowledge prior to March of 2016 that Global management personnel had considered a Section 8 referral for Ms. Bradshaw?" Robert said.

"Objection," Wendel said. "Asked and answered."

"Overruled," Judge Geraghty said. "Go ahead."

"I don't know what Captain Clark considered. I mean, I know that the e-mail that you're talking about but no one, Captain Clark, talked to me or told me what he was thinking or what he was considered with regard to Section 8. I never had any conversations with him about that. But yeah, I think that e-mail was one of the ones that was forwarded to me. Even sitting here, I'm not really sure what that email says, whether it says he's considering it or not."

"We're referring to one e-mail dealing with Section 8. Did you know there were two?" Judge Geraghty said.

"I did not, Judge. No," Wolfe said.

"Would you turn to exhibit CX-7?" Judge Geraghty said. "If you look at the email on November, it starts November 17th and actually goes down to November 16th, 2015."

"Okay," Wolfe said.

"It says, '*She could be a candidate for a Section 8.*' This is an e-mail from Captain Clark to Captain Wyatt," Judge Geraghty said. "So, we've got one from Captain Clark to Captain Wyatt on November 16th, 2015, a week after the one from Captain Clark to Oliver Miller."

"What I'm saying is, no. Captain Clark, Captain Wyatt and Captain Miller did not engage me and ask me about the appropriateness of a Section 8."

"Okay. So, you had the VP thinking about a Section 8 of a first officer for a week. And they didn't engage you on this?" Judge Geraghty asked again.

"That's correct. Yes. Yes, Judge. That's what I'm telling you," Wolfe said.

Then the fun began. Wolfe became evasive. Robert grew frustrated. Wendel objected more than he normally did. It turned out that it was Wolfe who had created the pretext of Darby's physical harm assertion in Abbott's report, despite Ms. Abbott stating she had inferred it. He then refused to answer yes or no, but instead attempted to argue his points.

"All right," Wendel said. "I understand it's late and there can be frustrations, but we've all tried to be professional to the witnesses. Mr. Wolfe doesn't deserve to be yelled at even though there's frustration. And there should be proper decorum when he's asked the questions."

"Mr. Allen?" Judge Geraghty said.

"This goes back to the goose and the gander issue in terms of the treatment of my client for an entire day and expecting 'yes' or 'no' answers. And when I'm asking this witness for a 'yes' or 'no' answer, he talks over me and doesn't answer," Robert said. "If I raise my voice somewhat, it's because this witness is not listening to the questions, not answering the questions, and not responding when I intervened to try to get him to answer the question."

Judge Geraghty listened to their arguments back and forth for ten minutes and then he said, "If the question is designed for 'yes' or 'no,' it can be cured if there is something that needs to be elaborated on, on redirect if that opportunity is elected to by Respondent's Counsel. Now I know the nature, one it's late, two you're a lawyer and you like to argue as well, it's the nature of the beast. Okay?"

"Maybe I'm just not understanding the question, Judge," Wolfe said. "But I'll focus, and I will … I will… I will limit that. I understand exactly what you're saying."

Darby stifled a yawn, and wanted to call bullshit into her hand, but she refrained.

"Ms. Bradshaw had written a blog in 2009 concerning a fatal Air France accident. Correct?" Robert said.

"That's correct."

And you provided Dr. Wood with that blog publication. Correct?"

"I believe I did. Yes."

"Your understanding was that Dr. Wood felt that this information was very important. Correct?"

"Yes. Dr. Wood was very interested. He was very interested in the response that Global had to that accident. He wanted to see the communications that were coming out of the 330 fleet to Global pilots. He wanted to understand how Global was reacting to that crash."

Robert asked him if he provided Dr. Wood with an FAA advisory circular regarding RVSM air space and manual flight, and how that related to Darby's mental health. Once again, Wolfe asserted that it was all Dr. Wood's request, and something that he was extremely interested in, but after some time he lost interest and dropped it.

Darby smiled at his response. Dr. Wood dropped it because she debated the subject with him for over an hour, as she schooled him that manual flight should not be an emergency, but a basic skill. And federal law required an autopilot in RVSM airspace.

But as it would be, her emergency low-level sleep light was now flashing a warning. They finally finished at 8:30 p.m. This had been a 12-hour day in the courtroom that concluded with, Attorney Joe Wolfe directed the play, which Rich Clark authored, and Ms. Abbott, Dr. Marsh, Dr. Wood, and Robert Dodson had all been actors.

Chapter 63

KATHRYN TURNED THE pages and shook her head. She then reached for her phone. She selected Darby's name to find her location. She was just minutes away to the courthouse. Kathryn pulled on her coat, grabbed the evidence, and headed downstairs.

She stood at the entrance to the courthouse and waited for Darby's arrival.

"Good morning!" Darby said, rushing up to her ahead of Tom and Robert. "What are you doing out here?"

"Waiting for you," Kathryn said. "Can we talk for a moment before you go in?"

"Of course," Darby said. When the guys approached, she said, "I'll be just a minute."

"Why don't you both go up with the escort," Kathryn said. "I'll bring Darby up in a few minutes."

"You're scaring me," Darby said once Tom and Robert were out of earshot.

"I'm a little scared too," Kathryn said, handing Darby her notebook. "At the very least, deeply concerned."

"My notebook!" Darby said. "Thank you. Where did you find it?"

"On a clerk's desk. I knew it was yours, so I picked it up," Kathryn said. "Then I made the mistake of opening it."

"Did you read it or look at the pictures?" Darby asked.

"Pictures," Kathryn said, sighing again.

"What do you think?" Darby asked grinning.

"They disturbed the hell out of me."

"I call it therapy," Darby said. "I decided that if I can't get justice, I could get revenge, if only on paper."

"But Wolfe's hands were strapped to a table and his fingernails were being dropped into his mouth," Kathryn said. "There was blood spurting."

"Did you see the pliers, and the pain in his face?" Darby asked with a smirk. "I'm also not sure if blood would spurt, but it added a little something extra, don't you think?"

"Darby, this is not funny," Kathryn said, trying not to laugh. "You drew a picture of throwing Abbott out of a plane into the mountains."

"The sheer terror on her face was a work of art," Darby said.

"It was," Kathryn admitted. "I don't know if you should be an attorney, an artist, or I should just lock you up."

"It's not my fault, it's my manic personality," she said.

"We'd better get inside," Kathryn said. "But if you want to express your creative ability torturing the bad guys, please don't leave it laying around."

"I promise," Darby agreed with a yawn.

"What time did you get out of here last night?" Kathryn asked.

"Let's just say from wake up to bed, it was literally a Sydney flight, but without the nap."

"It's almost over," Kathryn said, opening the door for Darby.

CHAPTER 64

I *CAN DO anything for one more day*, Darby thought as the judge swore in Dodson. Then this would be over, and she could start the progress for change. This also might be the most interesting of all testimony, because Dodson had sat through the entire trial and heard Global's conflicting testimony. *Did he even pay attention?* She had no idea. What she did know was that he was polished.

She listened passively to his flight hours, position, and all that he'd done in his career and what his job entailed. Today Narcea questioned Dodson, as Darby doodled in her notebook. But when they began discussing the meeting regarding inverse assignments, where the company could order pilots to take trips that violated duty times, she listened closely.

"The second issue had to do with crew rest or fatigue type issues," Dodson said. "And she was concerned that pilots would deviate, we call 'deviate from deadhead,' on the front end of the rotation.

"Our pilots have the ability to change their schedule if the first leg of their rotation is a deadhead leg. And they can go into the computer and say I'm going to deviate from that scheduled deadhead leg, but I will arrive on my own, somehow, at the station, in time for the flight that I'm actually going to be working.

With a calm, professional, laid-back tone, Dodson came across as sincere. He was also one of those guys who was disgustingly polite and respectful, and everyone just loved him. Completely relaxed, he expressed openness and honesty. Robert even thought he was a nice guy.

"Well, this guy lives in Phoenix," Dodson said, "he didn't want to go all the way to Oklahoma and then fly the deadhead from Oklahoma to Los Angeles, and layover and then fly to Sydney. And quite frankly, I wouldn't either. So, they would stay at home, rest, and then take the short flight from Phoenix to Los Angeles, and then work their flight to Sydney."

"Would that be non-rev?" Judge Geraghty asked.

"No, it's not. When you deviate from deadhead on the front end, they give you an option to book a positive space leg. So, you don't have to stress about non-revving and getting there.

"And Ms. Bradshaw brought up situations that, quite frankly, had merit. That what if a guy is doing that and flying a really, long deviate from deadhead leg, is he well rested when he gets to the location from where he is going to now work a flight? And that was the question that we discussed at length. And my position on it was that we also have pilots who commute to work, so would it be any difference if a pilot lives, for example, I know we have pilots who live in Hawaii, who commute to Los Angeles, is it any difference for them to commute from Hawaii to Los Angeles, and then work a trip?"

They never had that conversation. Yet, he spoke the words with a smile *and* stared at her while he did. He wasn't trashing her to the judge, but *what the hell?* she thought. She never said any of that. What kind of game was he playing?

"We don't have total control over what our pilots do before they report for work. But we do have some safety valves in there. One is that if for some reason their plan to get there and rested enough to fly the trip, if that doesn't work out, then they must, they are required by law really, to sign the release saying that they're rested enough to fly the trip. And so, they can call in fatigued and that's it, we're done. We take them off the trip and we will live with the consequences of that. But it's a contractual allowance that we give our pilots."

Darby's heartrate accelerated to the level of two Venti cappuccinos with extra shots.

"However," Dodson continued, "the situation we are aware that some people don't use it quite as responsibly as they probably should. And I know that in a flight operations meeting, prior to Ms. Bradshaw coming to my office, that this issue had come up. And we were quite actively looking at it and discussing it and trying to figure out a solution for that.

"So, I was aware of the situation. I could see the legitimate concern on Ms. Bradshaw's part, but I felt, to me, like it was already being looked at. The conversation was professional the whole time and at least from my perspective it was very professional and actually pleasant, as what I would expect. It was someone who walked into my office with a concern, and we had a good talk about it."

What they had talked about was the inverse assignment, where the company could force a pilot on a trip from anywhere in the country, to their base, and on the flight without logging it as duty time. It wasn't an option, the contract said they had to take it. What he was talking about was her concern that Global was giving green slips, double paid trips, out of base that required the pilot to travel positive space from Detroit to Los Angeles and fly to Sydney the same day.

All the union had to do was require that these trips be awarded the day prior, following federal regulations, and giving the pilot an extra day of pay and a hotel room. Then if the pilot opted to deviate deadhead, they could, and sleep in their allotted hotel room for 6-7 hours prior to the start of trip at 11 p.m. The pilot would get an extra day of double pay *and* be rested for the flight. Why the union was allowing the company to continue in this manner was perplexing. What Dodson was saying twisted everything.

The twelve-hour day in court the prior day had exhausted her, and she had too much caffeine in her system. Anger added to that mix would not be good. She reached for her bottle of water to mask her emotions.

"How would you characterize your relationship with First Officer Bradshaw at that time?" Narcea asked.

"Well, I thought I had a strong, a good relationship with Ms. Bradshaw. I mean my exchanges with her had been, at times, I would say maybe firm about whether or not, which protocol she should follow, going through me with her submissions. But we were both adults and it seemed like we went from that right back to normal communications about day-to-day functions. This meeting was a case in point, I thought we had a good relationship at that time."

"Ultimately, First Officer Bradshaw was returned to line and is flying currently. Are you comfortable with that?" Narcea asked.

"Yes, I am. You know, I trust the professionals involved and I did that from the beginning, trusted that Ann Abbott was concerned, and I trusted that Captain Clark and Dr. Marsh made a decent decision, or made a professional decision. I believe that Dr. Wood was being professional. But we have a process that says that two out of three doctors say that she's fit for duty, then we accept that. And so, I do. I think that's what I must do in this case. If I didn't think she was, I'd be screaming from the treetops."

Darby wanted to scream from treetops on top of a mountain. But when she paused for a moment and thought about it, she realized that this testimony was nothing short of interesting. Interesting that she and Dodson were friends. Interesting that he thought of her as a professional. Interesting that she had always been professional with him. More than interesting was that they shifted her concern regarding fatigue to align with theirs. This was completely opposite from Abbott's assessment. *What's their angle?* she wondered.

Then as if the lights to the runway turned on bright, she knew exactly what the hell they were doing and where they were going.

CHAPTER 65

W AS A PILOT a Level-4 threat if they were a threat to the flight? Robert had asked, and Dodson had no idea. He did acquiesce that the pilot should be removed from duty if they were a danger to the flight, but his overall lack of knowledge in his position was horrifying.

Fifteen months after Darby's retaliatory line check, she found a letter in her medical report that the check airman, who she had reported in the simulator years earlier, had said she had been a threat to the safety of a flight during that line check flight. That would have been a valid reason to place her in a mental health evaluation. Instead, they sent her to Abbott, five months later for something else.

She suspected that letter was an afterthought. She also supposed that the judge came to the same conclusion. Geraghty had also wondered why the check airman wasn't called to testify. Darby hoped he'd figure that one out himself, as well.

"Generically, you had correspondence in the last quarter of 2015, in which you expressed your appreciation to Ms. Bradshaw for her great energy with respect to the piloting profession, correct?" Robert said.

"Yes, that's correct," Dodson said.

"And was that a sincere comment?" Robert said.

"Absolutely."

Robert discussed Darby's request to wear her uniform and represent the airline at events such as Women in Aviation. Dodson agreed that she always asked, and that she was a positive example. Robert was documenting that Darby was a valued, professional employee, at least by Dodson's opinion. His opinion appeared to carry more weight than any other Global employee, thus far.

During her grievance meeting with Dodson, she kept stating that the Section 8 was unwarranted. He said that he did not order it. Darby had said, '*I know that, but it's still unwarranted.*' He became angry with that word. Darby finally asked him if he knew what unwarranted meant, and if he could explain it. He had said, '*I'm not going to give you a vocabulary lesson.*'

Darby suspected that Global was trying to prove that Dodson had nothing against her. That they were professionals. He respected her. They had great talks. Good buddies. All he did was give her the letter and had absolutely no reason to harm her.

"And would you agree with me that right up through the Section 8 you had what you would characterize as a good relationship with Ms. Bradshaw?"

"Generally. I think there were a couple times where she wasn't particularly happy with me," he said with a broad smile. "But other than that, yes."

Robert then challenged Dodson on duty time.

"Counsel," Judge Geraghty said, "I don't care, frankly, what Global thinks about its flight and duty time. I care about what the FAA regulations require to be the flight and duty time. I will tell you if there's a discrepancy I'm going to go with the regulations."

Shortly thereafter they broke for lunch and Robert pulled Darby aside.

CHAPTER 66

LUNCH

DARBY ASKED THE escort if she could take her back upstairs with her lunch. She agreed and Darby quickly gathered two turkey sandwiches. Robert had sequestered himself in a briefing room down the hall from the courtroom. He had wanted to focus. She dropped off his sandwich and told the escort she'd eat hers in the courtroom.

She entered the room and went to her table in the front. Darby opened her notebook and looked at Dodson's picture she'd begun drawing that morning, wondering if Kathryn would approve. Then decided to eat before she continued.

Struggling a moment with the plastic wrap on her sandwich, she opened the package and removed half the sandwich from the container. She ripped open a mustard, then a mayonnaise package, and added both on top of the turkey. She took a bite and startled at the noise behind her.

Turning around she saw Dodson sitting there. Staring at her.

"Why didn't you go to lunch?" Darby asked.

"I was in the bathroom," Dodson said. "They must have lost track of me."

"Do you want half my sandwich?"

"No thanks. I'm good. They'll bring me something."

Darby doubted Dodson was good. Due to his size, she suspected he hadn't missed too many sandwiches in his day. He would be hungry.

It didn't take a moment's thought before she said, "You need to eat. Even if they bring you something you won't have time before you go back on the stand. It's draining up there."

Pushing back her chair, she stood and grabbed one of the bottles of water she had brought for Robert. Then carried the other half of her sandwich in the container, the condiments and a bottle of water back to Dodson's table.

"Here ya go," she said, setting everything on the desk in front of him.

"Thank you," he said.

"Sure," she shrugged with a half-smile.

Darby returned to her desk and finished her sandwich. Despite her urge to ask him why he did this to her, she refrained. Only because of orders not to talk about the trial, and she did not want to jeopardize anything. Instead, she opened her notebook and drew how she would torture his ass for being part of this.

CHAPTER **67**

ONCE THEY WERE back on the record, Robert spent less than thirty minutes finishing up Dodson's cross-examination. Darby wasn't surprised that the morning session was the least hostile of all Global's witnesses. Dodson was a great actor. He spoke his lines well, and they had crafted his story as one of Global's professionalism and their concern for safety. But his saying he agreed with Darby was priceless. A spectacular ending to the show.

He got under her skin even more than Abbott. Perhaps because he could smile and lie right to her face without any remorse. It could have something to do with him being a pilot and stabbing her in the back. Maybe it was the end of the first step of an exceptionally long journey. Perhaps her feelings were simply a combination of all those reasons mixed with exhaustion.

Judge Geraghty assessed Dodson for a moment, and then he said, "You mentioned that the reaction that First Officer Bradshaw had when she received the Section 8 is that she was shocked or concerned. Did she cry?"

Dodson paused, and Darby thought *don't you fucking lie about this!* Maybe they hadn't told him how to answer. Perhaps he was thinking that if he said yes, then the judge would ask him why he hadn't reported her. Maybe he had a moment of conscience because she fed him.

"No," Dodson finally said, and Darby realized she had been holding her breath.

"Have you ever seen her cry?" Geraghty asked.

"No," Dodson said. This time his response was quicker.

"Now, you've sat for eight days in these hearings, when did you first see Ms. Abbott's rendition of her interaction with her in that hotel back in March of 2016?"

"Right here," Dodson said.

"Okay. Was her observation about First Officer Bradshaw's demeanor different than what you have ever seen her react in the past?"

"Yes, your Honor, in that I've never seen her cry."

Judge Geraghty then asked if anyone ever asked Dodson during this entire process, about his interactions with her after the Section 8. They had not. They discussed the gravity of the situation and the necessity of ALPO being present. The judge asked him why.

"I just felt like it was a very serious issuance," Dodson said. "And to be really honest with you, it never crossed my mind to do it without ALPO representation there for her. Part of that might have been vested in the fact that I had a solid relationship with the union rep there and I just thought it was best for everybody involved that she be represented. Quite frankly, I didn't know how Ms. Bradshaw might react, either."

Judge Geraghty queried Dodson's involvement of a Section 8 in the past, of which Dodson had participated in and was well versed, and affirmatively stated that he knew this could have led to the end of Darby's career.

"Based on your observations and the demeanor of First Officer Bradshaw at the time she was presented this letter, were you left with the impression she understood the gravamen of this letter?" Judge

Geraghty asked.

"My impression, and that is clearly what you're asking me, is yes, she did."

"Now, I'm a realist, okay, and I understand that what happens in this process was just not limited to the actors. Would it be a fair observation or concern that the word on the street for any pilot who has gone through a Section 8 for mental health reasons, someone is going to question them down the road if they want to fly with them?" Judge Geraghty asked.

"I'm a realist, too," Dodson said. "I just don't know how to answer that, because, you know, nobody has ever come to me and said word on the street is do you really want to fly with Ms. Bradshaw, no one has ever said that I've never heard that."

Judge Geraghty released the witness and said, "All right. So, I want to put this on the record so that we have the exact same story," and proceeded to discuss the binders.

"All right. So, we've addressed all the documents. Now I want to talk about a couple of things," he said with all the foreboding and concern that Darby had felt throughout the trial.

CHAPTER **68**

JUDGE GERAGHTY
CLOSE OF TRIAL

EVERYONE'S ATTENTION WAS at high alert with that statement. He was not pleased. How could he be? This had been a travesty of deception, and a waste of time in his courtroom and everything Global presented painted the picture of duplicity.

"I want to talk about the demeanor of the Complainant," Judge Geraghty said. "My observation is that... my impression was that she was alert, bright, engaging, confident, in some cases one could even perceive as being cocky. However, at no time, I saw any type of emotion that would indicate anything consistent with what Ms. Abbott observed.

"Now, I want to state that specifically for the record, because this is one point that bothers me in this case. Everything I've seen in this trial, with the exception of Ms. Abbot's report, is not what was being reported by Ms. Abbott. I don't know how to resolve that, but it is diametrically opposed to everything I've heard from witnesses and my observations of the Complainant during these proceedings.

"I'm going to notify the parties that pursuant to the authority under... if I can find it here... 29 CFR 22 1979.108(b), I am seriously considering issuing an order or a notice to the Federal Aviation

Administration asking them to separately file an Amicus brief in this matter. I am gravely concerned from the testimony that I've heard about the Section 8 and medical evidence not being turned over, upon receiving information that a pilot has a medical deficiency that results in a disqualifying for being entitled to continuing operating of any aircraft.

"I am specifically concerned because as I'm understanding this process, it only precludes an otherwise disqualified pilot from operating *its* aircraft as opposed to another aircraft. What immediately jumps in my mind is 91 subpart (k) with fractional ownership, which occurred post the development of the Section 8 process, as I understand this, and if this pilot has a first or a second class medical certificate, there's nothing to preclude them, absent not having the type rating, from getting in that plane and flying other passengers or flying general aviation aircraft.

"So, I just tell you that, it's gnawed at me since I heard the position that the onus goes on the pilot who might have a mental health issue. And I just want you to think about that. We're relying on a pilot who, and I'm not saying whether or not, you know, Ms. Bradshaw is going to win or lose, totally separate issue, but let's assume that this bipolar was in fact the case, we're asking a person with a mental impairment to make the determination about their mental deficiency, when we have someone outside of that who has affirmative knowledge of that, who is responsible for the protection of our public in our air space.

"Maybe that's the way the law is, maybe that's just it and there's nothing to be done about it. Somebody needs to know about that. If that, in fact, is the status of the law, and we've had testimony here about the Aviation Rule Making Committee, maybe the rule making committee needs to take a second look at that, whether or not… it just seems to me the high priority that we place the burden on the pilot to self-report, but we don't place the burden on the air carrier who has actual knowledge to report that to the FAA."

Judge Geraghty let that hang the air for a moment, then he said, "Let's talk about briefs." Then he explained that it was his understanding that Global conceded that Darby had engaged in protected activity by providing her safety report to Wyatt and Clark, and the room remained quiet.

"You may not agree with me," Geraghty said looking at Wendel, "but I believe I've already resolved the issue of adverse action referral to the Section 8 being an adverse action. It's not a disciplinary action, but it has adverse consequences. There's lots of case law that talks about the adverse consequences associated with that.

"So, I want you to take the page time in your briefs and talk about causation. I remind you of the criteria under Palmer, a *contributing factor* is all that the Complainant has to establish. And then the company is going to have to show, by clear and convincing evidence, that but for that protected activity, they would have taken the same action."

"'*But for*,' did you say that…'*but for the protected activity*'?" Wendel asked.

"But for the protected activity," Geraghty repeated.

"Right," Wendel said.

Judge Geraghty explained that the briefs were limited to 60 pages for each party, with ten of those pages dedicated to damages. The bottom line is, he would not allow more than 50 pages to summate the case.

"Given the length of this transcript, Complainant's brief is going to be due September 6th," Judge Geraghty said. "Respondent's brief, same thing, 60 pages, 50 substantive. Your brief is due October 11th. The Complainant has the burden, or at least the initial burden, therefore, I'm giving her a second bite of the apple. You will be limited on your reply brief, to 25 pages in that final transcript. That will be due November 8th."

Judge Geraghty explained the importance of a timeline, as to when things happened.

"The other thing that I will tell you, I'll just be up front, you are not going to like my findings, factually," Judge Geraghty said directly to Wendel's team. "If you really want this out there, I would think long and hard about this. You can settle at any point you want to, but the facts in this case, I'm going to lay it out, and from what I'm hearing it's not pretty.

"You've got a pilot that went through, I'll call it a 'gauntlet,' to get reinstated. And I understand the company is torn, the company has a hard decision to make, given the Germanwings scenario, but there's more to that than just the Germanwings scenario. And I am really troubled by some of these exhibits, about how this referral came to fruition. And it troubles me a great deal, I'll just tell you that.

"Please do not take this as, you know, Ms. Bradshaw, yes, you win. I would tell you, flat out, I could do a decision on the record, although it has to be a written decision, it doesn't mean I couldn't do it and use the transcript... but you all have to make a business decision if you want all this laundry out there.

"As far as the exhibits itself, if I noticed, you will note for the record I've got 'Confidential' all over the place in these documents, these are public records. I am not going to seal this stuff unless you've got some compelling reason. This is information that needs to get out about how this process was done with these documents. You can ask, but this is a public hearing.

"The long and the short of it, frankly, is no matter how I rule, this is a sad case. It really is. It's a sad case. And I would encourage the parties to think long and hard about settling this, before I write this decision, because you can't un-ring that bell."

There was a long pause, and Judge Geraghty said, "Any questions?"

"I have a question on the briefing," Wendel said. "You said that you were going to give the Complainant a reply brief, because they had the burden, if I understood?"

"Yes," Geraghty said.

"Their burden is only on the first prong, correct?" Wendel said.

"Right."

"So, is there an opportunity either for Respondent to have a reply on the part of the case for which Respondent has the burden on the second one?"

"No."

"That doesn't seem fair," Wendel said, "and I'll state that for the record,"

"It's noted, preserved for appeal," Judge Geraghty said, clearly at the end of his rope.

"You can count on it," Wendel snapped.

"It's your prerogative," Judge Geraghty said. Then asked, "Anything else?" When there was no response, he said, "All right. This hearing is closed."

Chapter 69

THE INFORMAL END of trial celebration party was at Darby's house twenty minutes after they'd left the courthouse. Tom was grilling steaks on the patio, and Robert was well into his third bourbon. Darby, Kathryn, Linda, and Jackie were in the kitchen making side dishes. What that looked like was, her friends were sitting at the kitchen table talking and drinking wine while Darby sauteed mushrooms. Everything else was prepared.

"I can't believe you have to wait a year for the ruling," Linda said.

"Whomever said justice was swift must have been pushing someone out of an airplane," Kathryn said grinning at Darby.

"The best kind of justice," Darby said with a wink. She then excused herself and returned moments later with her notebook to explain that comment to Linda and Jackie. Opening it to Dodson's picture she said, "It was pure therapy."

"I can see that," Linda said slowly.

"What's poking out of his uh... private parts?" Jackie asked. "And why's he on a boat?"

"They're cocktail umbrellas," Darby said. "He used to write and tell me he was cooling off with drinks with little umbrellas while fishing in the Florida Keys."

"Is that a shark fin?" Linda asked, tapping a finger on the paper.

"Yep," Darby said. "He's going overboard after he's bled enough to attract the sharks." She returned to the stove and picked up the spatula.

"This is disturbing on so many levels," Kathryn said, and turned to Dr. Wood's picture.

"I kind of like it," Jackie said. "They deserve so much more. I hope you win millions."

"Hardly," Darby said scooping the mushrooms into a bowl. "The award is only compensatory damages, and typically that's about fifty thousand. Robert also said I will only get reasonable attorney fees, not necessarily all of them. That's about 90 percent."

"But how is that fair," Jackie said.

"It's not," Darby said. "This also doesn't cost Global a penny because their insurance company pays for it. The longer they carry on, 90 percent of my attorney fees won't even cover the 50K award. As a matter of fact, we've already exceeded that, but I try not to think about it."

"They're doing this to drain Darby," Kathryn said, standing. She opened the oven and removed the dinner rolls. "It's called a war of attrition," she said over her shoulder.

Linda stood and removed the caprese salad from the fridge and handed it to Jackie. She picked up the Caesar salad, grabbed the bottle of wine, and said, "Shall we join the guys?"

"We shall," Darby said lifting her bowl of mushrooms.

The table had already been set and dinner was ready. They filled it with food and took their seats. It was Robert who made the toast, "To standing strong in all this."

Darby thanked him. She could not have survived the litigation without him. He'd taught her the law and peeled her off the wall when Wendel's motions put her there. They had done all they could, and now they would wait.

"Well, you did teach me about SMS," Robert said. "But I have to say that regulation, it's just…. it's such a girly law." His eyes sparkled as he spoke and emphasized girly in a long drawn out manner.

The table, once lively, fell silent until Darby burst out laughing. It wasn't long until her friends went from shock to laughing with her.

"He's right," Darby said. "Why do we need a law to tell airlines to mitigate risk and play nice in the sandbox? But I do take offense to the girly part."

"Says the woman who has bigger balls than any man," Robert said raising his glass and clinking it with Darby's.

When crew resource management began, called CRM, pilots referenced it as touchy-feely school. Those who didn't need it, thought it ridiculous. Those who did need it argued against it. But it worked and improved safety. Thereafter, CRM expanded to threat and error management. SMS was simply the next generation of risk mitigation to include the entire organization and all systems and processes. SMS was the regulation that covered everything a company did.

"Well, the CEO didn't even know what accountable executive meant when the FAA administrator who enacted the law sits on the Board of Directors, of which Croft is the Chairman," Niman said with a scowl. "How is this even possible?"

Kathryn and Tom exchanged a look and John said, "We can't lose sight of what brought us here, despite the Global shenanigans in trial."

"Exactly," Darby said. "Global's violations of federal regulations, their over reliance on automation, their lack of training, their forcing pilots to fly fatigued. They haven't changed anything and that's what this was all about." Then Bill's warning slithered into her mind.

"They definitely have kept you off their back for a while with this litigation," John said.

"Probably the reason we went to trial," Darby said. "And to keep me quiet, and to financially break me. But the truth is, I haven't really been quiet through all this. I've still been writing things up and reporting them to management when I see them, because I already have the noose around my neck, what else could they do?"

"They're placing passengers in jeopardy," Linda said. "That's bad enough."

"Yeah, it is," Jackie said. "But after listening to how bad training is, the near crashes, how many you've witnessed, I wonder how many more events there have been."

"That's what scares me," Darby said.

"And the fact the company is hiding mental health issues from the FAA," Jackie said, "I think that maybe planes should be operated by machines, and we should get rid of pilots."

"Sacrilege," Darby said. But if Jackie could be swayed toward autonomous aircraft, knowing what she knows, then the public could be convinced, too. *Fear is so powerful,* she thought.

"She might have a point," Robert said. "But I suspect they'll come to the table with an offer sooner than later."

"They haven't yet," Niman said. "Why now?"

"The judge scolded them," Robert said cutting into his steak. "Geraghty wagged his finger and told them it would be a business decision if they wanted to air their dirty laundry."

"But he also said he could have ruled for me, too." Darby said. "So why didn't he?"

"That could be in your favor," Robert said. "He knows if Global appeals, you'll need a well thought out, documented ruling, with case law and character assessments. I believe you're going to win, or should, anyway."

Darby smiled at the should part. None of this should have

happened. But it did. Whomever said life happened while you were making plans was correct.

"If they don't settle," Linda asked Robert, "will it really take a year?"

"Yes," Robert said. "One thing about Geraghty, he stands by his schedule."

Justice may wait a year, but passenger safety could not. Unfortunately, Darby was about to begin A350 training and needed to focus, putting her fight for safety on hold for a month or two. Especially, since she was unsure as to what they had in store for her when she showed up to headquarters for training. She had no doubt they were gunning for her. But passenger safety came first.

Darby emptied her glass of wine with new resolve and smiled. There was way more than one way to get justice than the AIR21 law.

CHAPTER 70

GLENMORANGIE HAD NEVER tasted as good as it did with freedom. Bill sat in an oversized leather chair in Drake's den and sipped a scotch as he watched the roaring fire. The temperature was still in the low 50's, and he appreciated the warmth of the fire. But more than that, the motion of the flames stimulated his synapses.

Bill loved aviation more than anything, but the industry was crumbling around him and destroying the pilot job. Fucking airline management cost his father's life. Bill had done what he thought was right to take control. That hadn't worked out as he'd planned, and now due to geography, he became part of the problem, not the solution. The transfer to San Quentin was for one reason only—to assist Drake. What else could he do? His options were minimal.

Drake and his predecessor, President Kohler, were meeting down the hall while Bill waited for the others to arrive. The doorbell eventually rang, and he heard voices in the entryway as Kohler walked into the den. Bill nodded in his direction.

"Can I get you a refill?" President Kohler asked, as he poured himself a scotch. Kohler had been the U.S. vice president under

Drake. Now he was just a tool that Drake owned.

"I'm good," Bill said as he stood.

Within minutes President Drake, George Wyatt, and Walter Croft entered the room. Bill shook hands with Wyatt and Croft. He couldn't stand those two assholes. His friends who had merged with the new airline were less than pleased. Had he not gone to prison, he, too, would have had to work for Wyatt, and would have been in the same predicament as Darby. Had they paid a doctor to call him crazy, he'd have shown them exactly what crazy looked like.

In hindsight, Bill was glad he had not been successful at ridding the world of Darby Bradshaw. He was quite proud of her standing up to the *Globeass boys* and defending the pilot job. He underestimated Kathryn as well. Now he wondered how he could use them.

After everyone was seated, Drake said, "So, you finished trial today."

"We did," Croft acknowledged.

"I heard the Judge gave you a little scolding," Drake said.

"He also said he wasn't going to rule for Bradshaw," Croft replied. "Of which he could have. He had the power, but he didn't exercise it."

Croft's defensiveness, and his justification were unbecoming. Tension filled the room, and Bill enjoyed Croft and Wyatt's discomfort more than he thought he would. He leaned back with one leg crossed over the other and sipped his drink.

"I'll tell you up front," Drake said. "I'm not pleased."

"But nothing's changed," Croft said. "This is a *delay*. Nothing more. Now is not the right time."

"I'll get into the FAA administration," Wyatt said, stepping to Croft's defense. "There will be a perfect time to pull the trigger, once I'm there."

"You'll get into position and keep that fucking MAX grounded in order to keep the profits rolling in for Global," Drake said in an even tone.

"That's not our only intention," Croft said.

Drake shifted his attention from Wyatt to Croft as they spoke. Then he nodded and asked, "What about Bradshaw? She appears to be the only pilot that you boys can't keep reigned in."

"She's attending A350 training next month," Croft said. "That'll keep her busy for a couple months. She's filed some grievances of which we got under control as well."

"You can't keep her busy forever," Drake said as he stood. He walked to the fireplace and lifted a poker. He thrust it into the logs, sparks flew, and more flames came to life. Drake stood that way for the longest time and then without turning from the fire, he said, "Do you plan to tell me when you think the time is right?"

"We do, Sir," Croft said, "absolutely."

"You do that." Drake said setting down the poker.

He then walked Croft and Wyatt out. Bill heard Drake wish Wyatt good luck at his hearing for the FAA administration position, and then the door closed. Within minutes Drake returned to the den.

"Those fucking assholes," Drake said. "Nobody tells me what to do."

"Now what?" Bill asked.

Ignoring Bill's question, Drake turned to President Kohler and said, "I want you to pull all our scientists out of the CDC factory in Wuhan. We're going to show Mr. Croft that I can give him maximum profits and I take them away."

"Sir," President Kohler said, glancing at Bill and then back to Drake.

"He's fine," Drake said. Then he turned to Bill. "And I have a couple jobs for you."

CHAPTER 71

May 2, 2019

*T*HE QUESTION IS—WHY? Darby thought, lying in bed after minimal sleep. Was it as simple as short-changing pilot training and violating regulations, to create a platform for autonomous aircraft? It worked on Jackie. But what if they pushed it too far and had an accident? That could not possibly be good for the airline. Autonomous airplanes could not be good for the union either, losing their sole source of income. So why is the union helping?

She yawned and then stretched. The sun wasn't up yet, but she needed to be. She would spend today at her computer. First things first, she needed to send an email, but that was not going to happen without coffee.

Dressed, Darby walked up the stairs with coffee in hand. As the sun broke free from the horizon, she settled at her desk with the intent to respond to a Global attorney, Marissa Spellings. Spellings had denied Darby's request for an investigation of those involved, months earlier, because of the pending trial. Pending was the key word.

Dear Ms. Spellings, Trial is complete, and we must now conduct a full investigation despite the AIR21 case. I appreciate your concern wanting to wait, but now it's complete. However, the AIR21 is not an ethical violation, but a federal regulation violation.

Within AIR21 liability you must demonstrate protected activity, an adverse action, and a causal link between the two. Prior to trial we had accomplished two out of three. However, ethics determinations do not require those multifarious determinations. Simply... they were bad, deceitful, dishonest, inconsiderate, unthoughtful, callous, mean-spirited, derogatory, and nasty. Any one of these adjectives should implicate the ethical rules. Simply reading our rules of the road and identifying the behaviors will support this investigation. I now have under-oath testimony of all witnesses, to prove what they did.

Global does not allow unethical behavior. An AIR21 case does not include ethical standards. Therefore, the two are different. Regardless, the trial is complete, as you requested. I look forward to an honest and sincere investigation, which should be nothing other than reading trial testimony, of which I will provide.

Darby sent the letter via email. Then she focused on two lawsuits. Despite everyone suggesting she should sue all those involved for what they did, she could not. There was no law to get them. She'd thought about a RICO charge because of the conspiracy. But Robert said that while she could win, he asked her *at what expense.* She would not win anything because she lacked damages. She had her job back. Therefore, they got away with what they did.

But not everyone. After a little research, her only hope were fraud charges against Dr. Wood and Attorney Joe Wolfe. They deceptively lulled her into the Section 8 process, which was not authentic, and she had relied on that premise. That's all she needed.

She had also filed multiple grievances against the company for the many ways they had violated the contract. Granted ALPO allowed them to do it, but the grievances were for all the pilots, not just her. She would not get anything by winning a grievance, but it wouldn't cost her a million dollars to pursue it, only her time. The grievance process would at least help to effect change.

Robert had given her an example of how to write the fraud complaints and she copied and pasted case law. By the time she was close to dying from starvation, not moving from her computer all day, she had finished both first drafts. Then she dialed Tom's number.

"What's your pleasure for dinner?" she asked, saving the drafts to a folder on her computer and logging back into her email.

"How about seafood at Anthony's?" he asked.

"Fuck," Darby said.

"That could be arranged," he said. "Before or after dinner?"

"No. Yes. I mean… I wrote to Spellings about the investigation this morning and now we have to wait until the ruling comes out," Darby said exasperated.

"Do you believe you'll ever get an investigation?" Robert asked. "Especially when the CEO was involved."

"Well… if we prove what they did, how can they *not* be held accountable?" Darby said.

"I wish it were that easy," Tom said. "I'll be there in ten minutes and we can talk about it."

Darby ended the call, walked to her closet and selected something black to fit her mood. *Nothing is ever easy*, she thought as she slipped into the dress. Then she thought about her pending training, and wondered what games they had in store for her. Her flight schedule was full until then, with three trips to Haneda. Then she remembered the little girl.

Darby had felt guilty for rushing to catch her flight instead of stopping to ensure she was safe. Global subsequently sent out a memo to all pilots directing them to notify dispatch if they suspected sex trafficking—pilots were prohibited from contacting the arrival station.

The company could simply be that fucked up, she thought, pulling on her shoes. Maybe they weren't criminal, just ignorant. But this trial and legal action had been a black hole, time suck, and made no sense. Regardless, and despite everything they were doing, the only reason for this trial had to be to attack her bank account. Winning was ego. God, she prayed they couldn't get to Geraghty. Money could be replaced, lives could not.

Chapter 72

HAVING ARRIVED FROM Los Angles on a 737 jumpseat after a Sydney flight, the thought of going out to dinner was the last thing Darby wanted to do. But this was important, and she loved her friend. Therefore, Darby changed into a pair of jeans, pulled a tee shirt over her head, and drove to Kathryn's house.

"What's going on?" Darby asked when she found everyone sitting in the living room.

"Dinner," Jackie said. "You're late."

"In the living room?" Darby asked. "Since when?"

"I want to watch Wyatt's hearing," Kathryn said.

"Oh yeah," Darby said, trying to forget it. She went to the dining room table and dished up a plate of food. Chicken and rice, green beans, and a garden salad with homemade dressing. Once her plate was full, she joined her friends and sat on the floor. With legs extended, plate on her lap, she leaned against the easy chair Jackie was sitting in.

"You can join us on the couch," Kathryn said, patting a seat between her and Linda.

"Not the way I eat," Darby said with a chuckle. "Really, I'm good down here where slopping on the floor causes less damage, and the three-second rule will never be noticed."

"Everyone ready?" Kathryn asked, and then pressed play.

As they swore George Wyatt in at the hearing, Jackie said, "I can't believe that it's possible for a retired airline executive to even be considered for the FAA administrator position. Talk about a conflict of interest."

"Even more than that, he's already violated a federal regulation," Linda said.

"He won't get it," Darby said, sipping her wine. "No way."

Kathryn raised the volume but made no comment.

Chairman Senator Roger Wenstrom began. "You consider the FAA as the global gold standard. If confirmed, what will you do to restore confidence of the FAA around the Globe?"

"There are 85,000 people that need leadership and need to be supported," Wyatt said. "We need someone to look at the 737 MAX to ensure recommendations are taken seriously."

What kind of fucking answer was that? Darby thought. Captain George Wyatt was nothing but a fucking suit that played with people's lives. No way in hell he would behave any differently at the FAA.

Senator Maria Albright asked, "Regarding flight and duty rules and a cargo carve-out, what do you think of that?"

"It's important to have one level of safety, both prescriptive and performance based. However, while it should be required to have a fatigue risk management program to include Cargo… we may have a different way to get to the same safety bar than we do for airline pilots."

The FAA certified cargo pilots with the same standards as airline pilots, and subject to the same FAA requirements of operation. Captain Wyatt's response was crap, as there was only one answer to that question—*any* pilot operating a commercial aircraft, which shares the airspace and is subject to impacting the ground and potentially people, should be subject to the same fatigue rules as all other Part 121 pilots. There should never be a *carve-out* for safety.

"Well," Senator Albright said, "regarding the flight attendant rest rule… will you help move it along quickly?"

"I don't have specifics," Wyatt said, "but I will be looking forward to discussing this."

"Bullshit," Darby said. "He has the specifics. The only answer should be that flight attendants, if fatigued, will be unable to perform their duties in an emergency and the current rest requirements are not sufficient."

Kathryn paused the video.

"Global Air Lines pushes their flight attendants to exhaustion," Jackie said, having been one she knew. "They have no recourse because they are not unionized."

"I was on a flight from Seattle to Shanghai and we diverted to get fuel due to thunderstorms and potential holding," Darby said. "The flight turned into an 18+ hour duty day. The lead flight attendant argued with scheduling for a new report time the following morning due to the entire crew's fatigue level. The company refused. When I questioned how they could do that, he said scheduling changed the crew's report time to later than they reported in the computer to make it legal. That crew was in no shape to work a return flight with minimal rest."

"They did that all the time when I worked there," Jackie said.

"Shall we continue?" Kathryn asked.

Darby nodded and said, "Sorry."

"Regarding the 737 MAX, preliminary findings, technology, and automation will continue to be part of these accidents. We don't want over-reliance," Senator Albright said. "How do you view the potential for over reliance and how do we best manage the human element in testing on technology?"

"This is one of the most important issues that has existed for a number of years," Wyatt said. "Automation provides benefits, workload management to get the job done. However, it can create risks that we must mitigate. We need to ensure pilots maintain manual flight skills. Training… to move various levels of training is essential."

Darby and Kathryn exchanged an incredulous look. This was the biggest load of crap Darby had ever heard, and the members of the Senate Committee on Commerce, Science, and Transportation committee were latching onto his hook.

"Do we have the adequate tools in place today?" Senator Albright asked.

"We do," Wyatt assured her. "Tools continue to be developed, but we need to focus. Focus on FPM instead of automation is a more holistic way to address the issues… to address the manual flight skills. It must be more strategic. The nice thing about newer airplanes in the last seven or eight years, it's easier to measure performance."

"FPM?" Linda asked.

"Flight path management," Darby said.

Global did not have the tools and practices in place to adequately train pilots. If they did, they sure as hell didn't use them. They trained by rote memorization. Simulator sessions did not afford repetition. Pilots taught themselves the systems at home and given the answers to the electronic tests to pass. The training philosophy was a push-the-button mentality. Some of the instructors even bypassed the required oral. *This is such bullshit*, Darby thought.

Senator Richard Brandt asked, "How will you restore confidence? The FAA is in crisis with confidence. How did the FAA determine that the agency failed to participate or monitor some of the crucial systems, and they simply delegated that and referred to Boeing? The company did not perform flight test with MCAS software malfunction, and disregarded complaints made by pilots. The question to you is… will you commit to reverse the ODA delegation? Safety on the cheap is what ODA does. Give perception of putting the fox in charge of the hen house. Will you review and reverse the excessive delegation?"

"ODA?" Linda asked.

"Organization Designation Authorization," Kathryn said.

"I will never personally or professionally abdicate my devotion to safety," Wyatt said, with sincerity. "I would never certify an airplane that I would not put my family on. I've seen media, it's hard to tell without being privilege to inside information. I will take recommendations of groups and whatever actions need to be taken, I will guarantee I will look into that."

"Oh my God, this is disgusting," Darby said, setting her plate on the coffee table. "He fucking abdicated all his responsibility and passed the buck on everything at Global."

"The Buck stops with you. I want your commitment that you will come back to us with results. And you will work with the committee," Senator Brandt said.

"You have my commitment," Wyatt said.

"His commitment is worth nothing," Darby said. "His words mean nothing." She went to the dining room to refill her glass. As she returned with the bottle, Senator Ted Jones was up.

"The FAA has long been referred to as the gold standard. The 737 MAX has drawn that reputation into serious question. Wallstreet from yesterday share many concerns. The FAA senior management did not monitor the process, and the MAX later crashed. There were process issues… Boeing didn't flag the stall system, that raises a concern… also at issue, whether agency officials performed any assessment. That creates a serious concern for me. Do you agree that these reports suggest a serious breakdown and what is the fix?"

"Hard to tell. If confirmed, I will look into this and group processes. We should not jump to conclusions. Joint authorities technical advisory board, whatever it takes. My highest priority will be safety for traveling public… U.S. or around the world."

"I agree with what you said not jumping to conclusions," Jones said, "but at the same time the easiest thing to do is to do nothing. Bureaucratic inertia is powerful. Natural instincts of the agency are to protect itself, protect status quo and admit no wrongdoing. Asking to be pissed off that 346 people died. Not a small matter. Not just those lives but those who get on planes every day. But also, the confidence of the flying public. I ask not to give into the natural bureaucratic reaction that defends what happened but ask seriously and vigorously what we could do because of agency mistakes."

"Please do not interpret my demeanor as satisfied with this. I will be the captain of the ship, steady hand on the tiller," Wyatt said.

"Will you vigorously figure out what went wrong?" Jones asked.

"I will," Wyatt said strongly.

The 737 MAX issue was not unlike Air France 447 where Global knew that the pitot static system was faulty, because they had 14 similar events, prior to AF447 crash. Under Wyatt's leadership they did nothing about them. Neither did the FAA. They knew the MAX had issues and did nothing until after *two* crashes.

"How the hell can they even contemplate making him the FAA administrator?" Darby said. "This is an embarrassment and conflicts with everything the FAA stands for."

CHAPTER 73

WITH HER HEART registering 120 beats per minute, Darby rode harder than she had in a long time. The more she thought about Wyatt, the angrier she became and the faster she rode. She could not figure out how to stop this FAA train from a catastrophe. Wyatt had lied on his testimony, asserting that he wasn't involved in any lawsuit. She needed to tell someone, but who would listen to the woman they called crazy?

She had argued with the union the day prior to no avail. They knew what he had done, but they would not stand up to him as an organization. Global's master executive council chairman said, *'I agree. He should not be there. But as a group, they're afraid if we go against him, and he gets in anyway, he'll go after us.'* They were National ALPO. *The gutless wimps,* Darby thought and pedaled faster. To look the other way when the union as a group knew of Wyatt's propensity for harm and his continued violations, was wrong on so many levels.

Forty-five minutes into her workout, Shakira blasting in her earbuds, her music stopped as a call rang in. She glanced at her phone. The word BLOCKED filled the screen. This wasn't spam, but whomever was calling didn't want her to have their number. Curiosity won and she slowed to a stop and answered, catching her breath as she climbed off the bike.

"Is this Darby Bradshaw?" the man's voice asked.

"It is," she said, grabbing her towel and her water bottle.

"This is Captain Hanks. Do you have a minute to talk?"

"I do," Darby said, her heartrate increasing again. She headed for an empty yoga room, where the gym's phone police wouldn't find her.

"I heard rumors of what happened at Global Air Lines with you. Is it true…was George Wyatt involved in some action against you?"

"He was," Darby said, and then she gave him the *Reader's Digest* version of what had happened as she paced, trying to cool down.

She explained how Clark told Wyatt what they were doing four months before they created the pretext, then approved of the action, and how he approved federal regulation violations when he was at Global regarding duty time.

"His testimony during the Senate hearing made me sick," Darby said. "Everything he voiced with training and automation, is exactly what Global is *not* doing."

"That's what I was afraid of," Captain Hanks said with a sigh. "I don't think he should be the FAA administrator."

"You and me both," Darby said, now sitting on an exercise ball. She wiped sweat off her neck and took a drink of water as he spoke.

"I want to do something about this. But this will put your name out there and I don't want to cause you any more grief," Captain Hanks said. "So, I'll leave it up to you."

"I have suffered so much grief over this already," Darby said. "I can take a little more. If he's not stopped, aviation safety will decline. If you can do anything to stop him, you have my blessing. I honestly don't care what happens to me."

"Okay then, I'll see what we can do."

They ended their call and Darby could not believe it. She called

Tom, but he didn't answer. Then she texted Kathryn—*Call when you can. I have news.* Darby was just about to call Linda, but the door opened, and a group of overly exuberant bodies walked in for yoga class.

She put the ball on the rack and grabbed a mat. *When in Rome,* she thought. The teacher began class and told the participants to close their eyes for a breathing exercise to clear their minds and relax. Darby breathed deep, but instead of clearing her mind, thoughts of the potential grief Captain Hanks spoke of took control, as she wondered what he meant by that.

CHAPTER 74

DARBY LAID IN bed feeling the warmth of his body against hers. They'd arrived at 0600, took a shower together, and slept the day away. She thought about Hanks taking on Wyatt, and knew if anyone could stop him, he could. Then her thoughts drifted to the man behind her. It had been a long time since she had layover sex.

As if he could hear her thoughts, he lifted her hair and kissed the back of her neck, and she moaned. He slid his hand from her hip and placed it on her left breast and massaged. His arousal made her smile. She turned toward him and said, "Good morning."

"It is somewhere," he said. "But I think it's dinner time."

"I'm hungry too," she said with a slow smile. "Ravenous."

"You're insatiable," he said.

She nodded smiling, and he threw back the covers, raised his body over hers and stared down assessing every inch of her skin that came alive beneath his gaze. This was exactly what she needed. She had forgotten that layovers could be so much fun.

Grabbing his waist, she pulled him toward her. He took it from there and pressed deep inside, and they became one, again. This time moving with the passion of a wildfire. The heat rushing closer, burning, darting, pushing, and finding a life of its own. It was a living growing beast that was completely uncontrollable, until they came and lay spent.

———⊹———

TWO HOURS LATER Darby and Tom were sitting in the Quay Restaurant overlooking the Sydney Harbor Bridge and the Opera House. A bottle of champagne sat to the side in a silver ice bucket. Glasses filled, and an order of raw Abrolhos Island scallops and Maitake mushrooms with Blacklip abalone lay in front of them.

"This is the most beautiful view I've *ever* seen," Darby said. "And this meal is beyond delicious." She dipped a scallop into the sauce then slid it into her mouth and moaned in delight.

"You normally don't dine like this on layovers?" Tom asked in jest.

"Hardly." Darby looked out to harbor as a cruise ship was approaching then turned to him and said, "Thank you."

"For this?" he asked, indicating the spread.

"For everything," Darby said. "What started out as the worst time of my life... wait, I'll change that to the worst time of my career, and receiving that bipolar diagnosis on Christmas, followed by my drunken stupor, turned out to be the luckiest day of my life because I met you."

"It was my luck," he said. "I can't say the best part was holding your hair back while you puked, but it was up there at the top."

Darby had a two-day layover and Tom had bought a ticket to join her on the trip. He didn't bother with pass travel, risking getting bumped or sitting in the main cabin. He must have been born into money, invested well, or was killing his life savings, because Global's first-class round-trip ticket was $23,000. She didn't ask and he didn't offer any explanation.

"You never gave up on me despite the hell I'd gone through with this trial," Darby said. "You were my rock. So, thanks."

"I love you Darby," Tom said. "I would never give up on you no matter what." He stuck his hand into his pocket and placed a box on the table. He then reached for the bottle of champagne and filled each of their glasses, as if he had not just given her hope of a future.

She stared at the box, then looked at Tom. Her heart pounding in her chest. "What's that?"

"What's what?" Tom asked with a wry smile.

Then he pushed back his chair and stood. He reached for the box, then walked around the table and knelt before her. He opened it, displaying the most beautiful ring she'd ever seen. A center diamond with swirls of gold, filled with smaller diamonds.

Tom removed the ring from the box and said, "Darby, will you marry me?"

"Yes. Yes. Yes! I will marry you," Darby said. Tears filled her eyes and she dabbed under them with a napkin. "Sorry, it's my mental health disorder."

He stood, as did Darby, and they kissed with more love than she'd ever felt in her life. For the first time in Darby's life, she knew that everything was going to be okay.

CHAPTER 75

DARBY REARRANGED HER schedule so she would have a full two weeks off to focus only on studying before A350 training began. Months earlier she had written flash cards and had been reading them at the gym. Now she would write a study guide to learn the plane. If she understood the A350 enough to teach it, she would be in her comfort zone. Despite Global providing pilots with the answers to the tests, Darby knew that the lack of understanding caused accidents.

While she was busy copying and pasting a hydraulic system photo into the document she was working on, her phone rang. She looked at the name and smiled. Appreciating the break, she said, "Hey Jackie."

"I still can't believe Tom proposed to you in Sydney," Jackie said without even saying hello. "He's so romantic."

"He said it gave him flexibility for remembering the date. If he forgets, he can claim it was due to being a date off."

"But isn't Sydney a day ahead of us?" Jackie said.

"It is," Darby said, with a laugh. "We were jetlagged, and he was confused on the dateline thing. It would only dig him a bigger hole."

They chatted about the trip, and Jackie told her she was thinking about going back to work as soon as JJ started school. She had decided to find a different career, instead of being a flight attendant. She told Darby she wasn't sure if she'd would ever set foot on a plane again. Her eldest son, however, still wanted to become a pilot, so Linda was going to help her work on that fear.

"I filed both my fraud lawsuits," Darby said. "I had to kill a couple trees because the court wanted seven copies of everything. The complaint and all exhibits for each case had to be in colored notebooks and snail mailed."

"I'm so proud of you fighting these guys," Jackie said, as a call beeped in.

"Jackie, Robert's calling. Can I call you back?"

"Of course. We can talk tomorrow."

Darby ended the call and clicked over to Robert.

"Turn on CNN," Robert said, "then call me back."

Darby ran to the living room and turned on the television and changed channels.

A photo of George Wyatt filled the screen as the commentator said, "*As Global's then-head of flight operations, Wyatt approved sending the pilot, Darby Bradshaw, to a psychiatrist weeks after she gave him and another flight operations manager a report that listed what she described as FAA violations by Global, according to documents.*"

Darby's photo in the flight deck then replaced Wyatt's picture as the commentator spoke. "*The psychiatrist diagnosed Bradshaw with bipolar disorder and the company grounded her for more than a year. Two subsequent examinations found that she does not have that disorder, and she is currently flying for Global. Bradshaw is suing Global in a Department of Labor administrative case that remains pending.*

Darby stared at her photo realizing that people worldwide were seeing this. With her face plastered on national television, she wondered how she felt about the reporter telling the world she had been diagnosed as bipolar. But there wasn't a damn thing she could do about it anyway. The commentator continued.

"In a deposition, Wyatt said he had ultimate responsibility over the decision to refer Bradshaw for a mental evaluation and called it a 'sound course of action.' Wyatt retired from Global last year. CNN made repeated attempts to contact Wyatt but could not reach him for comment. The White House has not responded to request for comments.

"On his Senate questionnaire Wyatt stated, 'During my Global employment, from time to time and in the ordinary course of business, Global was involved in various judicial, administrative or regulatory proceedings relating to its business, although I was not a named party in any such actions.' On another section that asked for 'additional information, favorable or unfavorable, which you feel should be disclosed in connection with your nomination,' Wyatt responded: 'None.'

"Global denies that the company retaliated against Bradshaw by referring her to a medical examination after she raised concerns. Wyatt, who is poised to lead the FAA in the midst of controversy surrounding the agency's prior certification of the Boeing 737 MAX, has decades of aviation experience as a former Air Force and Global pilot who became a senior Global manager responsible for flight safety and pilot training until his retirement last year.

"Bradshaw's ordeal began more than three years ago when she compiled a list of concerns about Global. She had witnessed a variety of events and practices involving Global employees, training, and scheduling practices that she believed violated FAA standards. She compiled her concerns into a report that described 'numerous areas where safety culture and ... compliance conflict with the FAA's (2013) outlined requirements and the airline's core values,' which

she presented to Wyatt and Global's then-vice president of flying operations, Rich Clark, in January 2016.

"A senior White House adviser tells CNN that Wyatt has been cooperating with the committee. 'President Kohler chose George Wyatt to head the FAA because of his almost three decades of experience at Global where he oversaw global flight operations,' a White House spokesman said in a statement. 'The White House has complete confidence in his nomination and expects him to be confirmed.'"

"Thank you, Captain Hanks," Darby said as she pressed off on her remote.

A false attack on a pilot and airline's lack of concern for mental health was of no interest to the public, as many have silently occurred over the years. Her story only became newsworthy because of George Wyatt's nomination as the next FAA administrator. The public now knew he violated the very rules he would be required to honor in that position, and he lied about it. The question was, would that knowledge deny him this position? Perhaps if the public had a vote it would.

CHAPTER 76

THE LADIES CONGREGATED in Darby's living room to watch what they called "the show." Chinese food cartons filled the coffee table. Red wine, the beverage of choice, filled their glasses. This was Darby's last day home before she headed to Oklahoma City for the better part of a month for A350 training. She was glad to spend it with her friends. Tom was off to detective training.

"Are you ready?" Kathryn asked.

"As ready as I'll ever be," Darby said. "We study and prepare, and there is always doubt if we missed something. But the truth is that the instructor can fail a pilot for anything."

"Nance, Steve, Joe, all said that too," Linda said. "But you'll do great."

"I'll be fine if they don't screw with me," Darby said reaching for the remote.

"I'm looking forward to the Senate committee chastising Wyatt," Jackie said.

"If we don't turn it on," Kathryn said to Darby, with a glance at the remote, "we'll miss the fun. Unless you want to record it."

"No way in hell," Darby said.

This time it would be live. As live as a delayed broadcast could be that is. Darby pressed the remote and Washington's Senator Maria Albright opened.

"Madam President, I rise today to speak in opposition to the nomination of George Wyatt to be the next administrator of the FAA. I have said that it is very important that, in this day and age, when it comes to aviation, safety must always be our top priority. We've considered Mr. Wyatt's nomination, his record, an ongoing case of whistleblower retaliation, and given all of that, it is clear to me he is not the right person for the safety culture that we need at the FAA.

"It is distressing to me that Mr. Wyatt advanced out of committee on just a party line vote. We've never had a partisan vote on an FAA nominee in the past, and I believe that we should have found consensus on a nominee for the FAA, given all of the concerns the public has about flying safety."

"Woo Hoo!" Darby said. "You go girl!"

Albright continued speaking but shifted to discussing Darby.

"She observed that there were issues she thought were putting both her and passengers at risk. So, what did she do? She did what all employees—we hope—would do. She informed her superiors and suggested possible solutions. She was persistent and wanted to make sure that these recommendations were met with by the leadership of the organization, Mr. Wyatt, and his second in command Rick Clark.

"And some of the concerns she raised about inadequate pilot training and not enough pilot rest were things that you thought would have maybe gotten her recognized for the great contribution to a safety culture that is so necessary today in an age of more and more automation. Whether you're talking about an automobile or an airplane, it's essential that automation and training go hand in hand.

"But, instead of Officer Bradshaw getting the attention she deserved, instead the company sent her for a mandatory psychiatric evaluation.

Can you imagine, as a whistleblower, bringing up concerns, and as a pilot flying for many years, and instead of being paid attention to, be sent for a psychiatric evaluation?"

They continued to listen to Senator Albright as she finished her testimony, their mouths agape at the strength of what the Washington Senator said about how proud she was of Darby. Darby never needed or wanted recognition, she just wanted to improve the safety culture.

"It's very clear that Mr. Wyatt did know, was involved with this pilot, did know what was happening and failed to disclose it to this committee," Albright said. *"We certainly can't have organizations threaten pilots with this kind of retaliation."*

Chairman Wenstrom followed Albright and said, *"The committee conducted an extensive review after we learned of the whistleblower case and found that Wyatt wasn't named in any lawsuits or administrative proceedings and was not accused of retaliating against employees who raised safety concerns. The committee studied hundreds of pages of legal documents.*

"That's bullshit," Darby said. "The AIR21 law doesn't allow for naming individuals."

"I believe Mr. Wyatt is an excellent nominee for this position," Wenstrom said. *"I think he will bring commitment, experience and expertise necessary to lead the FAA and fulfill its mission."*

The only other senator who spoke was the Connecticut Democrat Richard Brandt. He said, *"Wyatt is simply the wrong person to head the FAA. As far as I'm concerned, Wyatt's long tenure at Global makes it impossible for him to be independent of the airline industry."*

"The fact that Tommy lobbied against Wyatt's nomination, is the only reason they are here today," Darby said. "He has more courage than anyone I know."

"Who is Tommy?" Linda asked.

"Captain Hanks. He landed the plane without engines on the Hudson River in 2009," Darby said, and Linda nodded in recognition.

"He's been very vocal that the FAA needs an administrator who will act with integrity and independence to protect everyone who flies," Kathryn said. "*He* should be the administrator."

"But you work for the FAA," Jackie said to Kathryn. "Why can't you do something?"

"I wish I could," Kathryn said, "but not my department."

The hearing ended and Darby said. "Well ladies, I suppose, once again, we have to leave aviation safety in the hands of God and pray that Wyatt doesn't get this nomination."

CHAPTER 77

STEPPING OFF THE crew bus, Darby scanned the parking lot looking for her car. Then she opened her phone and located the photo she had taken a month earlier. She looked up and scanned the area, saw what looked like the location and headed that way. She found it hidden behind a suburban. The question of whether it would start was another story. Neither she, nor her car moved well after four weeks of inattention.

She slid into the driver's seat and turned the ignition, and it started up on the first try. "Good girl," Darby said and smiled. She backed out of the parking spot, then headed for the exit. Her destination was home for four days. Then back to Oklahoma City for her check ride.

The only dicking-around Global did to her was with her schedule. They scheduled her to train the late session on the night before her two-day break and the first session upon her return from that break. Meaning, she could not get home for even a day during her entire program. Then they gave her four days off to break the continuity and momentum before her check ride. None of this was good, but none of it broke her either.

She did not have a captain to train with, therefore she had seat support for all events. The instructors she worked with were great. Her seat support pilots were all retired captains or instructors who taught her some tricks. She only flew two hours each session instead of the four noted on the syllabus. But what the hell, this was train-to-proficiency, and she felt comfortable.

Darby sat at the longest light ever, drumming her fingers on the steering wheel. Traffic testing her patience. She glanced at her ring and smiled again. Tom had been in D.C. for a couple weeks of training himself, and therefore he only made it down to see her twice during the month. The next four days, however, would be getting to know each other and clearing her brain before the check ride. When the light finally turned green, she turned right instead of heading home.

Darby made a quick stop to pick up her mail that she had placed on hold at the post office, which turned into a longer ordeal than she had thought. But there was no way she would be going out of her house before she flew back to Oklahoma City. She climbed back into her car, tossed her mail on the passenger seat, and headed toward home.

She needed this break more than she could possibly describe. Living in a hotel room for a month reminded her how much she loved her home. Her plan was to review her notes on the flight back to Oklahoma City. She wasn't worried about the check ride. The Airbus A350 was the coolest plane she'd ever flown, and they soon became fast friends. On top of that, the instructors expressed pride and admiration for her taking on Global. Many had told her they wished they would have done something, too. But they feared losing their instructor positions, so they didn't. The consensus was that they supported her, and all hoped she'd win the case.

They also shared many stories of George Wyatt's evil ways and thanked her for putting her neck on the line to ensure he would not become the administrator. Darby explained they should congratulate

Captain Hanks for having the courage to stand up to him, regardless of the outcome. Something that ALPO refused to do. Nobody could believe that Wyatt would get the position now, and one of the guys even offered a case of beer if she got rid of Clark, too.

Darby pulled into her driveway and pressed the garage door opener, but the door didn't move. "Shit," she said under her breath, pushing it a couple more times. Sighing, she stuffed the mail into her computer bag, climbed out of her car, and removed her purse and suitcase. She dropped the suitcase at the front door and located the key on her ring.

She unlocked the door and moved all her bags inside the entry, and turned to deactivate the alarm system, but it was off. She turned and said, "Tom." But there was no answer.

Darby headed through the house and straight for the garage. She opened the door to see if there was power to the wall control and her eyes narrowed. The wall mount was black. And then she startled. There was a non-descript blue Ford parked inside. *Who the hell's car is that?* Darby wondered. Nothing registering as it should.

She closed the door and turned toward the kitchen and froze. Her heart slammed inside of her ribcage. Her mind ran through exit strategies, but there were none. He sat in the chair closest to the door she'd just walked in, and she could not exit through the garage. She was trapped.

"Hello, Darby. It's been a long time," Bill Jacobs said.

CHAPTER 78

DARBY DIDN'T MOVE. She just stared at Bill, wondering if she ran past him, how quick he would be. But she knew that answer. Having been lucky once, her luck appeared to be running out. Instead, she said, "I have a restraining order against you."

"You know those things never work." He turned the page in her trial notebook and smiled. That grin that had once endeared him to her ran chills through her body. Then he closed it and said, "I like this. Had I known, we could have done wonderful things together."

Darby glanced at the notebook and then said, "You're going back to jail."

"That is *never* going to happen," Bill said. "Sit down. Can I get you a beer?" He stood and opened her fridge and took one for himself and looked at Darby. She shook her head no and glanced toward the door instead of sitting. "I wouldn't," he said.

Darby waited until Bill returned to his seat, then she sat across from him. Keeping the table as a zone of protection. Wondering where Tom was.

"What are you doing here?" Darby asked, trying to keep her voice from shaking.

"I'm not exactly sure," Bill said and took a drink of his beer, his eyes boring into hers. "I have a directive to give you some information, but before I do that, we need to have a little talk."

"I'm listening," Darby said, trying to remember if Tom was waiting for her to call.

"Drake Industries was behind the MAX crashes. Drake has the technology to remove pilots altogether," Bill said, about to say something else, but he stopped.

"So does Airbus," Darby said to fill the space of silence. "But why crash the MAX?"

"To discredit pilots," Bill said. "Create a platform of fear so people will believe that automation is safer."

"But nobody in the U.S. crashed," Darby said.

"He tried," Bill said and sipped his beer, then continued. "Global has shitty training for one reason only, to increase pilot error to prove that machines are better than pilots. Walter Croft is working with Drake to ensure automation becomes a reality. Well, he was but—"

"That's exactly what I thought," Darby said, half under her breath.

Bill ignored her and said, "Global was to take one of their birds into the ground. Then Wyatt could sign off on autonomous planes once in office. It's kind of a brilliant idea. But Croft is backpedaling on the timing. But there will be a crash."

"A crash at Global?" Darby said. "They're going to force a crash?"

"Crashing planes creates change," Bill said, having enacted the same tactic years earlier.

"What happens if Wyatt doesn't get into office?" Darby said.

"He will. But it won't matter either way," Bill said, twisting the bottle in his hand.

"I think I'll have that beer now," Darby said, and pushed back her chair. She went to the fridge, grabbed a beer, and opened the bottle, then took a long drink. This all made sense now. This was the proof she needed.

The airlines and FAA were allowing for substandard training to prove pilots were inadequate. But a crash as the result of pilot error would solidify automation.

Leaning against the counter, Darby said, "Why the mental health accusation against me? I get why Clark's pissed, but why the trial? They know they can't possibly win."

"Control. Fear. This is all about keeping the pilots quiet as to airline's safety lapses. You were the only pilot who had the balls to say anything. They had to do something to set an example for the others. To ensure everyone remained quiet. To make you shut the fuck up."

"Global owns the union," Darby said, "and the reason they didn't help."

"That fucking ALPO," Bill spat. "It's not like when I was running the union and we supported pilot jobs. These guys are nothing but purchased extensions of the company."

"Why are you telling me all this?" Darby said. "Will you come forward?"

Bill sipped his beer and stared at her for a moment. Then he set his bottle on the table and walked into the laundry room, opened the electrical panel and clicked a circuit breaker into place. Darby watched him from her spot at the counter. He closed the panel and returned to the kitchen table and sat.

"Please, join me," Bill said extending a hand to the chair she had been sitting in.

Darby hesitated, then moved to the table. She could see he was torn about something. One thing Darby knew, Bill loved the industry more than anything, so much so that he was willing to kill for it. He was a whack job because his father had killed himself and Bill had blamed the industry, but he had the passion to keep the piloting job alive.

"My boss is a powerful man. He enlisted my support to remove pilots. Personally, I'd rather see you win. Those fuckers at Global are assholes, and if given the chance I would take each of them out. I also don't want the pilot job to disappear. I'm in unfamiliar territory."

He lifted the bottle to his lips, and then pulled a long slow drink, emptying it. Darby had seen this behavior before, and she knew Bill was calming himself. Bill Jacobs prided himself on being in control. He would show no weakness, but his weakness appeared to be Global.

"If you tell *anyone* about our conversation, I *will* kill the girls," Bill said.

The cold psychopathic eyes returned, and they bore into Darby's eyes and her soul.

"You just verified what I already suspected," Darby said. "So, what am I supposed to do with this? Not tell people what I already know to be true?"

"I doubt you knew they were planning to take down a plane," Bill said.

"True," Darby said, her blood running cold. "But how? Are they going to force it down or just keep cutting training until it happens?"

"You'll figure it out," Bill said. "But I want you to stop the bastards."

If only she could. "Was this the information you were directed to give me?" Darby asked.

"Hell no," Bill said. "I was directed to tell you your boyfriend works for Drake."

Her eyes narrowed as her brain tried to make sense of what he said. He could not possibly have worked for Drake. That was bullshit. "You're lying," she finally said.

"Ask him yourself," Bill said, looking past her with a nod.

Darby turned and Tom was standing in the doorway.

CHAPTER 79

DARBY TURNED FROM Tom then back to Bill. *What the hell?* Tom did not work for Drake. There was no way in hell that was possible.

"What the hell's going on?" Tom asked.

Bill stood and walked toward the garage. He opened the door and pressed the button on the wall, and the garage door came to life. He ignored Tom and turned to Darby. "Nobody, or I will keep my promise." He stepped out and closed the door.

"Nobody what?" Tom said. "What promise?"

"What the hell is going on?" Darby said standing. "What the fuck. You work for Drake?"

"No," Tom said. "I *worked* for him in the past. I was the head of security in the—"

"You didn't think it was important to tell me?" Darby said, tears filling her eyes.

"Darby," Tom said reaching for her, but she pulled back.

"Don't touch me. You knew what he was developing, you knew what he was doing."

"I signed a non-disclosure," Tom said. "I couldn't—"

"Bullshit," Darby spat. "Were you working for him when we met? Were you part of the legal attack on me?"

"No. I was hired to watch. To protect you. I quit Drake's company to take that job."

"Our love story was a fucking job?" Darby said, openly sobbing now. She stepped away from him and placed a hand on her forehead, while the other supported her back. How the hell could this be happening? How could Tom have lied to her? She had been such a fool.

"Sweetie," Tom said, placing a hand on her back, and she recoiled.

"Don't fucking touch me." She pulled the ring from her finger and slammed it on the kitchen table. "I'm leaving and I want you, and all your stuff *and* your bullshit lies out of my house and my life when I return. I never want to see you again."

"Darby, please," Tom pleaded.

She ignored him and grabbed her purse, wiping tears from her eyes, she rushed out the front door slamming it as she went. Tom was on the porch now, calling to her. She couldn't hear what he was saying and didn't care. One last look, over her shoulder, and he was on his phone.

KATHRYN ENDED TOM's call and tears filled her eyes. Bill's presence was the least of her concerns. *Darby must feel so betrayed*, she thought. She paced her kitchen and lifted the curtains to watch for her. In no time Darby pulled into her driveway. *Thank God*, Kathryn thought as she ran to the front door.

Before Darby could knock, Kathryn opened it and Darby fell into her arms and cried. Kathryn just held her and said, "It's going to be okay."

Darby pulled back and wiped her nose on her sleeve, and said, "It's not going to be okay. How would you know? How do you know what it is?"

"Tom called," Kathryn said. "He was worried about you."

"Worried about me?" Darby said. "He should have thought about that when he lied to me." Darby then narrowed her eyes and said, "Did you know?"

Kathryn opened her mouth trying to figure out what to say. "I learned later, but—"

"But?" Darby said. "Are you fucking kidding me? Did John know?"

Kathryn nodded and said, "Yes, but he, too—"

"So, all of you knew that my fucking relationship was a hoax, that I was just an assignment?" Darby said. "I am such fucking fool!"

"It's not like that," Kathryn said.

"No? Then what's it like?" Darby demanded. "Don't answer that. I don't want to know. But did Linda and Jackie know too?"

"No," Kathryn said. "Can we just sit and talk about this?"

"No," Darby said, now calm. "I don't think that I ever want to talk to you again."

"Please don't say that" Kathryn said.

Darby looked at her in disgust and then walked out the front door, not even bothering to close it. She stood at her car with her face to the sky for a moment, then wiped the tears from her cheeks with both hands and climbed into her car. Her movements were eerily slow.

Kathryn watched Darby drive out of her driveway and perhaps out of her life. She went inside and called Linda to ask for help.

CHAPTER 80

JULY 20, 2019

DARBY AWOKE TO pounding in her head and on her front door. She climbed out of bed and peered out the curtains and said, "Oh shit."

After pulling her robe on, she ran downstairs and tried to deactivate her alarm, but it wouldn't turn green. *Double shit,* she thought. She had changed the code last night. *What was the number?* She finally remembered, cleared the alarm, and opened the door.

The door-lock guy glanced at her attire then her hair, and said, "Did we have an appointment today?"

"We did," Darby said, "I'm sorry, I overslept."

"Would you like to reschedule?"

"No," Darby said. "You can start here, and I'll be back to show you the other doors. We'll key them all the same."

Darby ran upstairs to change. She assessed her blood shot eyes in the mirror and pulled a brush through her hair. After she had left Kathryn's house, she had driven down the street and pulled off to the side of the road and cried. That's when she blocked Kathryn, Tom, Linda and Jackie's phones from being able to track her. She drove around for a bit to ensure Tom was gone.

When she returned home, her engagement ring was still on the table. That's when her tears flowed even harder. Then she contacted a lock company and changed the security code on her alarm system. She had started her wash but didn't remember putting it into the dryer.

She did remember climbing into the tub with a bottle of Basil Hayden. She glanced at the empty bottle now and remembered killing it. During that time, she had listened to Kathryn, Linda, and Jackie's voicemail messages. Kathryn said she was sorry and explained what happened. She exceeded the limit, so she called back. Linda had asked her to call and told her that she loved her and said this was not the end of the world. Jackie called crying and told her how sorry she was that Tom was a lying sack of shit.

Darby now sighed. She had been here before, so why would she expect anything else? One thing she knew, you did not begin a life with someone that was based upon lies. You couldn't. She felt like a total fool that nothing Tom said, had been the truth. Did he even love her? Was he still on assignment? She wasn't sure of anything.

She dressed quickly and returned downstairs just as the guy finished the front door. While he was working on the other doors she put the ring into an ice cube tray, filled all the squares with water and stuck it into the freezer. She then put her laundry into the dryer. In no time, he had completed all, and Darby was alone again.

Plan B was to head back to training, focus on her check ride and earn an A350 type-rating. From there she would go directly to Los Angeles and fly her operating experience. She would push Tom's, Kathryn's, and John's deception out of her mind, and go into hiding for a month, and focus on herself. The only thing she had control over was her actions.

She packed her bag and despite trying to forget him, she found herself wondering who the hell had directed Bill to tell her about Tom and why. Why had Bill told her as much as he did? Bill working for

Drake was something that she and Kathryn already suspected when they transferred him to San Quentin, but they never suspected that Bill opposed Global and would be on Darby's side.

Drake was moving toward pilotless aircraft, also nothing that Darby had not suspected herself. She also suspected Drake and Bill were behind the MAX crashes. But she never expected, however, that Global wanted a crash. They were screwing with pilots to promote automation. Now with Airbus ahead of schedule and the uninterruptible autopilot, it was all beginning to make sense. The time for a crash was now, and she had to prevent it.

She zipped up her suitcase and thought about Tom again. If he worked at Drake Industries and left to protect her, who the hell would pay him for that? Tom was spying on her, but did he know why? Now she understood why he was not hurting for money. If her damn emotions hadn't got the better of her, she could have asked him. They had a lot to talk about, relationship or not. She sucked a deep breath and dialed his number, wondering if now was too soon.

CHAPTER 81

THE ONLY THING certain about plans is that they change. Darby did not study on the flight back to Oklahoma City. Instead, she watched a movie, drank bourbon, and ate dinner. Her extended hotel stay at the Hampton Inn would give her ample time to review.

Her forehead pressed against the window as the van pulled up to the front of the hotel. She found her way through the lobby and to the elevator, then pushed number 3. The elevator took her to her floor. *Home away from home,* she thought, sticking the key card into the slot. She opened the door and drug her bags inside.

The panel pictures of the A350 flight deck were still on the wall and provided a sense of comfort. Her only real relationship would ever be with a plane. Her exercise ball was lying in front of the wall, and she sat on it and dialed Linda's number.

"Hey Linda, sorry I missed your calls. All thirty-two of them."

"Ha. Ha," Linda said. "I'm sure it wasn't over thirty-one."

"I'm going to be okay. Remember… my life is not over; it's just going to be different," Darby said, trying to assure her she was fine. But doubting she'd ever be fine again.

"It doesn't have to be different," Linda said. "But now is not the time to discuss that. You've got to pass this training. I just wanted to tell you to not let this derail your check."

"I don't plan on it," Darby said.

"Have you talked to Tom?" Linda asked. "I know he loves you."

She knew that too, but love cut the hurt deeper. "I talked to him before I left. He refuses to tell me who he's working for. He says he doesn't know."

"Maybe he doesn't," Linda said.

"How's that even possible?" Darby asked.

"I don't know. I don't even know how any of what's been ongoing is possible. How is it possible that Bill could have convinced my husband to crash his plane and kill hundreds of people?" Linda said.

"Yeah," Darby said, knowing that nothing made sense in the world anymore.

"What about Kathryn?" Linda said.

"I told her I never wanted to see her again," Darby said closing her eyes for a moment. Not her proudest moment.

"I know," Linda said. "Kat fell into the middle of this without any choice. I'm not sure I would have done anything different myself."

"I don't think I would have either," Darby said.

The truth was, there had been a time when Darby had kept a secret from Kathryn regarding Bill, and Kat had forgiven her. They became closer than ever. It wasn't fair for her to have different standards.

"When will you be home?" Linda asked.

"Maybe a month."

"A month?" Linda said. "I thought your check was in a few days."

"Then I have to do OE, operating experience," Darby said getting off the ball, and wiping a finger under her eye. "I'll be home when I'm done, and we can regroup. Rewind. Make plans."

"I think that would be good for all of us," Linda said.

They said their goodbyes and Darby walked to the window and opened the curtain. As a Global 767 departed, she thought about what Bill had said and Drake's need for a crash. Could they possibly convince a pilot to crash his own plane? Bill was against a crash this time, and he wanted her to stop it. But how? Why didn't he do something? Darby rubbed her finger where her ring had been, wondering what Tom's involvement was, intentional or not.

CHAPTER 82

SMILING AND FLYING went together, despite the problems in life. Every time she climbed into a plane or simulator, she smiled. Darby and her captain had just departed Portland headed to Seattle. They were 32,000 feet over the Cascades. In another 30 minutes, she would have an A350 type rating, even though she was flying the check in the right seat, in a simulator.

Check rides in the AQP world were far easier than the actual training, and nothing compared to an old Appendix F check when the pilot was in the left seat, as the captain, and had to demonstrate their ability to fly. This was a choreographed play with automation engaged, that they had done many times before and knew exactly what to expect, in a controlled environment. However, if management directed an instructor to down the pilot, they could slip in a nuance or two, unnaturally overload the pilot, and make a speculative judgement to fail him, or her as the case may be.

Darby often wondered what would happen if there was a surprise for a new captain in real life who did not know how to think outside the training box. Those days would come, sooner than anyone would believe. Perhaps that's what they were planning.

Today she had three instructors instead of one. One was sitting in the left seat, playing captain, but he was a first officer instructor. The second was an FAA designee and the head of the A350 training program. He was a Global captain, certified to act on behalf of the FAA. Today he was giving the third guy his FAA designee checkout, while giving Darby her check.

Darby had worked with both instructors and had done well in their sessions. So much so, that this was the reason they had chosen her check ride to give the instructor his FAA designee checkout. It would be easier without a problem in the front seat.

"Global 350, we need you to reduce your speed to 210 knots. Cleared to descend 15,000 feet," the instructor said, playing air traffic control. He then transferred them to Seattle approach.

The speed they requested was below their flaps up speed, so Darby dialed the knob and waited for the plane to slow below the max flaps speed by a few knots, then called flaps one. She kept her hand on the speed knob until she verified the flaps were in position. But they didn't move. She increased her speed to ensure they would not stall.

"Captain, our flaps have failed," Darby said feigning surprise.

"Okay, you have the aircraft and the radios. Declare an emergency."

The first officer at Global flew and talked on the radio while the captain ran the checklists, figured out their landing distance and the brake setting, programed the computer for landing, then talked to the flight attendants, and contacted dispatch. Not necessarily in that order. But there was a lot he had to accomplish in the next twenty minutes.

All Darby did was fly and talk to ATC. Flying was easy, especially when they were on the autopilot. Talking had never been an issue for her, either. This process of the captain doing everything worked if they had time. But, this close to landing, if she were the captain she would exercise her captain authority and delegate the computer stuff to the other pilot and manage the operation, despite Global's training.

Darby contacted ATC and said, "Seattle approach, Global 350 is with you descending to 15,000. Declaring an emergency. Failed flaps. We'd like a long downwind."

"No," the captain said, "ask for a hold."

Over the mountains on an arrival? Darby thought. She glanced at the instructor and shrugged, then said, "Control, Global 350 would like to hold."

"Denied," ATC said. "Fly heading 360, we'll give you extended vectors."

Darby responded and dialed their new heading. They would be landing south and told them they would be using the center runway.

Darby said, "ECAM actions."

The captain began running the checklist, as Darby watched. He called *'status'* because he had arrived at the status page in the computer. Per Global's requirement Darby responded *'Stop ECAM,'* followed by saying *'After takeoff complete? Can we consider a reset? Should we consider a relight? Not? Okay. Continue ECAM.'*

Clearly, they did not have an engine failure and a relight was a silly thing to consider with a flap issue, 20 minutes out, screaming through the sky cutting into valuable time, but this is what Global required to pass a check. No thinking. Memorization. Granted, there could be an engine failure and the pilots might not think to restart it.

The captain reviewed the considerations displayed on the ECAM. When he was complete, he said, "Remove status?"

"Remove status," Darby said.

"ECAM actions complete," he replied.

His head was then back into the computer, while she had time to think.

"Approach," Darby said, "we're going to need the longest runway today."

"No, we don't," the captain said. "Look, I'll show you."

He pulled up the landing page on the computer and began typing data for the center runway and eventually said, "See, we're legal to land on the center runway."

Darby waited patiently for him to finish and then said, "We may be *legal*, but I am a new-to-the-aircraft pilot, and we declared an emergency. The left runway is 2,500 feet longer. We're going to be fast. Why would we want to leave pavement behind? I'm going to ask you if we could please land on the longer runway, even if we're legal for the other."

"Yeah, okay, but I wanted to show you that we could use it," he said, as they had just killed more valuable time in that discussion.

"Global A350, expect runway 16 Left," ATC said.

They finally accomplished the descent, approach, and landing checklists on final.

Then Darby said, "Did you talk to flight attendants?"

"Oh shit," the captain said. He then got on the radio to talk to them at about 900 feet.

Darby had not expected him to react to the flight attendants at that altitude. She thought he would speak to them once they were safely on the runway. He even forgot to call dispatch. At this point she said nothing about that because they needed to land.

Darby made a smooth landing because it was much easier to grease it on with a flatter angle without flaps. They taxied clear of the runway and taxied into the gate. After completing the shutdown procedures, Darby sighed and turned in the instructor's direction.

"Darby, excellent job!" The FAA designee said. "I watched how you held the stick with minimal pressure. Your decision making was excellent. No rushing. I cannot say enough about how impressed I am." He turned to the other instructor who was giving her the check, and said, "You two get out of here. Go debrief." To the first officer, playing captain, he said, "I want you to stay, we need to talk."

Darby climbed out of her seat and the FAA designee shook her hand. Then she and the other instructor walked out of the simulator. She had passed. They headed down the hall to the briefing room and she looked at her phone.

"Oh shit," she said and stopped.

"What? Is everything okay?"

Darby shook her head no, staring at her phone, and looked up. "I don't know if anything will ever be okay again," she said.

The U.S. Senate just voted along party lines 52 to 40 in favor of George Wyatt as the FAA Administrator.

CHAPTER 83

CHARLES SHULTZ HAD said to only dread one day at a time. If only she could adopt that philosophy. Training had cancelled her operating experience and rescheduled it for three weeks out. The time off would be great, but consistency from simulator to the plane would be an issue. She also had nowhere to go but home, so she did.

It was time to make amends. Her doorbell rang and when she opened it, the pizza delivery guy stood holding two large boxes. She paid him and brought the pies into the kitchen. Just as she set them on the counter there was a pounding on her door.

Sucking a deep breath, she headed that way again and opened the door. Kathryn was standing on her porch. Darby took one look at her friend and tears filled her eyes, then she spread her arms wide and wrapped them around Kathryn. "I'm sorry. I didn't mean anything I said."

Kathryn held on tight and said, "I know. I'm sorry, too."

"Get a room, you two," Jackie said as she walked up the path with Linda in tow. Then she hugged Darby and said, "Congratulations on the checkout."

"I knew you would do it," Linda said as she approached.

"I hope pizza is okay," Darby said, as she wiped a finger under her eye.

They went into the kitchen and sat around the table. With pizza boxes open, everyone filled their plates. Darby served Coors Light to help offset the calories. She then told them about her check ride, and the delay in the next stage of training.

"Do you think that guy playing captain was trying to screw up your ride?" Jackie asked.

"No. He was nervous and trying to show the bosses how much he knew," Darby said.

"That didn't appear to be much," Kathryn said with a chuckle.

"He's a product of the memorize to graduate program," Darby said. "Our next generation pilots who don't have the big picture."

"And he's an instructor," Linda said in dismay.

"I want to know how the hell Wyatt got the FAA position," Jackie finally said.

"They say it was political," Darby said. "Which may be true, but Global owns the FAA so I think it was more than that."

The women discussed the future of the aviation industry with Wyatt as the administrator and when he would put the MAX back into service. Darby doubted it would be anytime soon, because grounded it made Global extremely profitable. Then her thoughts drifted to Bill.

"Darby, are you okay?" Kathryn asked.

"Huh? Oh…I'm fine," she said, thinking about a pending crash.

"Time to raise our beers to Darby's success," Linda said.

They toasted and then Jackie said, "So what are you going to do about Tom?"

"Nothing," Darby said. "I think it's about time that I realize that love and commitment might not be in this life for me after all."

"Rethink that one," Kathryn said, and Darby shrugged.

"Okay, I rethought it," Darby said and tipped back her beer emptying the bottle. Then reached for another. She knew exactly what she planned to do, to get Tom out of her mind.

"That was fast," Linda said with a laugh.

"Brilliance can come before your third beer," Darby said opening it. She took a long drink then set the bottle down and paused, adding a little drama. She looked at her friends with a grin and said, "I'm going to screw the first good looking guy I find on my next flight."

Jackie started laughing. "Let me know how *that* goes."

"I will," Darby said. "But he's not going to be a pilot. He's going to be a total stranger."

"I know you're kidding," Linda said. "At least I hope so. But you need to be safe. The world is a scary place."

Darby stared for a moment and then started laughing, fearing that she would pee her pants. They had just made Wyatt the FAA administrator despite his violating Federal Law. Global was trying to induce a crash. Pilots were flying fatigued and lacked the training necessary for safe operations. They pardoned Bill Jacobs and President Drake and were trying to remove pilots altogether. And Linda just realized that the world is scary.

"Sorry. You're right, the world is a scary place," Darby said. "Speaking of which, I got you all a gift." She stood and went to the kitchen counter and opened a drawer and removed three small boxes and passed them to her friends.

They opened their gifts and Jackie said, "A key?"

"I changed the locks."

CHAPTER 84

THE FIRST DAY to fly the A350 finally arrived, but Scheduling changed the first leg to a deadhead, with a three-day layover in Paris. Unfortunately, Darby had packed for one day only, and she had commuted to Los Angeles for the flight. Regardless, it had been so long since she'd flown, it didn't matter if it was today or in three days, and she loved Paris in summer. She also loved first class international commutes.

If Global hadn't screwed with her, she could have commuted in her play clothes non-stop from Seattle and packed appropriately. However, she could not allow petty scheduling issues to get her, or she'd have to give up her career. *Don't get angry, get even*, she thought.

As she set her ID and passport on that counter, a man's voice from behind said, "Are you flying us to Paris?"

"No. I'm deadheading, so I guess I'll be sleeping with you to Paris," she said. Then she turned his way, with her mouth agape, and a slight flush. "That didn't come out right. I'm sorry."

"I thought it sounded fine," he said with a broad smile. "You're taking the suck up to the first-class passengers rather serious."

"You know about that program?" Darby said with a grin.

"We all do," he said with a nod.

God he was good looking. He was also on her flight. Then she flushed. If only in another fantasy world where she could be like a man who could hit on woman, romanticize her through the city of love and escort her to his room. Whomever said the sexes were equal was full of shit on that score. Then she thought of Linda's words of warning.

"I hope you have a great flight," Darby said with a wink and shifted her attention to the gate agent. Once he assigned her a seat, she went to the bathroom and changed out of her uniform and into commuting clothes. This was supposed to be her layover outfit, which would now need to last four days instead of one. *Ah, what the hell,* Darby thought. Trial was over, she would go shopping in Paris with the flight attendants.

When she returned to the boarding area, the gate agent waved her over.

"Remember that guy you were chatting with?" he said. "He change his seat to sit by you."

"Maybe he thought I was serious about sleeping with him," Darby said with a grin.

He laughed and said, "He's got good taste, but be careful."

Darby thanked him and boarded the plane. She was about to lift her suitcase into the overhead when the good-looking guy from the counter said, "May I help you with that?"

"Thank you," Darby said and allowed him to take it. She may fly planes, but she never discouraged the courtesies of a man wanting to open a door or help her with a bag. She stepped aside and he lifted it into the overhead.

"Nicholas Valencia," he said, extending his hand and she shook it. Then he asked her, "Where did you get the handshake?"

"My Dad," she said.

"He must be a good man," Nicholas said with a twinkle. "Knows a strong handshake."

"I wouldn't know," Darby said. "He left when I was eight. But I remember that."

"I'm sorry," he said, with sincere compassion that caught her off guard. "Shall we?" he said extending a hand toward their seats.

"We shall," Darby said.

They ordered bourbon for the pre-departure drinks. Then drank red wine with their dinner. They talked and laughed through the night, and Darby never knew a time she had so much fun commuting. She thought about Tom, and wished they could have shared this. Both had been so busy that they never went on vacation together. *Perhaps that wasn't in his budget*, Darby thought. They did have Sydney, but she forced that thought where it belonged—in a memory.

They talked for hours, ate together, watched the same movie, laughing at the same places.

"Do you have plans when you get to Paris?" Nicholas asked.

"I plan on sleeping," she said, "then I'll explore the city. And you?"

"Ah…spending some time on my boat," he said. He reached over and stroked a finger over the top of her hand and stared into her eyes, "I would love it if you could join me. No expectations."

She wasn't sure if it was the alcohol speaking, or feeling the loss of touch, but tingles that she hadn't felt since Tom surfaced.

"Unfortunately, I don't have boating clothes," she said. "I was supposed to fly this trip out and back. They changed me to a three-day layover So, I brought nothing to play in."

"Nothing works nicely," Nicholas said with a grin. "But not to worry. Whatever you have will be fine."

Darby's heart raced a little faster. This was one of those decisions that could either change the outcome of her life, take her life, or simply give her a memory to visit in her old age, tucked away with Tom's. But at the end of the day, the world she knew was in despair, and this might be a delightful day even if it did become her last one on earth.

"That sounds nice," she said. "I would love to." Besides, she had always thought about floating down the Seine. For all the years she'd walked the paths above, this would be a fun experience and a first. How much trouble could she really get in?

"Then I shall pick you up at 6 p.m.," he said, just as the lights illuminated to bright and the flight attendants began their breakfast service before arrival.

They were arriving at the gate at 6 a.m., only 9 p.m. her time zone. She would get a full night's sleep during the day, set her alarm to find clothes, then whatever the night would bring, she would allow fate to determine where her adventure with Mr. Nicholas Valencia would take her.

CHAPTER 85

THE BEST DAY of sleep in her life ended with pounding on the door. She looked at her phone. She had slept through her alarm by two hours. More like she forgot to set it. The pounding on the door continued and she threw back the covers.

"Coming," she yelled. The rooms were tiny, and she did not have far to walk. She looked through the peephole and who appeared to be a hotel employee stood outside. She opened the door. "Yes?"

"I have a package for you," he said. "Mr. Valencia's car will be waiting at 1800 prompt."

"Thank you," Darby said, accepting the package. She carried it to her bed and opened the box. Inside were a pair of white capris with navy leather accents over the pockets, a red form-fitting tank top with soft navy colored leather-straps, and matching Riomar leather boat shoes. There was also a lightweight white leather jacket. Even a matching leather purse.

"On my God, this is so cute!" she said. Checking the tags, she confirmed everything was her size. Then she saw a note and opened it.

I would hate to see the most beautiful woman in Paris
without her boating clothes on. I would feel overly protective

of that beautiful body. See you soon,
   Nicholas Valencia

Darby had Googled him when she arrived at her room that morning. Nothing but dead ends had popped up. *Who is this guy?* she wondered. He was about her age, maybe a couple years older. She glanced at her phone and realized she had less than 40 minutes to get ready. She jumped out of bed and headed toward the shower.

WITH FIVE MINUTES to spare, dressed in her new outfit, she threw her new purse over her shoulder and carried her jacket through the lobby. The crew she had arrived with was standing in the lobby, the meeting place to head across the street to the Canadian Embassy, the bar where they plotted where to have dinner.

"Wow," the captain said. "You look hot."

"Thanks," Darby said as she approached. She glanced at her watch.

"Have a date?" one of the first officers said.

"Actually, I do," Darby said stopping for a moment. "I'm going boating. But if I turn up missing for my trip in three days, blame it on a better offer than this job, or that I've been chopped up into little pieces and thrown into the river."

"I want one of those little pieces," the first officer said, with a grin.

"Should we know who to blame?" the captain called out, as she headed toward the door.

"The guy I sat by in 3A," Darby said over her shoulder before she went outside.

As she stepped outside the doorman said, "Ms. Bradshaw, your ride is this way." He extended his hand to the right.

A black Mercedes limo, parked by the exit to the street in a no parking zone, took up two spaces. The back door was open, and

Nicolas stood holding a single red rose, wearing a pair of black jeans and a polo shirt. He kissed her on each cheek and then helped her into the car. The driver closed the door. Champagne glasses were full, and a platter of cheese and crackers rested on a table.

"This is quite a ride for a couple blocks to the Seine," Darby said.

"Ah, Darling," he said with a wide grin. "I'm not sure my boat would fit in the river."

"Where are we going, then?" Darby asked, accepting a glass, her heart racing a bit faster.

"Le Havre Plaisance," he said, helping himself to a slice of cheese. "A nice little marina that houses my European boat."

"You have more than one boat?" Darby asked. "What is it that you do?"

"Yes, I also have one in the Pacific." Then he smiled broadly and said, "As to your second question, as little as possible. But when duty calls, I *am* the best."

"I searched you on the internet, and found nothing," Darby said.

"I did the same, but your results were quite different." He sipped his champagne and then said, "Would you like me to kill some people on your behalf? I'd be happy to."

Darby laughed, and almost spilled her drink. "Not at the moment, but I think you and I are going to be very good friends."

"I'm counting on it."

CHAPTER 86

TWO AND A half hours after they left Paris, the limo parked at Club Nautique Le Havre, and the driver opened the door. They climbed out of the car and walked down the pier. Darby felt a little woozy from the champagne and wished she had eaten more cheese than she had.

"Holy shit," Darby said. "That would definitely *not* fit in the Seine. She's beautiful."

"Let's go take a look, shall we?" He said, as they passed her bow. Her name, *The Little Redhead*, was painted on the side.

"Ah…You named her after me," Darby said jokingly, and flicked her hair.

He smiled and he held her hand, assisting her up the ramp to climb aboard. Once inside he took her on a mini tour until they reached the stern. The sun was low on the horizon. A table was set for two, with candles and exquisite gold and silver embroidered placemats. The crystal looked expensive, and the space amazing.

The boat was large enough to comfortably have a dinner party for twenty, with several couches and easy chairs to accommodate all guests. The covered space hosted the gorgeous teak wood, with tiny ball lights floating above.

"You must be hungry," he said.

"I'm actually starving," Darby said. "I should have eaten more cheese but was enjoying the conversation and the champagne so much, food seemed to get in the way."

"That it does. I ordered a Caesar salad, and grilled salmon with asparagus," he said. "I hope that's fine. If not, we can prepare anything your heart desires. The kitchen is full."

"Are you kidding, that's my all-time favorite meal," Darby said.

He opened a bottle of cabernet and filled their glasses, as they continued their conversation. Not unlike during the drive to the pier, Nicolas dodged the question about what he did for a living, yet he asked Darby many questions about her and Global. She filled him in on all the dirt, her fear they were trying to get rid of pilots, and the concern with automation.

"Would automatic planes be so bad?" Nicolas asked, as their salads arrived. "Beyond taking your job." He winked when he said the last part, with a glimmer in his eye.

"Imagine a warehouse with five hundred employees. Each managed 30 aircraft at a time. What would happen if the terrorists accessed that building?"

His eyes narrowed. "Thousands of bombs in the sky," he said, "at the control of the… *bad guys.*"

"Exactly. If we can keep the bad guys off the plane, we're safe. But allowing that control on the ground, nobody would be safe."

She ignored his teasing her with term bad guys. He listened intently to her concerns and what would happen to aviation and passenger safety, and perhaps the world, as they ate the most incredible salad she'd tasted in ages.

"Despite the terrorists, thousands of jobs would be lost," Nicholas said, "History and passion of the sky would become extinct."

He gets it, Darby thought. "That's exactly what would happen."

Their main courses arrived as the sun dipped below the horizon. Then she told him about Tom, and what had happened between them. She talked about their proposal as she stared out over the English Channel. Darby was not over him, and it was Tom she wanted to be sharing this moment with. Nicholas was not pretentious, and he made her laugh. She hadn't done much of that in a long time. He was also handsome and kind. But he wasn't Tom. Tom may have ruined her for enjoying any other man. At least for the time being.

"Have you ever had anyone special in your life?" she asked. "Been married?"

"No." He stared at the candle that flickered with the light breeze and said, "I thought perhaps once, but my life choices have not afforded me the luxury of a family. The life I have selected requires me to do things... But it's my choice. We cannot turn back time."

"I'm not going to ask you what those things were," Darby said. "But I know that we can change who we are. We can make new choices. Reinvent ourselves. We don't have to define ourselves by our past. If we find someone we love, we have to fight for them. Maybe you can still have that chance. Maybe you can't turn back time, but you can start the clock again."

"Is there anything more important than love?" he asked, staring into her eyes.

"I don't think so," she said. "Well, maybe this salmon?"

He grinned. "It's delicious, No?"

"It's delicious, yes," she said, and they both laughed.

Then he asked about her dad leaving when she was eight. Darby explained the volatile home life she had grown up in, and how he had left for his survival. The only real memories of him from that time were those her mother had created fueled by her hatred. But the counselor had explained how childhood memories are often implanted, either by our imagining the way we want to perceive ourselves, or those things people tell us over and over.

"So, I don't really know the truth," Darby said. "For some reason the worst is easier to believe in people when you see too much of it."

"How long have you been seeing a counselor?" he asked.

"She's actually a psychiatrist," Darby said. "A couple years now. Most of the time on Zoom calls, unless I'm in town." Darby twisted the stem of her glass between her fingers, and then said, "You know, you're the only person I've told that to."

"Why the secret?" Nicolas asked.

Darby shrugged. "My friends would understand. But one of them works for the FAA. I guess it's just easier keeping quiet. Also, if I reported it on my medical form, I would risk my medical license."

"If those idiots at your airline had that doctor conduct an authentic analysis requesting your medical records, they might have been able to pull you legitimately," Nicolas said.

"I know. They are idiots, right?" Darby said and smiled.

They finished their meals and moved to one of the couches, where chocolate mousse with raspberries and whipped cream taunted her to the point of giving in. He poured Darby a snifter of brandy, and she was feeling no pain. She sighed and said, "You know Nicholas, I thought this is what I wanted to do. But ..."

"What, may I ask had you wanted to do?" he asked, his eyes dancing with mischief.

"Oh, I planned on screwing the first good looking guy I met."

His eyes twinkled even more. "And I was that lucky chap?"

"You are kind of good looking," Darby said with a wink. "But. I can't. I love Tom."

"Are you sure?" Nicolas said, placing his hand over hers with a gentle squeeze, staring into her eyes.

"I am," Darby said.

"Then Tom's a lucky man," he said.

They stayed on the yacht for the night and Nicolas promised to be the perfect gentleman. He gave Darby the suite on the opposite side of the ship and away from his stateroom. He had bought her a pair of silk pajamas and had them delivered to her room with a bottle of water. Once dressed, she climbed into the king-sized bed and snuggled under the covers, alone. The room spun from the alcohol, but she was more at peace than she had been in a long time. Closing her eyes, she fell fast to sleep. Nicholas slept soundly in his stateroom across the yacht.

Shortly after midnight, Darby's door opened. The footsteps were barely audible as he walked quietly to the side of her bed and stared. A sliver of moon shone through the window illuminating her face. He bent down and kissed her forehead ever so gently. She stirred and rolled to her side. He froze. When he was sure she was sleeping, he turned and walked out of the room, closing the door behind him while wishing things were different.

CHAPTER **87**

ONE OF THE worst days in history and Darby decided to spend it at home. The check airman signed her off after her first three legs of OE—Paris, New York, Tel Aviv, and New York. Then she tried to get consolidated to no avail. She only got one additional trip. She needed 100 hours in 120 days from the day of her check ride and was many behind.

Darby arrived at SeaTac and jumped on the crew bus thinking about her Paris trip. She and Nicholas had breakfast the following morning and she took the limo back to the hotel, wearing her new jogging suit, alone. She'd never had anybody buy her clothes before, even when she was young, and it was fun. He had great taste and knew her size.

He also gave her his business card that only had a number on it and told her to call if she ever needed anything. She jokingly said, '*Like a new outfit?*' He had replied, '*If you need help.*' Emphasizing the word help as he stared into her eyes. He explained that his research identified those she was battling at Global were more dangerous than she could imagine. Then he told her to memorize his number and destroy the card. She did just that.

Within no time she arrived at the parking lot and found her car. It started on the first try and she headed for the exit. She hadn't spoken to Tom for almost two months. She loved him but didn't know how to approach him and did not want to do it on the phone. She had been cold during their last talk and had said they were over. Now enough time had passed that she could talk to him. She would text him in a few days to see if he was available. For now, she just needed a bit of time for herself to think about life.

Turning the corner, her heart slammed into her chest, and she lifted her foot from the gas pedal. She and her damned plans. Tom's car was in her driveway and he stood on her porch. He looked her way and half raised a hand. Darby pulled the car into the driveway beside his, opened the garage door and drove inside. She turned off her car and closed the door.

She was scared. Scared to allow him to hurt her again. She never wanted to feel that kind of agony. But her short time with Nicholas made her realize there could be nobody else. She saw Nicholas's ache giving up his true love. She did not want that. Love was not pain free. She jumped out of her car, hoping Tom hadn't left due to the length of time she sat in her car. She went straight to the front door, deactivated the alarm and opened it.

He was still standing there. "You changed the locks."

"I did," she said stepping back. "Want to come in?"

"More than you will ever know."

They went into her living room and Darby asked if she could make him a drink. She added ice cubes to two crystal glasses, filled them with bourbon and a splash of soda and a couple cherries. She returned with a bag of potato chips and their drinks.

"A cherry?" he said, with an odd look.

"I'm hungry," she said. "And I won't open those if you don't eat some."

"Darby, I'm sorry," he said.

Tom told her how he had worked for Drake and was approached for a security assignment of a different kind with another company. Drake had been furious when he quit and forced him to sign an NDA. He was paid a small fortune to work on a local police force to monitor Darby. Whomever his boss was, had access to the police department database.

That police department lost its usefulness when they required him to monitor George Wyatt and Rich Clark, too, so he became a detective that forced him into training. A ruse because he simply had to travel back East. But nobody in the detective academy knew.

"I don't understand," Darby said finishing her drink. The bag of chips was empty by the time he finished talking. "Who is it?"

"I have no idea," Tom said. "I swear. I've spent a great deal of time trying to figure this out. But I can't."

"How are you paid?"

"Deposit into an account," Tom said emptying his drink. He jiggled the ice in his glass and then ate the cherry.

"Can I get you another?" she nodded toward the drink.

"Please," he said lifting the bag of chips. "I can't believe you ate the whole thing."

"Yes, you can," Darby said as she headed to the kitchen. She added more ice to the glasses and smiled as she did. Then the bourbon, a splash of soda and one cherry for him, three for her, and a splash of cherry juice. She grabbed him a bag of chips, promising herself not to eat even one.

She returned with the drinks and gave Tom the chips.

"There's something else," Tom said, after he sipped his drink. "For some reason, whoever this is, wanted me to tell you about my monitoring you before trial. I refused. He threatened to fire me. I didn't care. You didn't need one more thing on your plate. But I couldn't figure out, if he wanted me to protect you, why do something that could harm you?"

"But why did Bill tell me, and *after* the trial?" Darby said. "Maybe to screw with my mind before training?"

"Bill works for Drake. If there's a connection to Global, the timing could have been to make you fail your check out."

"Do you think there's a connection with Global and Drake?" Darby asked.

"There are no coincidences. I think the reason they selected me was not because of my skills, but the fact that I worked for Drake. But I don't think that anyone at Global would have the funds or brains to pull this off. Whomever it was got nothing."

Tom was correct about the lack of brains. Then she asked, "How do you communicate with this guy?"

"Phone. Text," Tom said. "Untraceable. He uses burner phones."

"But you've never met him?"

Tom explained what happened when he had flown to D.C., and then said, "But I never got a glimpse of the man in the car. He sat in front and I wouldn't know him if he walked in the room right now."

"Well, we know he smokes cigars," Darby said with a slow smile. "And he resides in the D.C. area, or why would he make you go there?"

"Or he was flying out," Tom said opening the chips.

Tom ate a chip and extended the bag to Darby, and she shook her head no. They sat in silence, other than the crunch of the chips as Tom worked on them.

Then Tom said, "I was giving you your space and planned to wait for you to reach out to me. But I received a text as to what flight you would be on today, and was advised to be here waiting for you. No explanation."

"This is kind of freaking me out," Darby said. "The last trip I flew, I picked up on short notice. Then I deadheaded to Seattle. It's got to be someone at Global because this was not a planned flight. And how would they know my commuter flight?"

"That's what worries me," Tom said with sincerity. "I want to protect you."

"Like a damsel in distress," Darby said.

"Or as your husband," Tom said, without removing his eyes from hers.

"I thought you would never ask." Darby reached into her glass. She ate one of her cherries then stuck her fingers in again and pulled out the ring. There was still ice on the diamond, so she sucked on it for a moment then handed it to Tom.

This time, it was he who cried, as he dropped to a knee. "Will you by my bride?"

"For better or for worse," she said, and threw her arms around him. "But no more lies of omission between us."

He carried her upstairs and set her on the bed. He undressed her, and then removed his clothes. They made love with such passion, as if they were making up for days lost or days that would never come. Darby wasn't sure which, and she didn't care. Lying in his arms, as he stroked her hair, she was thinking about lies of omission.

"I have to tell you something," Darby said.

She would tell him about Nicolas another day. But now she had to tell him what Bill had said to her about the pending crash.

After she'd finished filling Tom in on the details of her and Bill's conversation, Tom remained quiet for longer than usual, stroking her back. Then he said, "He won't harm the girls. I'll see to that. But do you think Global will take a plane down on purpose?"

Tears filled Darby's eyes from the pressure release, finally able to tell someone and not carry the burden alone. But also from the reality of the truth as to what was about to happen.

"I do," she said. "I've been warned that people have been killed for a lot less."

Chapter 88

JOE WOLFE, GLOBAL'S attorney, was nothing but a hired gun for the Global Air Lines. A gun who shared a pulse with the union, and when the airline wanted something, ALPO complied. Global wanted this badly. Hell, after the fiasco they called a trial, they needed it.

Wolfe greeted his guest as he walked into the office. "Thank you for joining me on such short notice."

"Of course," Patolee said.

Joseph Patolee was the ALPO National president, and the first president that was not a Global pilot since the previous three administrations. It was Wyatt who recommended a change of airlines. It would not look good if the president of the largest pilot union and the FAA administrator, both worked for the same company. Patolee held no illusions as to his purpose.

"What do you need?" Patolee asked.

"Bradshaw's pending grievances. We need to win."

"We'll get an arbitrator to rule for the company," Patolee said. "That won't be an issue."

"We need more than a loss for Bradshaw," Wolfe said. "I also want you to provide Bradshaw with a national attorney, someone who has been camping out with you guys for over twenty years."

"I know just the guy," Patolee said. "But why?"

"I'm going to tell you," Wolfe said with a slow smile.

CHAPTER 89

NOVEMBER 15, 2019

DARBY NEVER IMAGINED she would be back to training so soon. She had already spent three days in a trainer, two hours for each event with an 0500 showtime, 3 a.m. her body clock. She visited the simulator for a two-hour warmup, equally as early. Tonight was her check ride that would begin with effing 9 p.m. brief. Not a normal check, but two. The first half being a full maneuvers validation, MV, and the second half an LOE, or line-oriented check ride. Technically two check rides. Four hours in the seat, in the middle of the night, was not something she had signed up for. If all went well, they wouldn't even be out of the simulator until 2 a.m.

She plastered a smile on her face and sucked a deep breath as she walked into the briefing room. "Hi, I'm Darby," she said extending her hand. "I'm sorry about this late hour."

"This is bullshit," the check airman said after they shook. "I only volunteered because I thought it was a two-hour session."

"I thought the same thing. To make matters worse, I'm only here because I couldn't get consolidated. They keep giving green slips to Detroit and Oklahoma guys, and flying them out to Los Angeles on the same day, to avoid giving me the flight."

Darby needed to get 100 hours of flight time in 120 days from the time of her first check ride. They delayed her OE by three weeks and that made her finishing in time problematic. Furthermore, with the four-person crewed flights, she only got credit for half the flight time due to the mandated breaks.

"They're going to screw with you for the rest of your career," the check airman said, in an expression of disgust against Global.

"So, you know who I am?" Darby asked.

"Hell, yeah," he said. "I also know that you are not one of our problem students, so I'm going to combine these events and we'll be out by midnight."

"Sounds good to me," Darby said.

"We'll do a Portland to Seattle engine failure scenario. I'll give you an engine failure with a windshear on takeoff. Seattle will be our takeoff alternate. Plan on a TCAS enroute," he said. "That should cover it."

Darby had no questions and the brief was over quickly. While they waited for the simulator to come down, they discussed Wyatt becoming the FAA administrator. They were both less than thrilled.

Apparently, Wyatt was not the most respected man by those who had shared a career with him. Darby had thought he retired early to get out of the line of fire of her lawsuit, but her instructor said that Wyatt had embezzled money from the company. Wyatt didn't take it for himself, but to pay his buddies to do side jobs in training. He had called it his slush fund.

True or not, Darby still believed he retired because of her case. If the company had any animosity toward him, they would not have paid a corporate attorney to fight the battle on his behalf in D.C. when Captain Hanks challenged him.

They took a restroom break and Darby wandered down the hall. *There would always be rumors*, she thought. But the fact is, the FAA administrator position should be non-biased, of complete integrity, and place passenger safety at the highest level. If Bill was correct, and Wyatt was to approve fully automated aircraft instead of pilots, the next level of terrorism would prevail. There would be no stopping it.

Bill had said that Croft was backpedaling. For what, she wondered. Tom said that nobody crossed Drake. That, she could believe. And Wyatt was part of this, but where was his alliance—with Drake or Croft? She wondered what Rich Clark's purpose was while she washed her hands, then smiled knowing he had none.

The real question was how they got so many employees to participate in the action against her. Maybe she would never know. One thing she knew to be true, this company was similar to a cult, and despite a rational mind seeing what they were doing, people believed the bullshit that was blown up their skirts.

Darby finished in the restroom and headed back to the briefing room. She yawned as she walked in, fighting fatigue. She had awoken at 0400, same as she had done the previous few days, but unlike the other nights she wasn't sleeping.

"Looks like you're ready to fly," the check airman said with a grin.

"With hard work, dedication, and exhaustion," Darby said, "anything is possible."

"Keep climbing higher, by lying, cheating and stealing," a voice said from the door. "Hi, I'm Frank, I'll be flying seat support tonight."

It amazed Darby how all the instructors knew what was ongoing at Global and nobody said anything. Nobody revolted. Bill was absolutely correct—fear was a powerful force. More controlling than she ever believed possible. Fear controlled people. Global counted on that fear, and soon the FAA would use the same tactic to scare the public from flying with pilots.

CHAPTER 90

TWO MORE CHECK rides complete, and she now had another four months to get her 100 hours. Darby tossed her purse onto the bed, wondering if she would really be going through this for the rest of her career. Global denying her flights and paying double for other pilots to take those trips was ridiculous. And setting her up for early training events followed by late-night check rides contradicted learning. Was it worth the fight? She wondered.

Darby climbed out of her clothes and took a quick shower. She made a cup of tea and sat on her bed Indian style with her tea on the nightstand and her laptop on her lap. Then she wondered if it were politically correct to say Indian style. *Criss cross apple sauce*, she thought lifting her cup and sipping the warmth, might be more politically correct. The world was trying to be so politically correct, it was becoming politically incorrect.

While the government was creating fights and unrest amongst the masses, pitting them against each other with colloquial sayings that meant no offense, they were placing people in harm's way on airplanes. Maybe that, too, was nothing but a distraction. Smoke and mirrors of distraction while the real crimes were occurring right before everyone's eyes.

Darby logged into her email account and was deleting the spam, and then she froze. There was an email from Rich Clark's replacement, Senior Vice President Bob Burms, in response to her concerns for Global violating duty time regulations placing pilots on a deadheaded the same day of their international flight. Dodson's testimony flashed into her mind as she opened the email.

"He's such fucking idiot," Darby said, realizing there was nothing these guys wouldn't do for money. But writing his ignorance in an email surprised her.

Burms argued that it was okay to fly across the country the same day of a 14-hour scheduled trip, *if* the pilot had received a green slip, because a green slip turned the deadhead into a commute. A green slip was a double paid trip that enticed pilots to fly fatigued, and part of Global's fatigue-inducing activity. Burms was just another idiot on the payroll of corruption.

Nobody should ever respond while drunk, tired, or angry, but she could not help herself or she wouldn't sleep. Besides, she hadn't had anything to drink. She began her response by explaining that commuting was when the pilots got themselves to their home base, and finished with telling him she would notify the FAA and allow the agency to decide.

Her neck already lay across the chopping block, so what the hell could they do to her now? One thing she would learn, was whether Captain Wyatt would take action against his own airline for a federal regulation violation, which he himself violated while working there and received his own violation for the same thing. This might be fun watching him squirm.

CHAPTER 91

THE DAY HAD arrived when Darby could finally litigate her grievances and take this off her plate. Everyone deserved the benefit of the doubt, and she was giving it to her union. She knew select members had been part of the action with Global. Even the good guys looked the other way, but many apologized afterward. They had given her an ALPO national attorney to use, which was better than the incompetence at the local level. Besides, he was an okay guy.

The representative who was supposed to be on her side had picked her up at her hotel and dropped her off at the front door. He said he had to make a call, so she should hang tight in the lobby while he parked the car during his call.

Darby walked through the entrance of the building and looked at the reader board. Doctor Marsh's office was down the hall from the ALPO offices. The last time she'd been here was to visit him and thought that to be so convenient. For what, she wasn't sure. The rep finally arrived and she followed him into the elevator, and he pressed the button for the fourth floor.

Darby followed him down the hall and he showed her into a

conference room with a large table and stacks of binders and asked her to wait there. As she assessed the binders, she wondered, *Does the legal world live by binders?* There had to be a dozen from her trial in her closet at home.

"Darby," a man said entering the room. "I'm Jeff, it's nice to finally meet you."

"Nice to meet you, too," Darby said turning to meet her ALPO National appointed attorney.

"The rest of the team should be here shortly, and we can start going through the documents," Jeff said.

"What are these?" Darby asked, waving her hand toward the binders.

"What Global intends to use tomorrow," Jeff said, just as the others walked in. "You know Greg and Ryan, don't you?"

"Yes, Greg gave me a ride today. Good to see you again, Ryan," Darby said looking up.

Jeff was pouring himself a cup of coffee and Darby walked to the end of the table and opened a binder. "What the hell?" she said.

"What?" Jeff said turning her way.

"These are the binders from our trial," Darby said. "There is no way in hell I am going into a grievance to retry my AIR21 case. That is not what this is about."

"Well, we can discuss this with the arbitrator," Jeff said.

"No, I'm not doing it if even one of these are admitted as evidence," Darby said. "The grievances have nothing to do with the AIR21 complaint. The trial was about the company putting me into the Section 8. The grievances are about Global union contract violations." She glanced at Ryan and his eyes dropped to the table.

Darby opened another binder, narrowed her eyes, and said, "Why is there a binder of my emails to my ALPO attorneys in the company's documents?" She looked up at Greg, Ryan, and Jeff, posing the question to each. When nobody replied, she said, "Aren't my communications with my ALPO attorneys supposed to be confidential?"

"They are," Jeff said apologetically.

"Maybe reps are exempt from that confidentiality," Greg suggested, looking at the emails.

"No," Jeff said. "All communications with *any* union representative are as confidential as if they were with an attorney."

"What am I supposed to do now?" Darby said.

"Let's prepare for our case," Jeff said. "We can investigate the rest of this later. But now let's focus on winning."

He was correct. They needed to win. Not for herself, but for her fellow pilots. There was nothing she would get out of this process, but she could ensure the violations would go on record and save someone's career in the future. She knew the exact sections of the contract they had violated during the process, and it was up to her to stand on behalf of the pilot contract. The rest of this nonsense, they could deal with tomorrow.

CHAPTER 92

IT WAS GLOBAL'S idea to go directly to the five-man board for the grievance. Darby had no objection because the sooner this was over, the better. This five-person board included two company pilots, two union pilots, and one arbitrator. The company pilots were also part of the union, but they voted for the company regardless. Darby was unsure why all the hairs on her neck were standing at attention, but she felt like a lamb led to the slaughterhouse. She wanted to scream.

The room soon filled with the remaining participants, to include the four pilot representatives, Global's three attorneys, and arbitrator Whales. Darby's National attorney spoke first. None of the pilots looked her way, and she wondered if she could interpret that as the same as when the jury didn't look at a defendant before sentencing. Darby did not trust this process in the slightest.

Arbitrators were businessmen. Robert referred to them as prostitutes with two masters, and they had to keep both johns happy. Therefore, they took turns at winning. And yet there were times that it depended upon who wanted to win the most. At Global, any job loss action typically went to the company to set precedent. The little stuff they threw to the union.

Robert had told her that years ago, as a young attorney defending a pilot at an arbitration, his case was so-so, but he won. Then he came up against the same arbitrator on the next case, and that case was not that strong, but he still won. Then, he finally had a case with a pilot so strong there was no way he could lose. Robert said that the pilot had all the facts in his favor, and it would be a slam dunk.

As it turned out, Robert was up against the same arbitrator as the previous two times.

They greeted each other, and then the arbitrator placed an arm over his shoulder and said, 'You do know, you're going to lose today.' Robert said, 'But you haven't even heard the facts, and we have a very strong case.' The arbitrator said, 'You don't understand. Today is your turn to lose.'

Darby wondered if it was her turn to lose, or if ALPO would understand that this was for the pilot group. She prayed that they would realize the success of this hearing was for her fellow pilots.

"Your honor, we'd like to address these binders that Global presented. These are from the AIR21 trial that could be open for appeal, so we object to their being admitted," Jeff said.

"This would take far too much time to address each document before we begin," Global's attorney said. "I'd suggest that we discuss each as they come up. We can determine at the time."

"I have no problem with that," Jeff said.

"On a case-by-case basis," Arbitrator Whales said. "Okay. I'm fine with that." Then he explained that he had no idea what AIR21 meant, so he had to look it up before the hearing. Darby wondered who brought that to his attention in the first place, and why.

Global's attorney began with opening statements. He rambled on about the timeliness of grievances and how Darby had manipulated that timing. It should be evident by all if there had been any manipulation, it was at ALPO's hands. He then spoke of the proceeding that was about to begin.

"This proceeding here, in the view of Global Air Lines, is not a proceeding in which the Association and Global are necessarily opposing parties," he said. "First Officer Bradshaw has repeatedly criticized, and I would suggest even defamed representatives of the Association, including representatives of the national organization for ALPO, local counsel for ALPO, and other ALPO representatives, including what's known as ALPO Aeromedical."

What the hell? Darby thought and looked at Jeff, expecting him to object. He did not. He just sat there with a placid face listening as any bystander would.

Once Global's attorney finished with his opening statement, Arbitrator Whales said, "I think I need a ten-minute break. I would like to think about what I just heard."

You need to take ten minutes to think about what you just heard, Darby thought. *Are you a fucking idiot?* She could tell him what he had just heard—that Global and ALPO were on the same side. Anyone listening just heard that all her grievances were going to the company.

Ten minutes later the hearing was shut down. The arbitrator said that all her grievances were time barred. ALPO did not throw her under the bus, they just threw their 14,000 pilots on the tarmac and provided clearance for the A350 to taxi over them.

CHAPTER 93

ONLY TWO MONTHS to go, and she would have the Decision and Order from her trial, and it could not get here soon enough. Darby could do anything for two months. Hell, she'd been calling ALPO for the previous three months to get the official ruling for her grievances, to no avail. She had finally consolidated on the Airbus A350, and loved flying it. As time went, by she decided that Bill had been wrong about the intentional accident. She and Tom were planning their wedding. Life was good, and then her phone rang.

"Robert," she said. "Did we get it?"

"No. But I have a bit of bad news," Robert said. "I just sent you Global's latest motion."

Darby headed for her computer. "Motion? What are they up to now?"

"They filed a motion to reopen the case as a result of your arbitration ruling."

"We don't have a ruling," Darby said, sitting at her computer and logging in.

"Global has it," Robert said, "They filed a motion to stay the proceedings of the AIR21 claim and admit new evidence. Their argument is that Global won that first grievance because you withdrew it."

"In what world does that make sense?" Darby asked scanning the document that she had just opened.

Robert said, "Page three says, '*The System Board held that Complainant's withdrawal of the grievance 'means the grievance was resolved, the withdrawal constituted [her] acceptance of the Company's denial [of her grievance].' Accordingly, the System Board explicitly rejected Complainant's contention that Global invoked or adhered to the Section 8 process under the PWA as 'retaliation' for her raising alleged safety concerns.*'"

"That was Rich Clark's denial of my grievance," Darby said. "What does this mean?"

"They're claiming collateral estoppel," Robert said. "Meaning, because you already tried and lost that first grievance, that Global in fact won, and that you cannot try the same case twice. The first grievance being they didn't have the right to place you into a Section 8."

"*That* grievance was not part of my grievance hearing because I dropped it, so how did it get into this motion?" Darby said, pulling a hand through her hair. "Second, they all agreed that the trial binders would *not* be admitted because we could be open for an appeal. Besides they didn't even have a grievance hearing. The arbitrator shut it down when he learned Global and ALPO were on the same side."

"You're preaching to the choir," Robert said. "We'll file our response. This is nothing but a pathetic tactic, and Judge Geraghty will see through it."

Her life was a game to them. Her union was more criminal than the company because they were supposed to be protecting the pilots. Instead, they were playing on the side with Global and placing the pilots in harm's way. Even now after they apologized, they still did this.

Robert calmed her down the best he could under the circumstance and told her the possible outcomes. The worst being she paid for a nine-day trial that should never have gone to court. After they said goodbye, she called Tom.

Darby explained the motion. She told him how the company used the grievance process with ALPO's assistance to buy a decision from the arbitrator, which enabled Global to challenge the validity of her trial. If the judge agreed that Captain Clark's decision, that he had the right to do what he did to her, was legal and binding because she dropped her grievance, and went to court instead, she would lose everything. The contract stated if grievances were not complete in two years, the win would go to the company.

"If they want a fight, I'll give them one," Darby said.

"This is bullshit," Tom said. "What are you going to do?"

"File a DFR."

"A what?"

"Duty of Fair Representation," Darby said. "They're hard to win because the union technically works for me. And it's not illegal if I employ incompetent attorneys. You can only win if you have proof that they refused to represent you."

"But they work for National," Robert said. "You didn't employ them."

"I know. But it's a technicality that the courts overlook," Darby said. "And in this case, they gave me a friggen national attorney to make it look like they were on my side."

Darby headed downstairs to make herself a protein drink. This would be more than a fueled-by-coffee effort. "Regardless, there is no way in hell that any judge would agree that a union attorney who remains silent and doesn't object while the company's attorney tells him they are on the same side, could not possibly rule in my favor."

"I could kill them for you. It might be easier," Tom said.

"That it would," Darby agreed. Then she thought of Nicolas

and his offer.

At the time she thought Nicolas was kidding, but the look in his eyes and unwillingness to discuss what he did for a living, she suspected he wasn't joking. Tom had also offered to kill a participant or two on her behalf, and he did have a gun. She smiled. If only justice were that easy.

She and Tom planned a playdate and ended their call. Darby opened her pantry and removed the canister of protein drink mix and dumped a scoop into the blender. She added water and yogurt and thought about what this latest motion meant in the big picture. Time and money she realized. It was not arms and legs, just her bank account and her sanity. *Fucking Global and ALPO*, she thought, adding frozen fruit to the blender. She would take them to the mat.

"Battle on bastards," she said and pressed blend.

CHAPTER 94

PREPARING FOR A flight to Shanghai, Darby saw the writing on the wall as she walked into the briefing room. Tom had begged her not to go to China, but she told him she wasn't planning to live in fear, despite what her ophthalmologist had said. There was a virus that was killing people.

"Gentlemen," the chief pilot said. "I want you to know that there is no validity to this Corona virus coming out of China."

"That's not true," Darby said, ignoring the *gentlemen* comment. "I just talked to my eye doctor who said that it's very real. People in China have been getting pneumonia-like symptoms since December. And that this virus came out of a lab in Wuhan. He has family there and I suspect he has more information than we do."

The chief pilot gave her a dismissive smile and said to the other pilots, "The company said we are safe to go. But we'll be providing you with boxed lunches instead of regular meals. There will be enough to take to your rooms."

"What about the beagles?" Darby asked.

"The *what*?" the chief pilot said looking her way.

"The vegetable, fruit, and nut beagles. The dogs search for those illegal foods."

"I don't know anything about that," the chief pilot said.

"Regardless of your lack of knowledge," the captain said, "you might not want to tell crews to take food off the plane, unless you want a healthy fine for the pilot and the company."

———oo◆oo———

THE FLIGHT WAS long and by the time they arrived, they learned that their flight would be the last flight from the mainland into China. All flights were cancelled indefinitely due to the Corona virus. The airport was a morgue. Darby had never seen anything like it. The absence of bodies looked like nuclear war. But this was scarier, because other than no people, there was no damage. The emptiness was haunting. It was like that book where people just disappeared.

People in full body suits and masks tested the crew for the disease, then the equally clad driver drove them to their hotel. People dressed in a comparable manner greeted them. Then three hours later, they were locked into their rooms. This now would be a four-day stay until their flight could depart. No gym. No fresh air. Food would be delivered at regular intervals and left on the floor outside her room.

Darby thought how easy it would be for Global to get rid of her in China under these circumstances, but they were too busy dicking around with the legal world. She now had four days to write up the DFR and file that complaint. Then she would formulate a plan to address Bill's warning without placing the girls in harm's way.

She suspected that Global would continue to push pilots to fly fatigued and with shitty training, were just hoping for an accident, not actually forcing one as Bill had. But an accident was inevitable unless she did something.

CHAPTER 95

BILL SMILED PLEASANTLY at Croft's secretary while he waited. He assessed the room and wondered what life would have been like had he not made the choices he did. *This could have been my office*, he thought crossing one leg over the other. He leaned back and extended both arms over the back of the couch.

Rose smiled sweetly at him, clearly nervous. Bill did not think he looked like the thug he was playing today, but perhaps she recognized him from the news. Either way, his days of killing people was over. Unless they deserved it.

He thought about his threat to Darby and wondered if he truly could kill the kids. Then Rose said, "Mr. Croft will see you now."

Bill walked into the CEO's office and scanned the room, his eyes immediately landing on Walter Croft.

"Mr. Jacobs," Walter Croft said, "This is a surprise. What can I do for you?"

"Probably not a hell of a lot," Bill said walking to the window and glancing out. He wondered why the hell this building and office overlooked the worst part of town. Then he turned. "Mr. Drake wanted me to tell you that nobody backs out on a deal with him."

"I didn't… I just delayed it because profits—"

"Your profits are about to end with the rest of the world," Bill said. "That little virus that has just been released will impact your bottom line."

"Drake did that?" Croft said incredulously, as he stood and walked around his desk. "I… I don't understand."

"Is the coffee fresh?" Bill asked but didn't wait for an answer. He walked to the credenza and poured himself a cup. He then moved to the couch and sat. "Please, join me," he said extending a hand to a leather chair across from him.

Croft hesitated a moment, and then joined him. Bill sipped his coffee and watched the reality of the virus work through Croft's brain.

"He fucking released a virus against the world to get back at *me*?" Croft finally said.

"Don't flatter yourself," Bill said with a grin. "I would call it a little social world experiment as how to control people. You might be in that group, but for a different reason."

"What the hell," Croft said standing. "This is ridiculous. He's already cost me millions. All my widebody flights have been cancelled."

Bill set his cup on the table and stood. "Looks like it."

"What the hell does he want me to do now?" Croft said, also standing.

"Join him for dinner. How does Sunday the 22nd sound?" Bill asked.

"Do I have a choice?" Walter Croft asked, his face red, and his body language suggesting that he wanted to kill the messenger.

"We always have choices," Bill said and walked toward the door. He placed a hand on the knob, then turned. "Shall I tell him you'll join him?"

"I'd be happy too," Croft said, with no pleasure in his voice.

They stared at each other a moment, and then Bill said, "Be there at 1800."

Croft had no choice. Bill knew that the revenue since the grounding of the MAX was making Global shareholders wealthier than they ever believed. Profits that also dictated Croft's bonus. But that was not Croft's concern now. Those revenues were chump change, and Drake just closed Croft's pipeline.

"I'll tell Drake that you'll join him," Bill said and closed the door.

Bill smiled at Rose, nodded, and walked through the lobby toward the elevator. He passed Rich Clark who was stepping off the elevator as he stepped on. Clark took a few steps, then turned and gave him a double take and began to say something, but Bill had already pressed the button to leave. Now he pressed the closed button multiple times. They shared eye contact and Bill smiled and gave him a nod as the doors closed.

CHAPTER 96

CROFT STEPPED OFF the elevator precisely five minutes *after* the hour. Perhaps it was childish to intentionally be five minutes late. But Croft was furious that Drake induced a virus into the world because he wouldn't crash one of Global's planes on his command. He had always planned on honoring the deal, he just wanted to reap the rewards a while longer.

Croft knocked on the door and waited. He looked at his watch, and then thought *Touché*. He wouldn't wait all night, but he would wait as long as it suited him.

"Good evening," a man said finally opening the door. "Please, come in."

Croft stepped through the doorway and removed his coat. The room was warm in contrast to the temperatures outside. He knew Drake was angry at him, and the chill cut him to his soul. But he never imagined that Drake would inflict a war on the world to show his power. Or perhaps only to teach him a lesson. Either way, this was ridiculous. *What lengths would he go to?* He had to undo the damage at whatever the cost.

Drake's butler led him through the ornate home and into the dining room. A table for eight with enough floor space for double that, was set for two. One setting at the head where Drake sat, and the other off to the side. Caesar salads with jumbo prawn cocktails awaited.

"What's your pleasure?" Drake asked standing, extending a hand to two open bottles of wine off to his right. He gave a nod to the butler who exited the room.

"White," Croft said slipping into a chair, as Drake poured him a glass.

"You're not having any?" Croft asked, lifting his glass.

"No. I realized while in prison that I think more clearly without it."

Croft considered that sentiment but suspected that he may need the entire bottle to get through this evening. The only thinking he needed was that of creativity, which wine would enhance. The more the better.

As they ate their salads and appetizers, Drake talked about the weather, Wyatt's successful nomination, and the challenges he overcame to reach the position at the FAA. Croft then shifted the conversation and explained the corporate strategy to ensure Bradshaw would lose her case with the collateral estoppel claim which would stop any further litigation. Drake appeared impressed but made no verbal comment. Yet Croft knew that none of this idle chatter was what Drake wanted to discuss. Yet they did.

"What about the union?" Drake asked.

"Her DFR will go nowhere," Croft said. "We've taken care of that."

"And the fraud charges?"

"Both will end before they begin."

"My concern is Dr. Wood," Drake said. "But nothing I can't take care of."

Croft assessed him for a moment then decided not to ask. He finished his first glass of wine, then set his glass on the white linen tablecloth. Picking up the last jumbo prawn with his fingers, he wiped up the remainder of the sauce and stuffed it into his mouth. He licked his fingers and then reached for his napkin.

"So, to what do I owe the pleasure of this evening?" Croft said, patting the edge of his mouth with the napkin, then setting it on the table. He was tired of being the mouse in this game and it was time to force the issue.

"I think we both know the answer to that," Drake said, setting his fork onto his salad plate. "The question is how we move forward and regain trust."

"Trust is easy," Croft said. "You *can* trust me. But this virus is killing our schedules."

"Perhaps. But aviation will continue," Drake said with smugness. He then rang a bell. "It may cut into your profits overseas for a while, but time and my assistance will cure that."

Croft refilled his glass. *My profits overseas?* He wondered how much Drake knew. Perhaps it was true, that there was nothing that went on in aviation that Drake did not have a finger on. The only flights Croft cared about were those coming from and going to Asia. He was making a shitload of money, but then so was the board due to the grounding of the MAX.

"How the hell will we get anyone on a plane breathing recycled air, if they won't even go to an outdoor restaurant?" Croft asked. "Nobody will fly again."

"Tell them the aircraft filter system removes the virus. Passengers will believe it because they want to," Drake said.

"Why did you do this?" Croft finally asked, and then fell silent as the waiter delivered their main courses. Perhaps this was nothing but a game to him, and if that were the case, Croft couldn't win. He needed Drake as an ally.

"I hope prime rib, rare, is okay," Drake said as the waiter set plates in front of them.

Drake lifted his knife and sliced into the meat, then stabbed a chunk and dipped it into horseradish. He stuck the bite into his mouth and chewed in pleasure, as if Croft hadn't asked the question. "Eat before it gets cold," Drake said waving a hand at Croft's plate.

There wasn't a hell of a lot he could do now, so he ate. After his first bite, he realized what an excellent idea that was. "This is delicious," Croft said. He was halfway through the meal, thinking how to go forward. Then he said, "I simply can't figure out how a virus cutting down flights could benefit our goal."

"Everything has a purpose," Drake said, focusing on his meal as he continued to eat.

"It's not that I wasn't going to keep our agreement," Croft said, setting he fork on the plate. "It's just that—"

"You were making money hand over fist, and I was locked up and couldn't react," he said without giving him a glance.

"It was simply the profit," Croft argued. "Nothing else. I had no idea the fear the public felt flying on the MAX." Had he known, he would have financed taking a MAX down himself, years earlier. This was the most brilliant money maker of all times. Discredit an aircraft that his competition flew but wasn't on his property. Wyatt could now keep it grounded for years.

"Fear is a powerful motivator," Drake said, setting his silverware on his plate before pushing it aside. "It will be interesting to see how far we can take the public. Would they be willing to get vaccinated without knowing what's in the vaccine? Would they allow us to inject a product into their bodies without proper testing? Will they care if we close small businesses for their safety while corporations prosper? We can play with the mental health of all our fine citizens, and the pilots."

Drake stared into Croft's eyes with such intensity that he felt fear he'd never felt before. He also understood brilliance. The combination was powerful.

"What happens next, will determine how much control we hold over the public," Drake said, breaking his stare.

"But how will this help us rid the industry of pilots?" Croft asked.

"That answer belongs with an after-dinner drink."

They pushed away from the table. After a short walk, they entered his den. The fire roared, and two cognacs awaited their arrival. They sat across from each other in easy chairs by the fireplace. Croft felt the warmth of the fire, and the knowledge that Drake was drawing him onto his team, once again. Drake had forgiven him.

"You *will* use this opportunity to let go of pilots," Drake said. "Not just any pilots, the most senior pilots with the most experience."

Those with the most experience were Croft's highest paid, having been there the longest. *That's not such a bad idea*, he thought. If they could divest the airline of the most experience, that would improve the bottom line, and an accident would be in the making. Naturally.

"We would have to buy them off," Croft said. "A year's pay and keep them on insurance for three years or until normal retirement."

"Do you care?" Drake said. "It's chump change, and a write-off."

He shouldn't care. Because of the contract, Global was paying those pilots even when they were not flying. Everyone who flew international was grounded due to the Corona crisis, but all were still on the payroll. All that money was flowing out the door and nothing was coming in. Why not offer them the opportunity to leave and get them the hell off the payroll in the long run.

"That's actually a brilliant idea," Croft said. "I'll cleanse Global of 2,000 of the most senior pilots."

"You do that, and I'll open Asia," Drake said.

This meeting could not have had a better outcome. As soon as Drake's social experiment was over, he'd turn the pilot funnel back on. Increase training. Push new and inexperienced pilots through the funnel. This process would find new hires without experience in the left seat. The accident Drake wanted would happen naturally and he would not have blood on his hands.

Most importantly, Drake would open the Asia market. That's all that Croft really cared about. Drake's concept of pilotless aircraft would help Croft immensely in more ways than one.

CHAPTER 97

HIS ARMS SLIPPED around her at the same time a chill found its way inside, and Darby shivered. She could not believe that she was doing this. But her captain had assured her this was the making of a real airline pilot. She'd laughed at the time and thought he was joking, but here she was. With time on her side, why not make the best of it?

"Hold it a little tighter," he whispered. She could feel his breath on her cheek even with his mask on.

"I'm trying," she said to the man half her age. She didn't have to wear a mask because this was a private club, and the very reason she could even be there at all. Especially with the world shutdown. But, still, this was kind of ridiculous. If anything, she should be playing with someone her age at least. But how would she get into it, if she thought he was a kid dressed like spiderman. She grinned at the thought.

"Now, I want you to come down hard," he said, and Darby giggled.

He dropped his arms and said, "*Seriously*?" when she began to laugh, just as her phone rang.

"Excuse me. I've got to take that," she said. She didn't care who it was, but the ringing saved her from embarrassment. This was the most humiliating thing she had ever done in her life.

When she answered, Robert said, "Did I catch you at a bad time?"

"No. You actually saved me," Darby said. "I'm taking a golf lesson and it's cold and wet and this kid is telling me to go down hard." She held a finger up to the kid and mouthed she'd be a minute.

"They're allowing you to play with the Corona outbreak?" Robert asked.

"Private club," she said. "But I suspect they'll be closed soon, too."

"I've never played golf," Robert said. "It's like crack cocaine. Equally as addicting, and just as expensive."

"Well, if Tom hadn't bought me the lessons, I couldn't afford it myself."

"Then I'm sorry for what I'm about to tell you," Robert said. "You might want to be sitting."

Darby glanced at the bench, but decided to sit where she was standing. She slid to the ground and then leaned against the golf bag. She wasn't sure how much more could go wrong. "I'm ready. Lay it on me." She closed her eyes and waited.

"That motion we filed to get you attorney fees was denied."

Darby sighed a breath of relief. These days she envisioned the worst of everything, but that wasn't so bad. Robert had filed for advanced attorney fees due to the length of time this case was taking. He presented case law that justified why she should receive them. Darby had thought Judge Geraghty would have allowed it based upon what he had witnessed in trial, and the additional evidence, to include Global's frivolous motion and collateral estoppel claim.

"Shit," Darby finally said, after she realized what this meant. "If Geraghty planned on ruling for me, then why not allow it?"

"I just sent you the decision," Robert said. "He didn't back it up with case law, just made a determination. I'm not pleased, and quite surprised."

"Thanks," Darby said. "I'll check it out when I get home."

They ended their call and Darby stood. She dusted off her butt and picked up her club. The instructor was now on the bench texting, so she walked to the tee and set a ball on it. Gripping her club firmly she turned her body and came down hard on it. The ball flew, but sideways and into the trees,

The instructor approached and said, "That was rather good. But you don't want to kill it. The trick is to let the club do the work."

Darby turned and assessed him for a moment with visions of allowing the club do the work on Rich Clark's head, and then Croft's.

"Would it be justifiable homicide if I claimed that my golf instructor told me to let the club do the work?" Darby asked. "That I wasn't really trying to kill them, it was the club's fault."

"You're talking about the balls," he said, looking a bit frightened.

Darby stared for a moment and then decided that she needed a different instructor. At the very least one with a sense of humor. After she assured him that she was *only* talking about killing balls, and not mentioning the entire leadership team at Global Air Lines, they continued with her lesson. But she couldn't focus on the game. She could only think of the many ways Global management and ALPO were screwing with her, and how she would gain retribution.

CHAPTER 98

APRIL 7, 2020
SEATTLE, WASHINGTON.

HER ALARM RANG, giving Darby a ten-minute warning. She made a fresh cup of coffee then moved to the living room with her laptop for her meeting. FAA inspector David Westrom scheduled the call. He had written to her explaining that their investigation regarding Global's alleged duty-time violations was complete, and that he and inspector Amy Hatters were going to speak to her and explain their findings. But a verbal explanation made no sense. This was a first.

Within minutes of the scheduled time, the phone rang and Darby answered. He carried on some small talk for a few minutes, and Darby finally asked him if he could share his findings.

"I want you to know that we took your concerns to heart, but we have found no violation," Mr. Westrom said.

"Are you kidding?" Darby said incredulously.

"No, I'm not. There is no language in Federal Regulations for commuting."

"As there shouldn't be," Darby said. "This is about a scheduled company deadhead."

"But since the Corona virus has impacted flight schedules," Ms.

Hatters said, "The company is giving positive space to all commuters."

"To their base. Not to another base that exceeds duty time," Darby said.

"We know this is a workaround by the company," Westrom said. "But there is nothing we can do about it."

"Yes, you could," Darby said. "Any company who creates a *workaround* of a fatigue regulation designed to reduce risk, but is increasing it due to a loophole, is violating safety management systems. You could get them for an SMS violation."

"I'm sorry this is not what you want to hear," Ms. Hatters said.

"Not what I want to hear?" Darby snapped. "I don't know if I should laugh or cry."

"It's not a perfect world, or a perfect system," Westrom said.

Perfect? Darby thought and then she let her anger blow. "You're supposed to be protecting passengers. Nobody expects perfect, they simply want to know that they are safe when they walk on an airplane, and their pilot hasn't been awake for 26 hours."

"We do our best, Ms. Bradshaw," Ms. Hatters said.

"I'm sorry, but with all due respect if you're doing your best then maybe you need to get another job." Darby was furious and she continued. "I get that you're afraid of speaking out against Global Air Lines because your new boss is aligned with them, but this is ridiculous."

"This has nothing to do with Mr. Wyatt," Westrom said.

"Okay, then answer one question," Darby said. "In 2016, Global Air Lines received a violation of order regarding a situation exactly like this. Duty time violations. Why then and why not now?"

"Uh… well," Westrom stuttered. "I can't answer that because … uh, that file is missing."

"A missing file?" Darby said. "This is ridiculous. If there's a missing file, I would suggest you look in George Wyatt's desk." She pulled both hands through her hair in frustration and then said, "I gave you the FOIA request, you know what happened."

"We read it, and I know it existed, but the entire file is missing. This is the first time this has ever happened, and I'm angry about it," Westrom said. "It will go into my final report."

Darby remained silent for a moment, fearful of what disrespectful thing she may say next. These two were nothing but flunkies and doing the bidding of their boss, George Wyatt. But if nobody stood up for right and wrong, then what good was the system. What good was the FAA? It wasn't worth anything.

"I hope that nobody dies while either of you are on watch," Darby finally said. "Because if there is a fatigue related accident at Global, you'll both be responsible."

"That's not fair," Ms. Hatters said.

"Fair? Are you fucking kidding me? Tell *that* to the families of the survivors," Darby said. "I don't want to hear about fair. I know what fair and just is, and I haven't seen either for an exceptionally long time. Especially not with the FAA."

Darby ended the call and carried her cup of coffee to the kitchen and threw it into the sink. Then she began to cry. She slid to the floor and buried her face into her hands. Her emotions were more than anger. It was the deep-rooted fear of Wyatt's absolute corrupt power without any checks and balances. Her tears were of frustration, that perhaps there was nothing she could do about any of this.

CHAPTER 99

THE SHINING CAME to mind as Bill walked down the long, minimally lit, hallway to Dr. Wood's office. This was one of the older buildings in Skokie, Illinois, and Dr. Wood had either purchased it on the cheap or used it for his higher goal. The elevator was decrepit enough, but this walk could put anyone on edge. He chuckled to himself with the thought of a nut job forced to enter this building for an evaluation. If they weren't crazy before they saw Wood, this walk could do it.

He located Dr. Wood's door and tried the knob. Locked. Then he knocked. Rustling came from inside, and he waited. Bill was a patient man when he wanted to be. Within minutes the door partially opened. The good old doctor appeared to be showing signs of paranoia.

"May I help you?" Dr. Wood said. Peering through the crack, then he looked up at Bill.

Bill stuck his foot into the opening of the door, then pushed it all the way open, shoving Dr. Wood back a few steps. He closed the door and latched the deadbolt.

"What is this?" Dr. Wood said. "Who are you?"

"You did some work for Global Air Lines," Bill said. "Today, I'm a messenger."

Dr. Wood backed up a couple steps until he reached the wall. "What do you want?"

"I want you to have a seat," Bill said, looking around. "Are there chairs in this dump?"

Wood glanced toward the door, and then he said, "In this room." He walked through an entrance to an inner office, which was equally as disorganized, but at least it had two chairs.

Bill directed Dr. Wood to sit. Wood's hands shook ever so slightly as he reached for the desk to lower himself to the chair. Then Bill removed Wood's landline from the cradle and set it on the desk. He moved the other chair in front of the open doorway and sat.

Instilling fear had always been his pleasure, and it somewhat aroused him. He enjoyed putting this asshole on edge. This pathetic example of a person who called himself a doctor had cost a couple of his airline buddies their careers. There would be nothing he would like more than to put a bullet into this son of a bitch's head, other than throwing him out the window. But that would be too easy. Then he thought of Darby's notebook, and smiled. That would be the perfect ending to Dr. Wood. Instead, he crossed one leg over the other and folded his arms.

Bill said nothing. Playing with a shrink had an entertainment value all its own. He simply stared at Dr. Wood, thinking how much he despised the man and how appropriate it would be if Wood were locked up in a nuthouse and sodomized by the cleaning crew.

"What can I do for you?" Dr. Wood finally said.

"I thought you'd never ask." Bill uncrossed his legs, and then leaned forward placing his forearms on his thighs as he clasped his hands and stared at Wood. "I've got a little business deal. You're going to forfeit your medical license in response to the Bradshaw case."

"No. I'm not," Dr. Wood said standing. "I did nothing wrong.

They requested—"

"Sit!" Bill demanded, and Wood returned to his chair. "You will forfeit your license because you did *everything* wrong," Bill said.

"But I can fight this," Dr. Wood said. "It was my opinion. At worse I get a suspension."

"This will not see the inside of a courtroom. Ever."

"But I won't say anything."

"You have no choice," Bill said leaning back in his chair again.

"Global can't do this," Dr. Wood said. "They owe me."

"They owe you nothing," Bill said standing, throwing the chair against the wall as he did.

Dr. Wood jumped, and Bill closed the door between the two rooms and turned toward the weasel, his eyes filled with fire. "You fucked up," Bill said. "You gave a diagnosis that could have been discredited by a first-year med student. You were a fucking idiot at trial. You're a wild card. I should just get rid of you and save us all the trouble."

"I'm not…I'm, I promise," Wood stuttered.

"You will be paid an early retirement," Bill said. "But if it were up to me, I wouldn't give you shit and bury your sorry ass in the first hole I could find."

"You work for Global?"

"Not exactly," Bill said.

Bill proceeded to tell Dr. Wood the terms of the pending forfeiture of his medical license. Then he grabbed him by the front of his shirt and pulled him to his feet. Wood was now standing on his toes, as Bill brought his face close to his and spoke in a low, deep voice.

"I told my boss it would be much easier to kill your sorry little ass. I even told him that I'd do it with pleasure. But he's a nicer guy than I am." Bill pushed him back down.

Hitting the side of the chair, Dr. Wood fell to the floor.

"You do *anything* other than what is offered," Bill said, "and I will return."

Bill ripped the phone cord from the wall, then with his palm open he said, "Cell."

Dr. Wood reluctantly gave it to him, and Bill slipped it into his pocket. Then Bill opened the inner door and walked through the outer office and turned the deadbolt to leave. Dr. Wood remained in place on the floor. If Bill wasn't mistaken, the scent of urine filled the air.

Chapter 100

TO HELL WITH *regulations*, Darby thought. If it works for the company the FAA will approve it. Due to Covid, which started as the Corona virus, she had not flown for three months and 22 days. However, despite federal law requiring that all pilots have three takeoffs and landings within ninety days, the virus changed those rules. Now it was okay to not see the inside of an airplane for four months before they needed to become current. To hell with safety.

Time off was great, but it felt so good to be back to work.

They were conducting their preflight, but something didn't look right because it wasn't. There was an amber EFOB with an associated eleven thousand pounds. EFOB was the expected fuel on board at landing, and 17,800 pounds should be displayed in green today. Instead the figure displayed 10,000, and was amber.

"There is close to a 7000-pound fuel discrepancy," the captain said. "I can't figure this out. All the numbers look fine."

"I was just looking at that," Darby said, pushing buttons and glancing at the map display. "I think I found it. Look at this, the plane thinks it's going to burn 6.8 thousand pounds in less than a mile to this first fix."

"If I remember right, there was a memo about that about six

months back," the third pilot said, "that says we can ignore it."

"Ignore what?" a mechanic asked, as he arrived to sign off the logbook.

"Our fuel is apparently showing less because the computer thinks we're burning 6,800 pounds in a mile," Darby said. "The reason we have this amber fuel warning."

"I don't like it," the mechanic said.

"Do you want to go?" the captain asked Darby.

"I'm willing to depart. If it sorts itself out on climb-out, we'll press on. If it shows 7,000 pounds light, we'll continue to Honolulu and land there for fuel," Darby said. "But it would only be right to ground the plane in Hawaii."

"I like the way you think," the captain said. "Did you bring your bikini?"

"Always, but I'd have to wear it in my room," Darby said. "With a mask."

"A vision I'd like to see," the captain said. "You good with that?" he asked the mechanic.

"Departing? Or the bikini with a mask?" he asked.

—o◆o—

THEIR FLIGHT EVENTUALLY made it to Haneda, with a total of eight passengers. The authorities administered the crew's Covid tests at the airport, the masked driver in a full bodysuit escorted them to the hotel, and security staff in similar dress, escorted them individually to their rooms to lock them in. She awaited her turn, looking forward to taking the damn mask off.

Darby didn't care about the lockdown. This would be a three-day sit due to the reduced schedules, and she planned on a staycation of bubble baths and a mystery that she had been planning to read, but never found the time. She also intended on writing to the company about the fuel issue. Why the had not not fixed the problem when they had time was a mystery.

Ignoring an amber warning before takeoff bugged the hell out of her. If the company was telling pilots to ignore the computer when it said they were thousands of pounds low, she knew what would happen when a plane really was low on fuel. The perfect storm.

Once in her room she stripped off her uniform and climbed into a bubble bath with a cup of tea, dumped a mini bottle of apple whiskey into it with a splash of melatonin. A long day, the warmth of the water, and the alcohol melatonin cocktail tugged at her eyelids. As the water cooled, she climbed out of the tub and into her pjs. Shortly thereafter she fell into a deep sleep. Albeit a short sleep, as she awoke in the middle of the night.

Flipping channels on the television produced nothing, so Darby decided to write Tom a love letter, and opened her computer. When she logged into her email account there was something from ca9_ecf-noticing@ca9.uscourts.gov. She narrowed her eyes and opened it. Then quietly said, "Fuck."

Darby lost her Duty of Fair Representation lawsuit against the union. Judge Landers approved ALPO's motion to dismiss it. She opened the file and began to read. An hour later, she learned it was because Judge Landers thought her union attorney's silence was just a subjective decision, and not nefarious.

Everything else the union had done over the years would have proven ALPO's pattern of behavior of working with Global. This event was the last straw. But now she could do nothing. None of the previous events against her could now be used. If Landers had allowed her to proceed and collect discovery, the years of ALPO's deception could have been allowed as evidence.

ALPO would get away with assisting Global, and there was not a damn thing she could do about it. Darby wished she would have filed a conspiracy charge against ALPO and Global instead of a DFR. That's exactly what they did—conspired together to harm her.

She wasn't sure why this felt like such a defeat, nothing short of a physical beating. She knew the DFR was a crapshoot. But still, she'd hoped Judge Landers would see through their behavior. *He's a pro-labor judge, for God's sake*, Darby thought. That's when it hit her.

Pro-labor did not mean for the pilot, it meant for the union. The fucking organization. Not the pilots. "Who is defending the pilots then?" Darby asked to an empty room with walls that were closing in by the minute, pressing the air out of her lungs.

Leaning back on her pillow she closed her eyes and took a deep breath, dumbfounded as to how a judge could make a decision that was so blind to the truth. Perhaps there was no justice, and at the end of the day those who had power and the money won the game.

CHAPTER 101

G*ROUNDHOG DAY* WAS underway aviation style. Darby returned to Tokyo, and the routine was the same. Except this time, they carried 18 passengers. *Why the hell are they flying these planes empty*, Darby wondered. More than likely, they needed to retain their landing slots. Either way, she wasn't going to complain because they were paying her to do it. While the flight attendants loved the low workload, she was wondering what the hell happened to the career she had loved so much. There was also a shift in attitude among the crews, with an unsettling anxiety as a result of the isolation.

The best part of the job had always been hanging out on layovers with coworkers to decompress. Darby suspected mental health issues were not too far off on the horizon for airline flight crews. While the flight attendants enjoyed the easier job enroute, isolation would eventually take its toll. She logged onto her computer to see what Tom had sent her today.

She opened Tom's email. Today it was a news clip of Wyatt and his promise to the public that he would be the first to fly as a passenger on the MAX. If he didn't fly it, it wouldn't go. Tom wrote—*If the plane's not ready to fly and he takes it, perhaps we can kill two birds with one stone.*

Darby responded—*That's funny. And a fantasy to get me through the night. Miss you.*

Then she opened the next email from an author in the UK who was investigating medical fraud. He wrote—*Did you know Dr. Wood forfeited his medical license to avoid prosecution?* This occurred two months earlier, but the first she heard of it. "Holy shit," she said.

Darby pressed forward, sending the email to Robert, and then asked him how to file a Freedom of Information Act request, known as FOIA. The medical department would have to disclose the files related to Wood's case. The prosecuting attorney had assured her that he was going to court. This was interesting. She wanted the little bastard prosecuted, so he could never harm anyone again.

As she scrolled down, she found two emails from a government email address tied to the court system, awaiting her review. She sighed and opened the first. "What the hell," she said.

The document was short and bitter. The court had reassigned her fraud case against Global's attorney, Joe Wolfe, to Judge Landers. The exact same judge who ruled against her DFR. She opened the next document, and the court did the same thing with Dr. Wood's case. They reassigned Judge Landers to both her fraud cases. "How is that even possible?" she said.

Darby pushed her laptop aside and climbed out of bed. She stared at it, then pulled a hand through her hair. "How the hell can they do this?" she said. "Why would I think I could solve anything?" Darby said, now pacing. "Those fucking bastards." There was no way the same Judge who ruled against her DFR would give her a chance. The blatant hypocrisy of it all.

Darby grabbed her phone and dialed Tom. When he answered, she said, "Global Air Lines bought a federal judge."

"Not Geraghty," Tom said quickly.

"No. Landers. The guy who ruled against my DFR. Both of my fraud cases were transferred to him."

"That's a bullshit conflict of interest," Tom said. "Are you going to fight it?"

"I could, but then they'd give it to one of his buddies," she said. "I'm screwed."

Tom told her how sorry he was, and Darby told him she planned to appeal the decision. She almost forgot about the news regarding Dr. Wood. Somehow that news did not feel as sweet as it should. She wanted justice for what they had done.

"Why didn't the prosecuting attorney tell you?" Tom asked.

"I don't know. I was thinking that myself. The last time I spoke to him, he had said that Dr. Wood was fighting it all the way, and we were going to trial."

"And then he just gives up?" Tom said.

"Yep," Darby said. "My question too. Why would he do that? He says he did no wrong, so I can't see him just giving up."

She and Tom discussed the many reasons Dr. Wood might forfeit his license, and why Landers held both her cases. The bottom line was— Global was behind it. They owned the legal system. With that much power, she feared that hers was a losing battle.

CHAPTER 102

PASTA GREW COLD in front of Darby as she pushed it around her plate. If it hadn't been for the virus, they would be sitting at their favorite Thai restaurant. Darby hoped her friends at the Mango Thai would weather the storm and sustain the substantial loss thanks to the government shutdown. It made no sense that a national furniture store was a necessity, but a local restaurant was not. Maybe she was just angry at life, and the injustice of it all. She feared the future in many ways.

She sipped herbal tea while Kathryn drank a red wine. Kathryn was deeply concerned about the girls, but since Covid had shutdown the college campus and the kids were at home it was easier for Tom to keep an eye on them. Regardless, Darby felt an impending doom or an unease that she'd never felt before.

"Who do you think is paying Tom?" Kathryn asked.

Darby shrugged. "We're both perplexed, but they're paying him a shitload of money."

"Are you sure it's to protect you?" Kathryn asked.

"No, I'm not." Darby set her fork on the plate. "That's *exactly* what's been bugging me. Whomever it is, could be after Bill, Global, or even Drake. Think about how many people died in the Colgan crash, AF447, and even the MAX crashes. There could be many wealthy disgruntled people who lost a loved one. I have been a target by Global for an exceptionally long time. I'm standing up to them, too. So, *what if* whomever is paying Tom to watch me isn't doing this to protect me per se, but... I could just be a pawn in someone else's game of revenge."

"Are you sure I can't get you something stronger?" Kathryn asked.

"No," Darby said, "this is perfect, thanks." She stood to add more hot water to her mug.

Seattle was dark and damp, typical of a winter day. Fatigue had also taken hold. She hadn't bounced back, having just flown in from Tokyo two days earlier. When she renewed her first-class physical the day prior her AME even told her she looked tired. But then again, the only time he ever said she looked rested was if she was wearing makeup. But she didn't have the heart to apply it.

"Just not feeling well," Darby said returning to her seat. "I hope it's not the vaccine."

The airlines had forced all pilots and flight attendants to get some loosely tested vaccine. Some were fighting it, but Darby didn't want one more fight on her hand, she wanted to fly. She complied like a good little soldier, to avoid the bigger battle. Maybe she didn't care anymore.

"Is everything okay?" Kathryn asked. "Beyond this shitstorm, I mean."

Darby chuckled. "No." She spiraled pasta onto her fork and took a bite. She then said, "This is really good." Avoiding answering the question.

"It's better warm," Kathryn said. "Can I nuke it for you?" Darby nodded.

She wondered how much she should she tell Kathryn. She trusted her to no end but more than that she loved her and did not want Kat to carry the weight of something that she could do nothing about. Playing it safe, she only told her the easy part, but now she wasn't sure this was fair.

"I received notice yesterday that I lost both my fraud cases," Darby said.

"Oh Darb, I'm sorry," Kathryn said setting the warmed pasta in front of her.

Darby held her cup with both hands feeling the warmth and sighed. "I knew when they transferred them to the judge who ruled against my DFR, the writing was on the wall. But I still hoped it would be different. I hoped that he would step up and do the right thing. I wished that there would be some form of justice."

Kathryn reached for the bottle of merlot and refilled her glass. Then she asked, "Is there anything you can do about it now?"

"File appeals. Pray there is a higher court that would change it. I don't know," Darby said. Then she held Kathryn's gaze and said, "I have to tell you something else."

Kathryn set her glass on the table. A look of sheer terror crossed her face.

"That's quite the look," Darby said almost laughing. "Save it, you'll need it."

"Am I that transparent?" Kathryn said with a half-smile. "It's just every time I hear one more thing, I question how much more I can take."

"I feel the exact same way. Every time my attorney calls I wonder what next," Darby said, "But I need your help." She stared into her mug, then played with the teabag, bobbing it up and down in the cup. Finally, she pushed the mug aside.

"Bill *is* working for Drake, just as we thought," Darby said. "Global is also on Drake's payroll. I'm not sure who is in the driver's seat, but I suspect it's Drake. Regardless, they are all in bed together. Global isn't providing the training pilots need on purpose. They want to induce an accident. They *are* going to have an accident, on purpose. They want it to appear to be a pilot issue. An accident is the goal, and they want it to come across as pilot error."

"There have been enough pilot error issues too take down a plane already," Kathryn said. "And all the events you reported in your report, and those pilots falling asleep could have killed everyone."

Darby nodded and wiped a tear from under her eye.

"This is good," Kathryn said, placing a hand over Darby's "Now I have something I can take action on and we can stop what ever it is they are up to. I can go to my boss and..."

"But you can't," Darby said. "Bill said if I tell anyone he'll kill the girls."

"What the hell?" Kathryn said removing her hand. "Why didn't you tell me?"

"Nothing you could have done," Darby said. "You know Bill. If you did anything, he might just do something to prove his point. My not saying anything was the safest course for the kids. But Tom now knows and he's doing what he can."

Kathryn listened and calmed down with each word. Then she said. "I wish you would have told me sooner."

"I was just worried," Darby said. "Bill told me that I needed to figure out what to do with the information he gave me. He doesn't want Global and Drake to destroy the profession. Regardless, instead of figuring it out, I'm simply proving *repeatedly* how corrupt the legal system is and how much control they have."

There was no worse feeling than not being in control of your life. The stress of everything was finally taking its toll on her. She was at a loss and had no idea if she could stop whatever they were doing. With Wyatt as the FAA administrator, nobody was safe. Why couldn't the public see what was happening?

"You don't have to worry about this alone," Kathryn said.

"Kat, I'm getting tired," Darby said. "I've fought and fought and have a gut feeling that this is not going to end well. I'm scared."

"Maybe it's time to step aside," Kathryn said, "and focus on your life."

"And let them crash a plane?" Darby said. "I don't know how I could do that."

Chapter 103

RICH CLARK DIDN'T mind waiting, he had a great deal of paperwork to keep himself busy. His wife wasn't so happy, however, that he gave up Saturday evening before Christmas. But it got him out of her family Christmas party. Unfortunately, he could not tell her he was meeting with the former President of the United States. It was late, and Clark was beginning to think something came up when his phone buzzed.

"Meet me in the parking lot by your car," President Drake said.

Clark glanced at the time. It was 11:15 p.m., and there was nobody in the building except the cleaning crew, and a security guard probably sleeping in the backroom. His car, however, would be alone in the executive lot. He pulled on his coat, grabbed his keys, and locked the door.

The wind was brisk when he stepped outside. There was another car beside his. He headed that way. As he approached, he saw that the back door to the other car was open. Bill Jacobs stood to the side, holding it. Clark stopped about ten feet away from the car. This did not look good.

"Climb in and slide over," Bill said.

Clark shook off his hesitation and stepped to the care and climbed inside. He slid across the seat. He hadn't expected Jacobs to be here too. Bill slid in after him and closed the door. The locks engaged with an audible click.

"Good to see you," Drake said, sitting in the club seat across from him. Black glass blocked their seating area from the driver.

Drake made some political small talk and then told Clark how much he admired him. They discussed Drake's concerns about Croft and Wyatt taking their time. Everything that Clark already knew. Clark also knew Drake would come to him.

There was a mutual dislike between Clark and Walter Croft. If it weren't for Clark's knowledge, he would have been gone years earlier. There was power in knowledge. But now he was in the fold of President Drake, and Croft's usefulness as an alliance was in question. He was beginning to wonder if he should clean house and tie up all the loose ends.

Bill Jacobs sat beside him not saying a word. Clark wasn't sure if he trusted Bill. Perhaps it was nothing more than envy. It was true, the guy had balls. There was also something about Bill Jacobs that drove just enough fear for Clark to show him respect.

"What can I do for you Sir?" Clark finally asked Drake.

"I'm glad you asked." Drake lowered a table between them. "I have a task for you." Drake removed a brown cardboard box, not bigger than a book, from a backpack. He placed the package on the table. He opened the box and gingerly lifted out a three-by-four-inch black plastic box, two inches thick, with a screen on the front, and set it on the table.

"Is this what I think it is?" Clark said.

"The solution," Drake said. "We need to make a plane disappear, like that triple seven did. To ensure the pilot is the suspect."

"How does this thing work?" Clark asked.

"Dial in the hours to countdown, here. It's connected to a burner phone." Drake removed a flip phone from his pocket and set it on the table. "Don't open this until you're ready. You call the programmed number, and the countdown begins at the time you've entered."

"What happens if there's an unexpected turnback?"

"You can't deactivate it," Drake said, "plan accordingly."

"Does it need Wifi?" Clark asked.

"Tied to a satellite for activation," Drake said.

It was so small. "Can this take out a widebody?" Clark asked.

"Place it by the fuel tank, and when she blows, the entire plane goes with her."

"I'd love to see that," Clark said under his breath. "But how will blowing up a plane be construed as pilot's responsibility?"

"Do it over the Pacific. It'll disappear off radar."

"But satellites... and won't controllers monitoring radar see it?" Clark said.

"You tell me when and where, I'll take care of the rest," Drake said. "The question is, can you get it on a plane *after* it's cleared into service?" Drake asked. "We cannot have it detected."

"That won't be a problem," Clark said. "How sensitive is this thing?"

Bill casually raised his arm and hit the box toward Clark. He jumped and caught it.

"Holy shit. Are you trying to kill us?" Clark said, his heartrate speeding.

"It only blows when programmed," Bill said.

"She's not sensitive," Drake said, with the smile not leaving his eyes.

Holy fucking shit, Clark thought. Then asked, "When would you like it done, Sir?"

"Might as well start the New Year off with a bang," Drake said.

Drake returned the device to the cardboard box and set the phone on top before he closed the lid. He placed the package into the backpack and handed it to Clark. Bill had already climbed out of the car and was holding the door open for him, once again.

Rich Clark climbed out with the non-descript backpack in hand. He stood by his car and watched the Sedan drive out of the lot. He reached for the handle on his car to head home but had a better thought. He put the backpack over a shoulder and headed toward the building.

He returned to his office. He gently set the backpack on his desk, then slipped into his chair and opened his computer to the January flight schedules. And there it was, the perfect flight. He would provide the flight number, date, and time to President Drake the following morning.

He removed the box from the backpack and set it in the bottom drawer of his desk and locked it. He hung the backpack on the coat rack. He stared at it for a moment, then removed it and stuffed it into the bottom drawer of the filing cabinet. He assessed his office and smiled.

Rich Clark was going to change history. He would be richer beyond any realm he could believe possible. That little thing called revenge would add flavor to make his victory all the better. He locked the door to his office and headed toward the elevator.

Chapter 104

THIS IS SERIOUSLY *getting old*, Darby thought. She picked up the note that had been slid under her door while she was in the bathroom getting ready for work—flight delay. Scheduling extended her 48-hour lockdown for another 24 hours of torture. She wanted to scream. Instead, she signed up for the movie channel for an additional 24 hours and ordered breakfast.

The bed was getting harder with each trip. The isolation felt overwhelming at times. There was so much to think about, and she wasn't sure she wanted the future that presented itself. She felt guilty with those thoughts. She swallowed her fears and selected *Four Christmases*, and in no time, her breakfast arrived.

By the time she finished breakfast, and the movie was over, she called Tom to wish him good night and tell him the unwelcome news. It was 8:30 p.m. in Seattle. Tom said he was looking for another job but would always spend his life protecting her.

They said goodbye, and she scrolled through the movies, and selected Elf. Then she reached for her laptop and logged into her email. There was an email from Judge Geraghty's assistant. *Oh fuck*, Darby thought as her heartrate accelerated.

The email came in at 8 p.m. in Seattle. *Why the hell would they be posting anything at that hour?* she wondered. Sucking a deep breath, she opened the attachment—Decision and Order Bradshaw versus Global Air Lines Case number 2018-AIR-00041. "Oh shit."

The report was 115 pages in length. She'd had read enough briefs and decisions to know that the punchline was at the end. Darby placed one hand to her mouth as she scrolled down to read the section. The fear was overwhelming, and her nerves fired on every cylinder.

Dropping both hands she screamed, "Oh my God! Oh my God! Oh my God!"

Her heart was racing so fast she thought she was having a panic attack. She could not believe it. How could this have happened? Robert was on the East Coast, and it was approaching midnight, but she called him anyway.

"Darby," Robert said. "Everything okay?"

"The ruling is in. We won! He awarded me $500,000, plus the highest pay of any first officer for the remainder of my career. And even my vacation!"

"Are you kidding?" Robert said dumbfounded.

"No, it's in your inbox," Darby said.

"Standby," Robert said. By the time he opened it and made a few exclamations of his own he said, "This is unbelievable. And Global must also post this ruling in every base and email it to every employee."

"We won," Darby said. "We won!"

"We won big," Robert responded. "This is ten times any AIR21 award in history. It's simply amazing."

They agreed to talk more when she returned to the mainland. He congratulated her, and she told him she could not have done it without him. Then she called Tom. Tears of joy flowed as she told him that this was over. She had proved Global violated federal standards.

She'd proven that she had reported in good faith, and they took an adverse action. This ruling cleared her name if there had ever been any lingering doubt with anyone.

"What time is it there?" Tom asked.

"Noon."

"Good, because I don't think you're going to be able to come down off this high for a few hours."

Darby laughed. "No kidding. I'm going to read the entire order, take notes, put on another Christmas movie, order lunch, and write a letter to HR to force that investigation."

Tom laughed. "That was a mouthful."

"I know. But while this is over for me, the traveling public is still in harm's way. I'm going to tell HR that Global lost. We have a non-retaliation policy and all those employees involved were found guilty, so now they have to do something. They have to get rid of them all."

"But I thought you couldn't name people," Tom said, "the reason Wyatt was able to become the FAA administrator."

"True, but…"

Darby explained that while you could not name people, Judge Geraghty gave a character assessment of each person involved. This document was a compilation of history, trial documents, character assessments, and testimony that showed each person's involvement. This was nothing short of an investigation followed by a report. While they couldn't name people in the case, everyone involved had been called out, and Global had a non-retaliation policy. Therefore, the AIR21 law had no relevance on company policy, but proved the guilt.

"The judge politely called Rich Clark a liar," Darby said, "and said I was an unwitting player in Clark and Wolfe's game of chess."

"That you were. But please listen to me," Tom said, his voice shifting to concern. "These guys are sore losers. If they try to delay you any longer than tomorrow, get yourself to the airport and I'll buy you a ticket on the first flight home."

"You got a deal," Darby said. She said good night for the second time.

Now that she won, she could use this as leverage to address the training and fatigue issues. She would ensure that an accident would never happen on her watch.

CHAPTER 105

THE BEST CHRISTMAS ever. Kathryn, Jackie and John, Linda and Niman, and Tom and Darby were sitting in the living room, laughing, and talking about the award. Darby looked at Tom with more love than she ever felt before and couldn't believe how wonderful life was. She squeezed his hand, and he smiled with a squeeze of his own.

"I'll be back in a minute," Darby said, and headed to the kitchen to see the kids. "Hey guys," she said. "How's college life?"

"Aunt Darby," Jennifer said and hugged her hard. Jessica pushed her sister out of the way and squeezed her.

Chris mumbled, "Hey."

"Get over here," Darby said, and then wrapped him into a hug. too. He turned a shade of red and the girls teased him, as Darby hugged Francine, Linda's daughter. "I'm so glad you were able to make it home."

When Covid hit, John had pulled some strings to get Francine out of Europe as soon as possible. He saw the writing on the wall and took action before they closed the borders.

"Me, too," Francine said. "There really is, no place like home."

"What are you party animals drinking in here?" Darby asked.

"Sparkling cider," Jess said rolling her eyes. "Want some?"

"Nothing could be better," Darby said. She loved these kids more than anything. And while she wasn't really their aunt, she'd always thought that playing aunt would be enough. But the worry they gave her with Bill in town held a new challenge all its own. She felt for Kathryn, and wondered how she handled it all these years.

Jessica grabbed a champagne glass and Francine was filling it for Darby, when Kathryn yelled for the kids to get into the dining room for dinner. Darby rolled her eyes, and they all laughed. She loved being one of the kids. It gave her a chance to divest of all adult responsibility, and a break from reality. But they were no longer kids, and that was sad in a happy sort of way.

Once everyone found a seat at the dining room table, Kathryn raised her glass and said, "We have so much to celebrate, and so very much to find gratitude in. I don't know what the future will bring, but the present is a gift. Merry Christmas to my family. I love you all."

They toasted, and Darby wiped away a tear. Then she extended her plate for a slice of turkey. It was hard to believe that three years ago, on this date, Dr. Wood had diagnosed her as bipolar. She had also cheated death. That's when Tom came to her rescue and into her life. Now, this battle was finally over, and life was about to begin.

They talked about the industry and Darby's case. The industry looked bleak, with honesty and integrity an illusion. Even her AME, who was a good guy, had feared helping her. If the good guys wouldn't stand up to injustice, then what hope did anyone have? But then, out of the blue, there was one person who changed her opinion of justice—Judge Geraghty. Darby would forever be grateful for his integrity and interest in aviation safety.

Maybe if a person held out long enough, fought hard enough,

maybe they could unearth justice. Darby wasn't sure if it took courage to do the right thing and stand up for others, or simply the ability to put others first. She closed her eyes and said a silent prayer, thanking God for being her navigator through this journey through hell.

"I'm so glad you won," Jackie said.

"To say she was excited was an understatement," Tom said. "I think she compiled a twenty-two-word sentence without breath when she told me."

"It was only twenty-one and a result of my manic behavior," Darby said, whacking his arm. "But the funny part was what my captain said the next morning."

"What did he say?" Chis asked.

Chris loved pilots and anything they said and did. The girls said it was his excuse because he had a crush on Darby. She knew otherwise. Sometimes flying passed through generations like a mutant gene that would not dissolve. Chris's father had been a pilot and died in a plane crash at the hands of Bill Jacobs. Now Bill was working with Drake and the CEO of Global to induce a crash. There was often no sense in the world. But history did repeat.

"Aunt *Darby*… what did he say?" Jessica said.

Darby glanced at Kathryn who shrugged.

"He said, 'Congratulations,' shook my hand and then said, 'Since you were locked in your room alone, I suspected you received good news with the trial, and I did a legal search.' Then he told me how happy he was."

"Why would being locked in your room alone lead him to a legal search," Linda said.

"I kind of yelled, 'Oh my God' 'Oh my God' 'Oh my God' rather loudly."

Everyone laughed and Chris said, "I don't get it."

"I hope you never do," Jackie said.

Darby glared at Jessica, who was about to open her mouth, and John jumped to the rescue of the young man and said, "So, what's Santa Claus bringing everyone this year?"

The baby squealed, "Santa," and they all laughed.

Darby must have been a really good girl this year because Santa had given her the best gift in the world. He had given her more than her share of gifts. It was no coincidence that Judge Geraghty released the ruling just before Christmas. He had been incredulous to learn that Dr. Wood gave her the bipolar diagnosis on Christmas Eve, especially when he notified Global months earlier. Then there was Tom. Forgiveness was a gift she gave herself.

As much as she loved Christmas at Kat's, Darby was looking forward to being alone with Tom to give him his real gift. *Soon, very soon*, she thought.

CHAPTER 106

LIFE IS A *blessing,* Darby thought. Through her ordeal she learned that it wasn't the lack of problems in her life that dictated happiness, it was an understanding that she wasn't alone to fight them. She'd thought about how angry she felt with Tom, but without forgiveness they would not be here creating a life together.

Darby sat across his lap in an oversized easy chair made for two. He'd poured them each a glass of champagne and told her that he didn't get her a present. She argued that point. He said she'd have to wait until morning to see what Santa would bring, but he got her nothing. She knew otherwise.

"Serious, question," Darby said, laying her head on his shoulder. "What kind of job are you looking for?"

"I'm thinking with Boeing," Tom said. "But, based on what you and Kat said about the airline industry and automated flight, maybe I'll go into automotive instead."

Darby furrowed her brow, thinking about that. Then she sat up and looked at him perplexed. "When you said you were in security at Drake, what did you mean?"

Tom returned her confused look. Then said, "Oh, no. I wasn't the security guard. I worked in security for automation. That's the one piece of the puzzle they haven't mastered, it's the security of wireless control to ensure nobody can hack it. I almost had it, too."

"Holy shit. You're a techy?" Darby said scrambling off his lap. "I thought you guarded the building and the reason you played cop. The two, kind of, go together."

"Yeah, but I…"

Darby walked away and stood by the fireplace and stared at the Christmas tree, thinking. *That explains everything,* she thought. From his programming her new computer to teaching her how to use her phone. He'd even written programs for her computer. More so, it answered her question as to why and who employed him.

"Tom," she began, and sat on the ottoman between his legs. "I was trying to figure out who cared enough about me to pay you that much money to watch me. One theory was a family member of a person on one of the industry crashes who knew I was fighting for safety. The evidence I dig up could be the proof they needed that the crash could have been avoided."

"That's a theory," Tom said.

"But not the correct one. I think this was a ruse, and someone wants to stop Drake's automation takeover," Darby said.

"Why?" he asked, now sitting forward.

"Competition," Darby said. "Think about it…why record Kat and me? She is the connection to the FAA, and we talk. Then Bill's warning and wanting me to stop the crash. But then again, what if it's not competition?"

"Now I'm confused," Tom said.

"Oh shit," Darby said suddenly realizing the truth. "What if it was Drake? What if Drake paid someone else to set up this ruse to pretend to protect me? What if he is simply watching me to know what I'm doing, what the FAA is doing, and what John is doing?"

Tom closed his eyes and multiple expressions crossed his face as he thought about what she had just said. When he opened his eyes he said, "That makes more sense than anything else. He would have reason to keep tabs on me too."

"Exactly, you know all Drake's secrets. He'd as soon kill you as let you go work for someone else."

"You're right about that," Tom said.

"This is great news," Darby said.

"How do you figure?"

"When you know who they are, you give them what they want." She grinned. "I said that incorrectly. You give them what you want them to have."

Darby and Tom talked about the situation for another twenty minutes and concurred that Drake was behind Tom's job. Then they retreated to her bedroom. It wasn't long until she lay naked on the red down comforter completely sated. He trailed kisses from her abdomen to her breast and then to her neck. He stirred all the emotions of new love, deep within. Then he slid on top of her again.

"I love you Darby," he said, slowly pressing himself inside her, as they became one. He carried her to the peak of ecstasy and back to earth again. Then he pulled her back up. He drove her wild and she couldn't contain herself. They came together in as much force as waves crashing to the beach, flowing, resisting, succumbing, and drawing back out, and slowly running up the shoreline.

When Darby thought Tom had fallen asleep, she sneaked out of bed and dug through her drawer for the golden-wrapped box she'd put together for him.

"What are you doing?" Tom asked, and she jumped.

"Getting you your present." She climbed back into bed and said,

"Do you know why Santa had two black eyes?"

"He laid the wrong doll under the tree," Tom said.

"You're pretty smart for guy," she said scooting beside him and pulling a comforter over her body. "How about, why Santa has no children?"

"You got me on that one," he said.

"He only comes once a year, and it's in a chimney."

Tom laughed hard. When his laugher subsided, she gave him his gift. He opened the box and stared. Then removed a pair of purple baby booties. His eyes wide, he said nothing.

"Purple, because that's what you get with blue and pink, and I have no idea... it's too early." She climbed out of bed and paced. "I know I'll be like 47 when the baby is born, but Janet Jackson gave birth at 59. And ... please say something."

"If you'll shut up," Tom said. "I will. What time is it?"

"Christmas morning, for the previous twenty minutes," Darby said.

"Good. Wait here."

Tom left the room and Darby could feel tears well up again. She knew it was the hormones, but what the heck was that all about? Within minutes Tom returned with a little red bike with training wheels and a big red bow.

"You knew?" Darby said.

"Hell no," Tom said. "It was Santa. I wrote my letter to him and told him I wanted a gift for you for...motivation. He brought you this."

"You're happy?" Darby said, placing a hand to her abdomen. She had been so scared that since he'd lived a solitary life for so long, that was all he wanted.

"I could not be happier," Tom said setting the bike aside and wrapping her into his arms.

"But you lied to me," Darby said with a grin. "You said you weren't giving me a gift, and instead you gave me the best one ever. A baby."

Tom held her tighter than she ever could imagine. "Thank you," he whispered.

The best gifts in life were those given in love. This baby was one of those gifts. Tom would not be like her father. Tom would stay and love them both until his time on this earth was up. He would teach their baby how to ride a bike and give unconditional love, no matter what.

"I'm going to have one rule only," Darby said.

"What's that?"

"The only way this kid's going to become a pilot is over my dead body."

"Yeah right. You're going to have her flying an instrument approach when she's five."

Chapter 107

DARBY WAS BUSY taking ornaments off the tree, and listening to Christmas songs when the phone rang. She glanced at the name and then answered.

"Is this a good time?" Robert asked.

"Of course," Darby said.

She stopped what she was doing and went to the kitchen, as Robert asked her how she was feeling and congratulated her once again. She poured whole milk into a pan and placed it on the stovetop. Real cocoa was her caffeine replacement for the baby.

"We have bad news," Robert said. "Global filed their notice to appeal this morning."

Darby moved to a chair and sat. "With what Geraghty wrote, I'm surprised."

"I've never faced such arrogant assholes in my life," Robert said. "It's that arrogance that is driving their decision-making."

"Do they have a chance?"

"No. Well, there's always a chance. But Geraghty's Decision and Order did us a great favor assessing the credibility, or lack thereof, of their witnesses."

Robert explained in the next level of review, Global could not challenge the facts. The judge's credibility assessment stood. They would have to show that Geraghty was a whack job and that wasn't going to happen. Therefore, the only way they could win was by proving he made a legal error. Which, he did not.

"Why are they doing this?" Darby asked. Suspecting it was to keep Wyatt in place at the FAA as long as possible. Until they lost an appeal, he was innocent as was Global.

"Wendel told me they've engaged in a war of attrition."

"Seriously?" Darby said. Kathryn had told her the same, but out of the mouth of Global's attorney, there was more truth than speculation.

"They're trying to bankrupt you," Robert said. "If you need any help, let me know."

"I'll be fine," Darby said, thanking him. They chatted a moment and said their goodbyes.

There was nothing she could do until Global filed their appeal. Rushing to the stove before she burned the milk, Darby added chocolate powder and stirred, thinking of what was to come. There would never be enough appreciation for Robert's generosity, his wisdom, and patience with her through all this. They had been fighting for years, and now it looked like it could be a few more. It pained her heart to think what would happen to a pilot who didn't get their job back and had a mortgage to pay and mouths to feed.

Darby was one of the lucky ones.

Justice was a slippery illusion. One minute you think she passed you by, then next thing she pokes up her head and taunts you, to only go back into hiding. If there was any justice at all, it was slow. Far too slow, that you never saw it. But one thing she knew, Global would never play this game with anyone again if she had anything to do about it.

CHAPTER 108

TOM CARRIED HER bags to the curb and set them on the ground. He kissed her long and hard, then wrapped his arms around her and held tight. She didn't want to leave his embrace. Flying wasn't what it used to be, and this fight with Global had taken something out of her. Despite winning, Global still wanted to battle. Then she thought about their baby and knew she could not give up now. She had to ensure that the skies were safe for everyone's families, not just her own. Too many people she loved had died in airplanes.

"You know, there's no hugging in the blue zone," Darby finally said. "So, I should probably go, or miss my flight."

"I thought there was no kissing in the blue zone. Hugging was in the red zone," Tom said, with a laugh. "And missing your flight is sounding better every moment."

Instead of being a derelict pilot, they said goodbye and Darby made her way through security and onto her commuter flight headed to Los Angeles. Tom would have come with her, but today she was flying to Shanghai, and the only people allowed in the country was the flight crew. The passengers had to stay on the plane as they continued to Korea with a new crew.

She watched a movie, declined the pretzels and tried not to suffocate wearing a mask on the flight. Darby had a tough time breathing when she wore it. Thankfully, as operating crew they could remove it in the flight deck. This Covid world was something that she never expected, but the government decisions on how to manage it were odd. Perhaps they had no idea either.

In no time she was walking into flight operations. She walked up to a computer beside one of the captains she was flying with.

"Hey Jack," Darby said, logging in to the computer. "Uh oh... I better be careful saying *that* at the airport."

"As long as you don't tell me hi, then you're safe," Jack said.

"Oh shit," Darby said. "We're delayed?"

"Equipment swap, I think. The other two live here, so we'll see them in a couple hours," Jack said. "Didn't they notify you?"

"Nope," Darby said. Not that it mattered because she would have taken the same flight down, regardless.

"Just like them," Jack said. "Can I buy you lunch?"

"I would love that," Darby said, as she was hungrier than usual these days.

They parked their luggage in the bag room, and then found one of the few open restaurants. Jack ordered a BLT and Darby a cobb salad. They both ordered large iced teas.

"I hear congratulations are in order," Jack said, after placing their orders.

"So, what are you congratulating me on *exactly*?" Darby said, extending her left hand and wiggling her fingers, flashing her ring.

"You're getting married? My heart be still," he said placing a hand to his chest. "I guess I waited too long to snatch you off the market."

"Yeah, not sure what your wife would have thought about that?"

He gave her a fake shiver with wide eyes. They laughed and he told her how happy he was that Global lost. Then he told her about the holidays with his grandkids. He was one of her favorite pilots to fly with, and this was the best way to start the New Year. Jack was also the senior captain on this trip, therefore, her being junior to the other first officer didn't matter. They would be the first crew to fly, which was preferable.

"I'm really proud of what you did," Jack said, as their meals arrived. "Nobody was willing to stand up to the Global boys. These guys don't play fair, and they have left a swath of bodies in their wake. Not sure how you did it. But good for you."

"Thanks," Darby said, pouring more dressing on her salad than she needed.

She wasn't sure how she did it either. It was as if the moon and the stars aligned with the best attorney, an uncorruptible judge, and her relentless fight for safety. She knew that nothing happened by chance, and that all the pieces to this puzzle came together with a higher purpose by a higher power, and everything was going to work out as it should.

"Unfortunately, they've already filed an appeal," she said. "They'll drag this on for years and cost me a few hundred thousand more."

She told Jack what Robert said about her chances with the appeal, and what the judge wrote in the ruling regarding his character assessment of Rich Clark, Abbott, Joe Wolfe, and others. She also promised to email him the Decision and Order when they got to Shanghai.

"The judge is also making Global send the ruling to all the pilots by email and post it in each base," Darby said. "Pure embarrassment for the almighty leaders."

"Yeah, I probably won't live to see that," he said, biting into his sandwich. With his mouth full, he added, "They don't seem to have the emotional maturity to do the right thing, even if it's court ordered."

"If you only knew," Darby said. "They refused to provide discovery, but we ended up getting it anyway from the dirty doctor, the very reason we knew they didn't give it to us. That doctor, by the way forfeited his medical license to avoid prosecution."

"You had something to do with that?" Jack asked, and Darby nodded.

"I called the Illinois medical department monthly, sometimes weekly, for three years before they took action against him. Then the prosecuting attorney said Wood was fighting it in court, but out of the blue, he up and forfeits his license to avoid prosecution. I thought that was weird, so I filed a FOIA request to see what happened."

"Any response?"

"Yep. They combined my case with another pilot. My case number only provides documents from the other pilot's case. It's as if mine disappeared. I personally gave them over 700 pages of material. Maybe more."

"Global had something to do with that," Jack said quietly. And then added, "This is just bullshit. I don't know if there is justice in our world anymore."

"I don't think there is," Darby said. "I filed a DFR, duty of fair representation lawsuit, against the union for telling the arbitrator that ALPO was on the same side as the company. The judge ruled against me. Then they removed my original judges, for both my fraud cases, against Wolfe and the doctor, and reassigned them both to the DFR judge who had ruled against me. I don't believe there is justice, either."

"Ever consider revenge?" Jack asked with a Cheshire grin.

"Oh yeah. With pictures and everything," Darby said, with a chuckle. Then she asked, "What *is* the difference between revenge and justice anyway?"

He thought about it for a minute as he finished his sandwich.

Then he wiped his mouth and said, "Huh. Perhaps justice finds a fair and rational resolution and revenge inflicts harm."

"Yeah, I'd like to inflict some harm," Darby said. "God knows they deserve it."

Darby was beginning to believe that there was no justice. Global still had substandard training, and it would get worse with the early retirements due to Covid and new pilots coming on property. Justice was elusive, despite her winning the lawsuit.

There was still a threat of Global intentionally planning to crash a plane, but Darby had come to grips with that. She realized it was Bill just inflicting fear. She had no doubt there would be an accident, but it would be due to substandard training combined with fatigue.

"Well, if there is no justice, they say revenge is sweet," Jack said with a smirk.

"That it is," Darby said. "But I think that retribution might be a better word. It sounds much more dignified, don't you think?"

"Retribution is a fancy way of saying the same thing," Jack said. "Like the fluffy tail on a squirrel, it's still just a rat. And people feed it."

Darby laughed hard, and then said, "So true. Ready to fly?"

EPILOGUE

KATHRYN STOOD IN front of the television with John and Tom at her side. Linda and Jackie sat on the couch crying. Linda's tears flowed silently down her face and Jackie openly sobbed.

Global Flight 92 from Los Angeles to Shanghai went missing. It fell off the radar and they lost all communication eight hours into the flight. They say the situation is like the missing triple seven, MH370.

Multiple microphones extended in front of Global Air Lines CEO, Walter Croft, while Rich Clark and George Wyatt stood off to the side.

"Sir, can you provide any information on your missing flight?" a reporter asked.

"We are deeply concerned," Walter Croft said. "One of the pilots was First Officer Bradshaw. We suspected she had a mental health disorder, and we did our best to keep her out of the cockpit. We feared this would happen. Unfortunately, the mental health system protecting our passengers has failed, and the system forced us to put a mentally unstable pilot back on the flight line, back into the cockpit."

"That's such bullshit," Jackie said, said between sobs. "How can they lie like that?"

"You think this missing flight was intentional?" another report asked, camera's flashing in the background, giving the news a more surreal effect. Katheryn was frozen in disbelief. This could not be happening. She fought to keep from vomiting.

With tears in his eyes Croft said, "It might be too early, but yes. Yes, I do believe this was a nefarious act and at the hands of a mentally disturbed pilot. My heart goes out to the families of our passengers. That's all I have." He held up a hand to silence the number of questions thrown his way.

George Wyatt stepped forward and patted Croft on the shoulder as they passed.

"Sir, as the FAA administrator what are your thoughts?" a reporter asked as all microphones pushed forward in his direction.

"We will always have the potential for a mental health breakdown in the cockpit," Wyatt said. "Sadly, the only option would be to replace pilots with computers."

"Are you saying that's a possibility, to have fully automated aircraft?" the reporter asked, "Would that have stopped this?"

"Yes, to both your questions," Wyatt said. "I want to extend my heartfelt prayers to the families. I wish I could give hope, but the only hope for the future is to ensure we have better mental health protections with pilots to improve public safety."

The reporter turned toward the camera and said, "There were 65 passengers and 18 crew members on board. We'll be following this story as it progresses."

Kathryn muted the television and said, "This is wrong. Darby would not do anything."

"I've made some calls to get the satellite footage," John said. "But it was down, and when it came up, the plane was gone."

"And no distress calls to any other flights?" Kathryn asked.

"None," John said.

"Those fucking bastards," Tom said. "I'm going to find out who the fuck did this and I will fucking destroy every last one of them."

"You and me both," John said, his eyes now watering.

"Stop this, you two," Kathryn snapped. "There is no way in hell Darby is dead. I don't know what happened, but I would feel it. I would know. She isn't because she can't be!"

Linda stood, and wrapped Kathryn into an embrace, quietly telling her it would be okay, as Tom dropped into a chair and began sobbing. Kathryn pulled away from Linda and knelt before him.

"It's going to be okay," Kathryn said, reaching out and touching his arm.

He looked up and wiped his hand across his face and said, "It's never going to be okay. They killed Darby and our baby."

"Baby?" Kathryn said. "Darby was pregnant?"

Tom nodded. "We were going to tell you all when she returned from her trip."

Kathryn stood, and the room swirled. This could not be happening. The world was a better place than this. Darby was a fighter. Her ears began ringing and tears flowed down her cheeks. She dropped to her knees covering her face with her hands crying, just as the front door burst open. She glanced up.

"Mom!" Jessica yelled, "We heard on the news. Is it true?"

Jennifer was balling and Linda placed an arm around her shoulder, pulling her in. Chris had fallen onto the couch, sobbing into his mother's arms. Jessica stood, with anger and fear etched into her face, demanding that her mother tell her it wasn't true. That this couldn't be happening. She stood like Darby would, with hands on her hips. Then she thought of the baby.

Kathryn wanted to lie to her daughter. She wanted to tell her it was going to be alright. But she knew that it wasn't. Darby and her baby were gone. Nothing would ever be okay again. Nothing could ever bring them back.

She sucked a deep breath and stared at Jessica, and said, "Yes, it's true, her plane is gone. But she did not do it. Don't ever listen to anyone who says otherwise."

"Darby is not gone," Jessica said. "Only her plane."

John stepped forward and pulled Jessica into an embrace, and said, "You're absolutely right, and we will find it."

GRATITUDE

A HUGE THANK you to my husband, **Dick Petitt**, for reading and editing the stories he has lived with me. His advice and suggestions are invaluable.

Thank you to **Carol Singleton** for taking the second editing challenge. She has been following this series from the beginning. Not only does she work in the industry, but her son is a captain at an international airline, and she has a personal interest in the safety and longevity of the pilot job. Her comments were amazing, and she is so much appreciated for her dedication.

A huge thanks to my sister, **Kristine Kassner**, for the second edit. There were some fun scenes that had real life, personal, events that included bourbon, a cherry, chips, and her favorite pastime that I included just for her. I appreciate Kris taking her weekend to read and edit this novel. We opened the door for discussion on the next.

Thank you to **Captain Eric Auxier**, known by all as Cap'n Aux, for his comments on the book. He took his time to catch up to Darby and the gang and read the book in a couple days. The comments he wrote were amazing, especially coming from an international B777 pilot with the expertise of piloting and that of an author. You can find Cap'n Aux at https://capnaux.com. I have read all his books and enjoyed all of them, and highly recommend reading his blog.

Thank you to **Kathy McCullough** for taking her time to read and comment. Kathy is a retired Delta Captain, an author working on her next novel, photographer, a new grandmother, and took the time to read and comment. We have worked closely for years on multiple books, attend conferences together, and her opinion is appreciated. Kathy is the author of the novel, Breakfast in Narita, where Cassie, an international airline pilot, takes on a group of senior pilots involved in a sex trafficking scheme. A must read. All her books are available on Amazon. You can find her at https://kathymccullough. photodeck.com/

Final thanks go to **Nathan Everett** at Elder Road Books. He has been a blessing in my life to put all my novels into a book format. He has worked diligently on my behalf, and I adore him. His talent is endless and writing incredible. He's written many books himself, in multiple genres, which can be found at https://nathaneverett.com. I cannot thank him enough for his commitment to excellence, and his follow through during the busiest and toughest times. For book design and editing, he can be reached at elderroadbooks@outlook.com.

KARLENE PETITT IS a retired
Delta Air Lines captain who is
type-rated, has flown, and/or
has instructed on the A350,
A330, B777, B747-400,
B747-200, B767, B757,
B737 and B727 aircraft. She
has worked for Northwest
Airlines, Braniff, Evergreen,
Coastal Airways, Prem Air,
America West, Guyana, Tower Air, and Delta.

Petitt holds PhD, MBA and MHS degrees and is working as
an Aviation Safety Expert and speaker. She is the mother of three,
grandmother of eight, and is working to improve her golf game.

KARLENE IS AVAILABLE to host aviation discussion groups, join book
clubs, or speak at your meetings. Please email her at Karlene.Petitt@
gmail.com to schedule your next event. Check out her blog for more
writings at KarlenePetitt.com

www.ingramcontent.com/pod-product-compliance
Lightning Source LLC
Chambersburg PA
CBHW032038090426
42744CB00004B/46